fandango

fandango

SANDY HILL
RECIPES BY STEPHANIE VALENTINE

Photographs by Eric Scott Smith, Luca Trovato,
Macduff Everton, and Roxanne Lowit

ARTISAN

To Tom,
who makes every day an occasion for me.

Published by Artisan
A Division of Workman Publishing, Inc.
225 Varick Street
New York, NY 10014-4381
www.artisanbooks.com

Library of Congress Cataloging-in-Publication Data

Hill, Sandy, 1955-
Fandango / Sandy Hill ; recipes by Stephanie Valentine ; photographs by Eric Scott Smith . . . [et al.].
p. cm.
Includes index.
ISBN-13: 978-1-57965-338-5
1. Entertaining. 2. Cookery. 3. Menus. I. Valentine, Stephanie. II. Title.
TX731.H45 2007
642'.4--dc22   2007007957

Design by Jan Derevjanik
Printed in Singapore
First printing, October 2007

1 3 5 7 9 10 8 6 4 2

CONTENTS

FOREWORD by Martha Stewart

I have known Sandy Hill for a very long time. When we first met we were both young magazine contributors: I was writing food and entertaining articles for *Mademoiselle* and Sandy needed some recipe advice as she was planning a bridal shower for a fellow editor. Since then, our lives have crisscrossed time and again, and I have been fortunate to attend Sandy's parties at her California wine-country ranch, and many other places over the years. She is a hostess with great panache and entertains her friends and family by opening her imagination to limitless possibilities. This is also how Sandy has lived her life.

She loves to make occasions special whenever she can. One of my fondest memories of Sandy's parties is one she threw in Africa for me and a few other friends following our successful ascent of Mt. Kilimanjaro. We hadn't been back in Nairobi for more than a few hours before Sandy had sent each of us a beautifully hand calligraphed invitation to dinner in a garden cottage at the historic Norfolk Hotel. While the rest of us were packing, unpacking, resting, and reorganizing in our hotel rooms after the rugged climb, Sandy was busily working on the menu with the chef and on décor and costumes with the hotel manager. At the appointed time, I was ushered into an incredibly lovely aerie of a room, with wild birds singing in the garden and waiters in fez and flowing robes moving about with gin and tonics, and for dinner, serving us heaping platters of creamy avocadoes, ripe mangoes, and delicate fish. While others might have been content just to have a roof over their head after camping for five days, Sandy transformed our last night in Africa into magic.

The best word to describe Sandy is intrepid. She is also adventurous, creative, energetic, organized, and generous. She is unabashedly the mistress of the moment. She adores the complexities of entertaining and always rises to a challenge, which is why each of her events is so out of the ordinary. Whether it's a theme party or a holiday, a rite of passage or a romantic dinner for two, she infuses the event with a vision unlike anyone else's. Everyone can learn from these uniquely "Sandy" events . . . they mark the occasions of our lives, and Sandy shows us how to celebrate with style. In *Fandango*, she shares her ideas, secrets, and recipes to help make your parties, like hers, delicious and memorable.

MARTHA STEWART

APRIL 2007

INTRODUCTION

I was preoccupied with the question of when to stuff the apple in his mouth: while he was still malleable, cold, and pink, or after, when his browned snout would be crisply roasted shut? So, until it was time to start cooking him, I had overlooked the even greater problem of how to squeeze fifteen pounds of piglet into the oven. It was, after all, the first time I had attempted to prepare such an elaborate feast. I was fourteen years old.

At the beginning of my ninth-grade English Literature class, the teacher explained that passing the course would require a final project that illustrated our reading, to be presented in May. Since the survey curriculum spanned a thousand years, from 800 to 1800, it seemed to me that there would be no end to the creative possibilities.

In *Beowulf*, I read that King Hrothgar threw two great parties for the soldiers, but the best one was the victory celebration held beneath a grim trophy, the bloody severed arm of the defeated monster, an essential detail that I didn't care to reproduce. But in the next book, *The Canterbury Tales,* I found a woodcut illustration of the pilgrims gathered around a dining table with a roast pig on a platter in the middle, and I just knew I could bring that medieval scene to life: I would recreate supper at the Tabard Inn in my classroom and require my classmates to attend dressed as their favorite pilgrim.

The mead wine was going to take months to ferment, so I concocted it in late November and stored the sweet liquor in glass carboys in the basement. While buying a whole piglet was unusual in the 1960s, it turned out that it was not very difficult to obtain, since we bought our meat from our butcher (who had the unforgettable name of Cactus Frank), and he simply ordered the animal directly from a local hog farmer.

I was thrilled to learn that forks and spoons were not used in England during the fourteenth century, because it meant that, for the sake of historical correctness, we all had to eat with our hands and a knife. And I discovered that the traditional way of serving the spiced mead was heated, by inserting a hot iron poker into the cool liquid, a dramatic finale I accomplished with the help of the teacher from the metalworking shop and his blowtorch. Needless to say, none of the other kids' projects—which included Beowulf's boat made from Popsicle sticks, a papier-mâché frieze depicting Lilliput, and a pen-and-ink portrait of Milton's Satan, which everyone but the teacher recognized had been copied from the cover of the Pink Floyd LP—managed to so completely engage the imagination of the whole class and the envy of all the other students.

This end-of-term feast established many of the themes that have defined my parties ever since, the most important of which is that I never hesitate to knock myself out for the sake of making a great occasion. Carrying a suckling pig—not to mention dressing up as the Wife of Bath in a hennin with a veil and smuggling mead wine into my high school—was certainly special for me. And it was special for my classmates as well, not merely because of what I did, but because of what they had to do: dress up and take part in the fantasy. When people have to actively participate instead of just sitting back to admire a model boat made from Popsicle sticks, they become more invested in having a good time.

Since then, I have learned a few other things about having parties. Making sure you have a good mix of people on your guest list is one of them. There's a place at my table for all sorts of people, as long as they're not all the same person. The liveliest parties are made up of the widest assortment of personalities, people with not only diverse interests but also different types of social skills. Every opinionated dynamo needs at least one thoughtful listener; every serious character is more engaging when there's a jester to provide a little levity.

I am fortunate because I almost always entertain with my husband at my side. Tom is a truly gifted conversation maker; he has something interesting and provocative to say about almost anything, but even more important, he brings out the best in everyone else. Besides the fun our guests have talking to him, this takes a lot of the pressure off of me as a hostess; knowing they are in his capable company enables me to attend to more of the production work.

Although I didn't really recognize it at the time, that Chaucerian feast included an element that I always pursue when planning a party: a focus. It can be dressing up as fourteenth-century pilgrims, dead poets, or a member of Elvis's entourage; it could be

tasting a flight of Australian shiraz or a whole menu that's scented with truffles; it could be as traditional as celebrating Father's Day or as unique as riding elephants through a vineyard. But no matter how grand or intimate the occasion, it's this focus that centers a party and provides a much more eagerly anticipated occasion than simply "dinner."

A large part of the focus is, of course, the food. It goes without saying that the food should be delicious and satisfying, but I also think it should be something more: a conversation starter. Whether the edibles are unusual or unexpected, whether they're sinfully indulgent or surprisingly simple, food can be—and I think should be—not only a visceral, sacramental experience but also a uniting one. "And for dessert, we made our own miniature hot fudge sundaes, and everyone ate more than one!" is more fun, and more memorable, than another slice of fruit tart served on a plate.

I think the same holds true for wine. It should be an adventure, one tailored to the interests of your guests. That could be anything from a single rare bottle to a carefully constructed flight. It could be that I seek out a Tasmanian shiraz to serve to someone who I know loves Rhône wines, trying to unearth a new twist on an old favorite. With luck, the Tasmanian bottle may be delicious—but it also may be awful. And that's okay: That awful bottle doesn't mean an awful experience—no one died, we laughed about it, we learned something, and we moved on to a safe pinot noir. No matter what, we shared an experience.

To me, great parties and occasions have never been about having the perfect everything: china, crystal, glass, silver, invitations, flowers, décor, music, outfit. Even if you have these things available to you, when they are all added up in equal measure, they just don't make an occasion go "boom." My favorite occasions are made by knocking myself out for a few atmospheric effects and allowing the high energy of my guests to fill in where I did not.

I am not a passive participant in my parties, sitting in a corner and waiting for people to entertain me. I am constantly making introductions and connections, serving drinks and food, ring-leading and scene-setting. And I don't hesitate to ask my guests to make an effort as well. I find that when you ask them to come in a costume, bring a covered dish, recite poetry, sing songs, dance, or compete in a sporting event, the collective energy rewards us all with a huge return on the investment.

I can't say that nothing good ever comes to she who waits; I haven't enough experience with that approach to comment on it. But I have found that the rewards in my life have been multiplied exponentially by the thought and effort I've invested in earning them. This book is not about quick and easy anything. This is about making any occasion as grand as you would if it were the last thing you would ever do.

STEPHANIE VALENTINE

Breaking bread over long, leisurely meals is the best way I know to form lasting bonds with family and friends. Before we had the vineyard, I cooked every meal that was served in my home, including dinner parties for up to fifty people. But starting our Oak Savanna label, we entertained many more people much more often, and cooking became a full-time job.

Stephanie Valentine is the chef for Oak Savanna Vineyard. She is a graduate of the Culinary Institute of America and worked with Charlie Trotter for six years, and was then chef at the raw-food restaurant Roxanne's, before joining us. For every occasion in this book, the food was conceived and prepared by Stephanie. I can attest to the fact that these recipes are within the grasp of anyone who is enthusiastic and passionate about cooking.

There are two hard-and-fast rules that Stephanie follows when gathering her ingredients for any dish. First, she is uncompromising when it comes to the integrity of every ingredient she uses: Each is the freshest and finest she can find, and that often means it is from a local source. Of course, here in California we have a seemingly seasonless array of fruits, vegetables, meats, and fish to choose from, but nowadays, fine fresh local ingredients can be found in season all over the country. Second—and here's the twist—she is also super-flexible,

willing to tweak a dish or even reinvent a whole menu if she finds that a certain ingredient is not currently at its peak. I have noticed that Stephanie's favorite challenge seems to be finding herself cooking in a new and unfamiliar place, discovering the freshest ingredient in that location, and adapting an "old" recipe to create something new and local at the same time.

Tom and I would rather eat Stephanie's food than go to any restaurant in the world. It is that good. My favorite thing about Stephanie's style of cooking is that her approach to creating recipes and menus is so often irreverent, forcing me to look at the familiar in a whole new way. Sometimes I think she must have forgotten to read the chef's rule book: olive oil and salt ice cream; potato chips, truffles, and lobster; Mexican street food at fancy occasions; a quail egg stuffed inside a squab; savory herbs in desserts—whoever heard of such things?

Thanks to Stephanie's cooking, delicious surprises like these elevate every occasion at Rancho La Zaca. When you serve dishes like the ones she has created here, your guests, like mine, will know you cared enough to prepare something thoughtful, original, and interesting in their honor. And when your guests feel special, they can't help but have a good time. You'll all be left with unforgettable memories.

A NOTE ON THE WINE SELECTIONS

For the wine pairings in this book, I relied on the expertise of the sommelier Andrew Bradbury. When I first met him, he was running the wine cellar at Aureole in Las Vegas, considered one of the finest in the country. The reason it has that reputation is Andrew's maverick approach to wine pairing—although the "cellar angels," gorgeous showgirls in Lycra cat suits who are electronically hoisted with ropes up the glass-enclosed wine tower to retrieve wine bottles from the stacked bins, may also have swayed some of the critics. I will never forget our introduction: It was with the winemaker Andrew Murray, who organized a twelve-course tasting menu dinner at Aureole, with wine selections by Andrew Bradbury. For the first six courses, he brought exclusively Austrian and German rieslings to the table. With the next two courses, we had a viognier and a chardonnay. It was only during the last two savory dishes that reds were offered—one American and the other Italian. Then he took us right back to white grapes, with a pair of sweeties for dessert. Since then, we have called on Andrew often to help us with wine pairings at our own vineyard occasions.

Andrew's accomplishments are impressive. While collaborating on Aureole's multi-award-winning wine program, he also conceived, developed, and implemented Aureole's first-of-its-kind electronic wine list, Vinio, which enabled guests to survey the restaurant's vast wine list on a handheld touch-screen computer.

While he was wine director at Aureole, Bradbury also conceived and developed 55 Degrees Wine + Design, a visually stunning wine bar and retail shop, at Mandalay Place, Las Vegas. This gave wine enthusiasts of all tasting levels access to wines they may never have experienced. The concept redefined the wine bar, an innovation he has taken even further with his latest venture, Clō (in which I'm a partner), located at the Time Warner Center in New York. Clō provides guests with state-of-the-art technology, from smart cards to interactive tabletops that provide information on wines, tasting notes, and winemaker profiles.

Andrew's wine pairings are a great match for Stephanie's menus because he shares with her a mischievous sense of adventure, a total disregard for all the rules that just don't matter, and a deep reverence for the ones that do. I think guests appreciate interesting wine pairings much more than they do the predictable, or worse still, expensive wines selected just for the sake of making a big impression. The most important thing in making a wine selection is to let your guests know that you thought about the wine *and* about them when you made the choice. Sometimes, offering a bottle that didn't cost much but was brilliant with the food, or deciding to offer a varietal few have ever heard of—anything that even slightly puts convention on its ear—says exactly that. A flattered guest is always having a good time at your party!

About the Wine Notes

Throughout this book, in the "Wine Notes," Andrew recommends an array of wines to go with Stephanie's recipes. As you'll see and taste, the process of pairing wine with food is part art and part science. There are no hard-and-fast rules, but Andrew does have a few guidelines for successful pairings:

• In wine pairings, there are two schools of thought: On the one hand, you can choose a wine whose flavors and textures contrast with those of the dish. Many of the best contrasting pairings are in fact textural, as when you use a tannic red wine to cut the richness of braised or well-marbled meat. Another approach is to match the flavor and texture of the food with the wine. If you have, for example, a summer salad with a fruit component, something sharply acidic like sauvignon blanc not only matches the acidity in the salad but amplifies its fruitiness.

• In general, alcohol and tannin in wine will exaggerate spiciness and saltiness in food. You'll notice that in many of the Mexican-themed recipes Andrew selects wines with some residual sweetness and lower degrees of alcohol. Rather than turning up the heat, these mellower wines offer a cooling contrast. With very pungent, garlicky, spicy dishes, almost any wine will get stepped on; sometimes the best option is to pick something that will cleanse and refresh the palate but otherwise stay out of the way.

• A great starting point in any pairing is to consider the scale of the dish and select a wine of similar intensity. If the food is delicate, you're not likely to score with a rich, oaky wine, much as you might want to pull out the big guns for your special guests. Save the richer stuff for a more luxurious dish.

We have listed the names and vintages of the specific wines we had with every meal in this book, but in reality you may not be able to locate the exact bottles suggested. Not a big deal. Think of these wines as stylistic guideposts for your party-wine search, read our Wine Notes to get a better idea of what we considered as we made the selections, and talk to your own wine retailer about those points to help him zero in on the perfect selection for you and your guests.

WEDDING PICNIC

Steamed Salmon with Nasturtium Mayonnaise

Asparagus, Artichokes, and Cèpes

Butter Sandwiches on Kalamata Kumquat Bread

Sweet, Salty, and Fragrant Panna Cotta

THE BRIDE'S FAVORITE COOKIES AND CANDIES:

Mexican Wedding Cookies

Coyotes

Caramels

IT WAS WHEN WE WERE PLANNING OUR WEDDING THAT WE FELL DEEPLY IN LOVE
with the Santa Ynez Valley. We had owned the ranch for less than a year, and even
though I was raised near San Francisco, I knew very little about this part of the state.
As I always do when I'm embarking on a big creative project, I looked first to history
for my inspiration. It didn't take much digging before I discovered that there was a tradition here, dating back to colonial times, of fantastic, over-the-top parties, and an
exuberant indigenous entertaining style.

Robert Isabell, the great New York florist and party planner (and a longtime friend
of mine), had already volunteered to "do" my wedding, and when I showed him accounts
of such historic events, we both agreed that this occasion just had to be inspired by
the Alta-Californio *rancho* style. We decided that it would be a mix of formal and outdoors elements: a proper church wedding followed by an elegant picnic luncheon.

Dressing for the occasion would be easy for me and my bridesmaids: I already
owned a tall tortoiseshell *mantilla* comb (an impulsive flea market purchase), and a call
to a friend who dances flamenco as a hobby put me onto a resource for a traditional lace
veil and more hair combs for the attendants, all of whom I otherwise asked to "just wear
dresses, long, Spanishy, and red." But I will admit that I was more than a little surprised
when Tom confessed that he'd always wanted a cowboy outfit. Throwing himself into
the spirit, he took our two grown sons to a tailor known for making elegant Spanish suits
and ordered flat hats, embroidered jackets, pants with silver *conchas* and chains down
the legs, and spurs with jingle bobs. Clearly, in Tom, I had met my match.

The ceremony was in a charming little chapel nearby, a state historic landmark built
in 1875. Afterwards, back at Rancho La Zaca, we proceeded on foot, by horseback, and
in horse-drawn carts up a hilly dirt road to a field of wildflowers we had planted just for
this occasion. It was our only décor, other than pillows and cloths strewn under the
craggy old oaks. A small orchestra performed the traditional music of the Californios.
Our guests lounged in the tall grass until well after the poppies had closed up for the day.

At our wedding, like other people do, we merged our lives, our families, and our
interests. We also discovered how much we love giving parties together. Our Spanish
forebears had it right: Include family and friends, hold it outdoors whenever possible,
serve the best food and wine you can, and whether accompanied by music or not,
always keep it spirited. Kick up your heels anytime. It's a fandango.

Steamed Salmon
with Nasturtium Mayonnaise

Nasturtiums are sunny and colorful annuals that often grow wild in the salad garden. The peppery flavor of their petals is tamed in this mayonnaise sauce, and their exuberant color is toned down to a sublime shade of saffron—a chic accessory to salmon pink. To make the banana leaves easy to handle, pass them quickly over an open flame until the color changes slightly from flat to bright green.

makes 4 servings

FOR THE SALMON

One 1 to 1¼-pound skinless salmon fillet

¾ to 1 teaspoon salt

¼ teaspoon freshly ground white pepper

8 very thin lemon slices, seeds removed

4 teaspoons extra virgin olive oil

Five 8½ x 12-inch sections of banana leaves (see Resources)

FOR THE NASTURTIUM MAYONNAISE

1 large egg yolk

1 tablespoon fresh lemon juice

1 teaspoon finely grated lemon zest

1 teaspoon red wine vinegar

Pinch of sea salt

⅓ cup extra virgin olive oil

½ cup grapeseed oil

2 cups nasturtium petals, loosely packed

1 tablespoon thinly sliced chives

MAKE THE SALMON: Make sure that the brown "skin" has been removed as part of the skinning and trimming process. Cut the fillet crosswise into four 4- to 5-ounce portions. Prepare a steamer. Season the salmon with the salt and white pepper and lay 2 slices of lemon on each portion. Lay out the banana leaves with the short side facing you, like a sheet of paper. Place 1 piece of salmon about 1½ to 2 inches up from the bottom and centered in the middle of 4 of the banana leaves, and drizzle each with 1 teaspoon of the olive oil. Fold the sides over the salmon and press down the edges. Fold the bottom over the top, and wrap the salmon firmly, but not too tightly. Tie the package with a strip torn from the remaining banana leaf.

Steam very gently, over water that is just barely simmering, for 5 minutes (this will vary depending on the thickness of the salmon).

MAKE THE NASTURTIUM MAYONNAISE: In a blender, combine the egg yolk, lemon juice, zest, 1 tablespoon of water, the vinegar, and salt. Pulse for a few seconds to combine. While the blender is running, slowly add the olive and grapeseed oils in a thin, steady stream. Once all the oils are emulsified, add the nasturtium petals and chives and pulse for a few seconds until just combined. The mayonnaise can be prepared up to 2 days in advance and refrigerated.

Unwrap the salmon and spoon a tablespoon or two of the mayonnaise on top. Rewrap loosely in the banana leaf and tie. The salmon may also be removed from the leaf and plated with the sauce.

LEFT: Butter Sandwiches
on Kalamata Kumquat Bread

ABOVE: Salmon steamed in a banana leaf and
topped with Nasturtium Mayonnaise

Asparagus, Artichokes, and Cèpes

Salmon is often paired with asparagus. Sometimes artichokes. Occasionally wild mushrooms. So, this dish is a combination of all three of the classic accompaniments. For our wedding dinner these were placed in a picnic basket in parchment paper cones. For a plated dinner, arrange the accompaniments to the side of the salmon.

makes 4 servings

3 large artichokes, leaves and stems removed

Juice of ½ lemon

1 teaspoon sea salt

1 pound thin asparagus, trimmed

4 ounces cèpes

1½ tablespoons extra virgin olive oil

1 small shallot, minced

1 garlic clove, minced

1 teaspoon lemon juice

1 tablespoon chopped parsley

⅛ teaspoon freshly ground black pepper

Place the artichokes in a large saucepan and add water to cover. Add the lemon juice and ½ teaspoon of the salt and cover the artichokes with a paper towel or clean kitchen towel to keep them submerged. Bring to a simmer over medium heat, then reduce the heat to low and simmer until cooked through, 15 to 20 minutes. Remove the artichokes from the liquid and allow them to cool. Remove the choke from the artichokes and cut each heart into 8 wedges.

In a large saucepan of boiling water, blanch the asparagus for 30 seconds; refresh under cold running water and drain. Clean the cèpes and slice them if they are large.

In a large sauté pan, heat the olive oil over high heat. Add the cèpes and shake to coat with the oil. Cook until they begin to get some color, about 3 minutes. Add the artichokes and continue to cook for an additional 3 minutes over high heat. Add the asparagus, shallot, and garlic and heat through. Stir in the lemon juice, parsley, the remaining ½ teaspoon salt, and the black pepper.

Butter Sandwiches on Kalamata Kumquat Bread

You won't find a lot of recipes for butter sandwiches. But a butter sandwich is really about the bread, and this bread is one of the more spectacular loaves that'll ever come out of your oven. For the filling, be sure to use the highest-quality European-style butter you can find, such as Plugrá. And be amazed at how such a simple sandwich could be so delicious.

makes about 10 sandwiches

1 package (1 tablespoon) fast-acting yeast

3½ cups all-purpose flour, plus additional for kneading

¾ cup whole wheat flour

½ cup plus 2 tablespoons cornmeal

2 teaspoons sea salt

2 teaspoons sugar

1¾ cups whole milk

2 tablespoons unsalted butter

¾ cup chopped kalamata olives

½ cup chopped preserved kumquats (page 129, as prepared for terrine)

3 tablespoons chopped mixed herbs, such as sage, rosemary, and oregano

8 to 12 ounces (2 to 3 sticks) high-quality unsalted butter, preferably Plugrá, for the sandwiches

In a large bowl, combine the yeast, flours, cornmeal, salt, and sugar, and stir together. Warm the milk with the 2 tablespoons of butter to 115°F, then add to the flour mixture. Stir with a wooden spoon until it becomes too difficult, then add the olives, kumquats, and herbs. Start kneading by hand. When the dough comes together, turn it out onto a clean surface and knead until elastic, 5 to 8 minutes. Cover the dough and allow to rest for 10 minutes. Divide the dough into ten portions and form into balls. Press the balls into 7 x 1½-inch rectangles, then roll each rectangle into a cylinder, pressing the ends under. Place on a baking sheet. Make 3 diagonal slits with a very sharp paring knife or razor. Let the dough rise until it has doubled in size, about 25 minutes.

Bake at 400°F for 10 minutes. Reduce the oven temperature to 350°F and bake for an additional 18 minutes. Let cool.

Break the bread open lengthwise and slather with 2 to 3 tablespoons of the high-quality butter. Wrap in parchment paper and repeat with the remaining individual loaves.

Sweet, Salty, and Fragrant Panna Cotta

Panna cotta is a fancy term for milk gelatin. It is simple, lightly sweet, and utterly divine.

makes 4 servings

2 teaspoons gelatin	2 lavender sprigs
½ cup plus 2 tablespoons sugar	1 thyme sprig
½ cup heavy cream	1½ teaspoons fennel seeds, toasted and crushed
2 teaspoons finely grated lemon zest	
2 cups whole milk	⅛ teaspoon sea salt
2 mint sprigs	4 medium navel oranges

In a small bowl, dissolve the gelatin in ⅓ cup warm water. In a small saucepan, combine the gelatin, ½ cup of the sugar, the cream, zest, milk, mint, lavender, thyme, and fennel seeds. Warm over medium heat until steaming. Remove the pan from the heat and let sit for about 30 minutes so the flavor of the herbs infuses the cream mixture. Pour through a fine-mesh strainer into a medium bowl and stir in the salt.

Slice a quarter off the top of each orange and reserve this "lid." Cut around the inside of each orange to loosen the flesh, then pull it out. Get between the pith and flesh with your fingernail (or the edge of a spoon) and carefully remove all of the flesh. Be careful not to crack or break the skin in any places or to make any holes. Squeeze all of the juice from the orange flesh and lids, working over a fine-mesh strainer into a small saucepan. Add the remaining 2 tablespoons of sugar. Cook over low heat until reduced to a syrup, about 2 tablespoons.

Place the hollowed-out oranges in a shallow baking dish so they sit upright and are ready to fill. Pour about ½ cup of the orange mixture into each orange shell, and refrigerate until set, 3 hours or overnight. Top with the reduced orange juice and serve.

Mexican Wedding Cookies

These cookies are small, so you eat them whole, in one bite. You won't stop at one, because they are so light and delicate that they just melt in your mouth. When you toast the nuts, make sure to use a low oven, around 300°F, to help toast them evenly all the way through.

makes 50 cookies

Generous ½ cup whole raw almonds, toasted

Generous ½ cup pecan halves, toasted

1¼ cups (2½ sticks) unsalted butter, cold and cut into pieces

¼ cup plus 1 tablespoon confectioners' sugar, plus more for dusting

2½ cups all-purpose flour

2 teaspoons anise seeds

½ teaspoon sea salt

Preheat the oven to 325°F. Line 2 baking sheets with parchment paper.

In a food processor, combine the ground almonds and pecans and grind to a fine meal, 2 to 3 minutes. Add the butter and blend until a paste forms, 1 to 2 minutes. Add ¼ cup plus 1 tablespoon of the sugar and blend until combined. Add the flour, anise seeds, and salt, and mix well. With floured hands, roll the dough into very small balls, using about 1 teaspoon of dough apiece. Place on the prepared baking sheets. Bake until golden brown, 15 to 20 minutes. Let cool for about 10 minutes, then roll in confectioners' sugar to cover lightly. The cookies can be prepared 2 days in advance and stored in an airtight container.

Coyotes

These are little buttery sandwich cookies, lightly scented with orange and filled with *cajeta*, a sweetened cow's or goat's milk that has been slowly caramelized into a thick syrup. It is available at most Hispanic markets.

makes about 24 cookies

½ cup (1 stick) unsalted butter, softened

1 teaspoon finely grated orange zest

⅓ cup plus ¼ cup confectioners' sugar, sifted, plus more for dusting

½ teaspoon pure vanilla extract

¼ teaspoon sea salt

1¼ cups all-purpose flour

1 cup goat's milk *cajeta* or cow's milk *cajeta*

In a standing mixer, cream the butter, zest, and sugar until light and fluffy. Add the vanilla and salt and combine. Add the flour and mix until well combined. Roll the dough into 1-inch-diameter logs and refrigerate for 1 hour.

Preheat the oven to 325°F. Line 2 baking sheets with parchment paper.

Slice the logs crosswise into ⅛-inch disks and place on the prepared baking sheets. Bake until just beginning to brown on the bottom, 10 to 12 minutes. Let cool before filling.

Spread about ¼ teaspoon of the cajeta on the underside of a cookie and sandwich with another cookie. Repeat with the remaining cookies until all are filled. Dust with confectioners' sugar to serve. The cookies can be prepared and filled 2 days in advance and stored in an airtight container.

Mexican Wedding Cookies

Caramels

Of course, you could buy caramels of some ilk at any candy shop. But these homemade caramels are softer and richer, they don't stick in your teeth, and they're simply irresistible. They're especially charming in their little wax paper wrappings.

makes about 100 tiny caramels

¼ cup (½ stick) unsalted butter, plus more for greasing the pan

1 cup granulated sugar

½ cup light brown sugar

½ cup light corn syrup

¾ cup heavy cream

¾ cup whole milk

1 tablespoon pure vanilla extract

⅔ cup walnut halves, toasted and chopped

Line a 9 x 5-inch pan with foil and grease generously with butter.

In a large heavy saucepan, combine the sugars, corn syrup, cream, milk, and the remaining ¼ cup of butter. Cook over low heat, stirring, until the sugars are dissolved. Raise the heat to medium and cook until the mixture reaches 242°F on a candy thermometer. For softer caramels, cook the mixture to 240°F; for firmer caramels cook to 244°F. Remove the pan from the heat and stir in the vanilla and chopped walnuts. Immediately pour this into the prepared pan and let cool. Caramels do not need to be refrigerated, but they are easier to cut if slightly chilled.

Cut into ½-inch squares and wrap in 4 x 3½-inch sheets of wax paper. The caramels can be prepared a week in advance and refrigerated.

WINE NOTES

Pinot Gris, Adelsheim Vineyards, 2005 (Oregon)
Viognier, Sanford & Benedict, Cold Heaven, 2005 (Santa Barbara, California)

There is some richness in this menu (salmon, butter sandwiches) along with some elements that can be anathema to wine (artichokes, asparagus). One of the qualities of good Oregon pinot gris is its combination of delicate, slightly floral aromas with a well-rounded, almost oily, texture.

With an oily fish like salmon you're wise to choose a white with some heft, but with all those assertive accompaniments you'll appreciate the clean flavors of pinot gris.

The nasturtium in the mayonnaise calls for something a little more aromatic, and viognier is one of the only wines known to lessen the bittering effect of artichokes and asparagus. The best viogniers have a magical combination of big fruit and a whiff of earthy smoke, and even when we tried the salmon with Cold Heaven's 2005, all of the fragrant-yet-earthy elements of the wine were on full display.

RANCHO LA ZACA

California was claimed by Spain in 1542, just fifty years after Columbus landed safely in Central America, but Alta California was not occupied by the Spanish until 1769. Planetary convergence triggered the settlement of Alta California: The Pacific Coast was one of the best places in the world from which to view a rare transit of Venus across the sun. Eighteenth-century astronomers believed this celestial phenomenon would give them important information that could be used to precisely calculate the distance between Earth and the Sun, a number so valuable that scientists risked their lives traveling around the world to ascertain it. Spain mistrusted the intentions of the visiting foreigners, even though the land was considered worthless, so Catholic missionaries were dispatched from Mexico to rapidly colonize the state from south to north.

Using local Indian labor, twenty-one mission settlements were built between 1769 and 1823, and the land, while still owned by the Spanish crown, was available for anyone to use during this pastoral period. Plots large and small were surveyed on horseback, typically using a fifty-foot riata to measure boundaries. Land grant sizes were approximate, and basically unimportant. There were no fences; at that time, a man's wealth was measured in cattle.

The La Zaca grant was awarded in 1838 to the Indian Antonino. It was distinguished as the first in the Santa Ynez Valley, and of the hundreds of land grants Mexico awarded in Alta California, it was also one of the smallest. La Zaca was located in the heart of Santa Barbara County, and it is believed that Antonino used it to graze a flock of sheep. He would not be the only *ranchero* to make a living this way: Benjamin Foxen's Rancho Tinaquiac grant was located just north of La Zaca on the *camino* that would later become known as Foxen Canyon Road.

The California Gold Rush of 1849, the conquest of Alta California by General John Fremont (in which Benjamin Foxen is supposed to have played a crucial role), and California statehood, which was fast-tracked in 1850, forced a change in ownership of many of the Spanish/Mexican land grant ranches. Some families who had held property for several generations were forced to produce proof of ownership on the spot to U.S. marshals anxious to seize properties on which they believed gold might be found. La Zaca was spared such a hostile takeover. By 1890, small parcels of it were being offered for sale, but this development scheme seems to have failed. About ten years later, the parcel was bisected, using the line of the stage road that diagonally halved the square 4,458 acres as the new property line.

The western, hilly half of Rancho La Zaca was intact until the late 1970s, when it was divided into four smaller lots, one of which is the site of our modern-day ranch and vineyard. The eastern half of the original grant is known by its anglicized name, Zaca Ranch. It is comprised of a flat mesa incised on the far boundary by a spring-fed creek that originates five miles away at Zaca Lake, the largest natural lake in all of Southern California.

RELEASING A NEW VINTAGE

Crayfish Risotto

LAMB THREE WAYS:

Grilled Rack of Lamb with Kuri Squash and Rainbow Chard

Braised Lamb Ribs and Shoulder with Hominy

Spice-Roasted Leg of Lamb with Wild Mushrooms

Point Reyes Blue Cheese with Cherry, Rose, and
Crushed Tellicherry Peppercorns

Bittersweet Chocolate Cake with Oaxacan Mole Sorbet
and Muscovado Ice Cream

EVEN THOUGH WE HAVE OWNED THE VINEYARD FOR A FEW YEARS NOW, RELEASING a new vintage still brings on a variation of opening night jitters. And this year the occasion was doubly daunting. The new wine was very different from any other we had produced: a blended super-red, which is considered the ultimate expression of the art of winemaking, and it was Andrew Murray's first attempt at such a masterwork. The fruit had been grown to Andrew's exacting specifications, and from vine to barrel each step of the winemaking had gone according to plan. Now all that was left to do was to create a fitting and grand debut, accompanied by fine food and an audience of good friends.

One Thousand Hills, as the wine is known, was the inspiration for this intimate wine-tasting dinner for twelve people dining outdoors among the very vines from which it was made. Assembling a group of discerning critics was important to both Andrew and me—we wanted to share the wine with friends who were articulate and conversational in food-and-wine speak, and comfortable enough with us to give their honest opinions.

We started with sample bottles of one of our white wines with the first course, then shifted into full gear with the new red for the duration of the meal. In Stephanie's typically thorough and well-researched way, her menu struck every flavor note in perfect harmony with the new vintage: lamb three ways, a cheese course that required eating with the fingers, and finally a decadent chocolate dessert. I will confess that I have never had a "chocolate tooth." But now that it was bittersweet, spiced like mole, and paired with red wine, this course received my standing ovation.

Considering the wine first and building a menu around it is an approach I am resolved to take more often, even when we are not debuting a vintage of ours. We could have just as much fun doing a similar taste test with any of the extraordinary and unusual bottles we have received as gifts from friends. The key is to serve a variety of food flavors—savory, meaty, acid, spicy—to invite experimentation in matching food to the wines.

Crayfish Risotto

This fresh, light course is paired with a lightly aged Oak Savanna Sauvignon Blanc that has some oakiness in it. The "oak" theme continues with an oak-smoked bacon in the olive relish and the risotto is garnished with a fresh herb and crispy fried shallot salad. You can substitute prawns or shrimp for the crayfish; you will want about five small crayfish or shrimp per serving.

makes 12 servings as an appetizer

5 tablespoons unsalted butter

1 small yellow onion, finely diced

1 garlic clove, minced

2 cups arborio or other short-grain rice

1 cup Oak Savanna Chardonnay or other high-quality chardonnay

3 cups low-sodium canned chicken stock

1 recipe Crayfish and Broth (recipe follows)

2 tablespoons grated Pecorino Romano cheese

1¾ teaspoons sea salt

½ teaspoon freshly ground black pepper

1 tablespoon minced chives or parsley

1 cup grapeseed oil

¼ cup all-purpose flour

¼ teaspoon hot paprika

1 cup thinly sliced shallot rounds (about 8 shallots)

2 loosely packed cups mixed soft herbs such as tarragon, salad burnet, nasturtium leaves, nasturtium flowers, calendula flower petals, basil, mint, and bronze fennel

¼ teaspoon fresh lemon juice

¼ teaspoon extra virgin olive oil

¾ cup Bacon and Olive Relish (recipe follows)

In a medium saucepan, melt 3 tablespoons of the butter over medium heat. Add the onion and garlic and sauté until translucent, about 2 minutes. Add the rice and stir to coat with the butter for about 30 seconds. Reduce the heat to medium-low and stir in the chardonnay. When the chardonnay is mostly absorbed, begin adding the chicken stock and 2 cups of the crayfish broth in half-cup increments as each addition of liquid is absorbed, continuing to stir gently, for 18 to 25 minutes (depending on the type of rice you are using). The rice is done when tender and the risotto is the consistency of a loose porridge.

Remove from the heat and vigorously stir in the remaining 2 tablespoons of butter, the cheese, 1 teaspoon of the salt, ¼ teaspoon of the black pepper, and the chives or parsley.

In a medium saucepan, combine the remaining 2 cups crayfish broth and the crayfish tails and heat gently over low heat while you prepare the fried shallots. In a medium saucepan, heat the grapeseed oil over high heat until it reaches 350°F. In a medium bowl, mix the flour, paprika, ½ teaspoon of the salt, and ⅛ teaspoon of the black pepper. Toss the sliced shallots in the flour mixture, then remove to a sifter to shake off the excess flour. Fry until golden brown, about 2 minutes. Drain on paper towels and let cool slightly. Toss the fried shallots with the 2 cups of mixed herbs, the lemon juice, olive oil, and the remaining ¼ teaspoon of salt, and ⅛ teaspoon of black pepper.

Spoon about ½ cup of risotto into each of 12 bowls. Divide the crayfish tails (about 5 each) among the bowls, and ladle a spoonful of broth over each serving. Top with 1 tablespoon of the Bacon and Olive Relish and 2 to 4 tablespoons of the shallot salad.

Crayfish and Broth

FOR THE CRAYFISH

1 tablespoon black peppercorns

4 bay leaves

1 tablespoon fennel seeds

1 tablespoon mustard seeds

4 whole cloves

2 tablespoons sea salt

3 tablespoons white wine vinegar or
  rice wine vinegar

½ yellow onion, sliced

1 celery stalk, sliced

1 carrot, sliced

4 pounds whole crayfish
  (about 60; see Resources)

FOR THE BROTH

Reserved crayfish heads

2 tablespoons grapeseed oil

1 small yellow onion, sliced

1 celery stalk, sliced

1 carrot, sliced

1 tablespoon tomato paste

¾ cup Oak Savanna Chardonnay,
  or other high-quality chardonnay

6 cups low-sodium canned chicken stock
  or water

MAKE THE CRAYFISH: In a stockpot, combine all the ingredients except the crayfish with 4 gallons of water. Bring to a boil, reduce the heat to low, and simmer for 15 minutes. Add the crayfish. Cook over low heat until they are cooked through, about 7 minutes. Drain and cool the crayfish.

Remove the heads by twisting and pulling gently to separate the tail meat; reserve the heads for the broth. Crack open the tail shells with your fingers and pull out the tail meat. Discard the tail shells.

MAKE THE BROTH: Place the reserved crayfish heads in a food processor and pulse for 10 to 15 seconds to break up the shells.

Heat a large heavy-bottomed saucepan over medium-high heat and add the oil, onion, celery, and carrot. Cook until slightly browned, 5 to 8 minutes. Add the tomato paste and cook for 1 minute. Stir in the crushed crayfish shells and add the chardonnay. Cover the shells with chicken broth or water and bring to a simmer. Simmer for 30 minutes, skimming off the foam. Pour through a fine-mesh strainer. Set aside 2 cups of the broth for the risotto. Separately set aside the remaining broth and the crayfish while you prepare the risotto. The broth and crayfish can be prepared a day in advance and refrigerated separately.

Olive and Bacon Relish

4 slices artisanal smoked bacon
  (see Resources), sliced into ¼-inch pieces

2 garlic cloves, minced

2 small shallots, minced

24 high-quality French green olives such as
  picholine, pitted and sliced lengthwise

1 tablespoon chopped mixed herbs such as
  parsley, chives, tarragon, and thyme

2 teaspoons fresh lemon juice

2 tablespoons top-quality extra virgin olive oil

½ teaspoon sea salt

¼ teaspoon freshly ground black pepper

In a small sauté pan, cook the bacon over medium-low heat until just crisp and most of the fat has melted, about 15 minutes. Drain all but 2 tablespoons of the fat from the pan. Add the garlic and shallots and cook for 2 minutes. Stir in the olives, herbs, lemon juice, and olive oil. Heat through for 2 minutes, season with the salt and pepper, and remove from the heat. The relish can be prepared up to 3 days in advance and refrigerated. Reheat gently before serving.

LAMB THREE WAYS

Each of the three different cuts of lamb pulls out different flavors of the One Thousand Hills wine. For this special dinner, we served all three cuts, with their accompaniments, on one plate, to compare how the wine held up to the different flavors of the meal—we were testing the wine's pairing abilities. If you want to try the same tasting-menu approach to the entrée to serve a party of ten or twelve, see page 32 for special plating suggestions using all three lambs and their accompaniments. But if you want to make just one of these lamb dishes, any of the three is fantastic.

Grilled Rack of Lamb with Kuri Squash and Rainbow Chard

This is the lightest, herbiest of our trio of lamb recipes for the new-vintage dinner. Many rack-of-lamb preparations include herbs, often in a crust, but here the herbs are just pressed onto the meat. Be sure to bruise and crush the herbs in your hands, releasing their oils and fragrance, before patting them onto the racks.

makes 4 servings

2 half-racks of lamb (16 chops total), chine bones removed and frenched

6 tablespoons extra virgin olive oil

1 teaspoon freshly cracked black pepper

8 oregano sprigs, crushed by hand

1 bunch thyme, crushed by hand

6 rosemary sprigs, crushed by hand

1 bunch sage, crushed by hand

2 teaspoons sea salt

1 recipe Roasted Red Kuri Squash Puree (recipe follows)

1 recipe Braised Swiss Chard (recipe follows)

1 cup Red Wine Sauce (recipe follows)

Marinate the lamb by rubbing with the olive oil, pepper, and herbs. Place in a 1-gallon zip-top bag and refrigerate at least 4 hours, or overnight. Remove the lamb from the refrigerator half an hour before grilling.

Preheat the grill to medium-high. Season the lamb with the salt and grill, fat side down, first. If the bones start to get too brown, cover them tightly with foil. Grill the lamb for 10 minutes per side for medium rare, until a meat thermometer inserted into the thickest part of the meat measures 140°–145°F.

Remove to a cutting board and allow the meat to rest for 5 minutes before cutting. Spoon about ½ cup of squash on each of four plates, and place the ¼ cup of braised chard on top of the squash. Cut the racks into individual chops, then fan 4 onto each plate. Spoon about 2 tablespoons of the wine sauce over the lamb and serve.

Roasted Red Kuri Squash Puree

makes 2 cups

1 small red kuri squash (also known as orange Hokkaido)

3 teaspoons extra virgin olive oil

½ teaspoon sea salt

⅛ teaspoon freshly ground black pepper

Preheat the oven to 400°F.

Cut the squash into 4 pieces, rub the cut sides with the olive oil, and sprinkle with the salt and black pepper. Place, cut side down, on a sheet pan with sides. Add water to ¼-inch deep, and place the pan in the oven. Roast until very tender, about 40 minutes. Remove from the oven and peel off the skin. In a food processor, puree until creamy and smooth. This may be done early in the day or a day ahead, and reheated in a small pan over low heat.

Braised Swiss Chard

makes 1 cup

1 bunch (about 1 pound) Swiss chard, stems removed and leaves sliced into ½-inch pieces

2 tablespoons extra virgin olive oil

1 small yellow onion, halved lengthwise then cut lengthwise into ⅛-inch slices

1 garlic clove, thinly sliced

1 tablespoon unsalted butter

½ teaspoon sea salt

⅛ teaspoon freshly ground black pepper

Wash the chard in a large bowl of water. Remove from the water but do not dry it well—the water is a part of the cooking process.

Preheat a medium sauté pan over medium heat. Add the olive oil, onion, and garlic and sauté until starting to brown lightly, about 2 minutes. Add the chard and cook until tender, 10 to 15 minutes, adding water if needed. Remove from the heat and stir in the butter, salt, and black pepper. The chard can be prepared a day in advance and refrigerated. Reheat gently before serving.

Red Wine Sauce

makes 2 cups

This recipe makes more than you'll need for the lamb, but the sauce freezes well for other uses.

1 tablespoon grapeseed oil

½ yellow onion, finely diced

½ carrot, finely diced

1 tablespoon tomato paste

1½ cups red wine

4 cups Veal Stock (recipe follows)

½ to 1 teaspoon sea salt

⅛ teaspoon freshly ground black pepper

In a small saucepan, heat the oil over medium heat. Add the onion and carrot and cook until caramelized, stirring often, about 10 minutes. Add the tomato paste and cook for 1 minute, stirring. Carefully—and away from the heat—add the wine. Reduce the heat to medium-low and simmer until reduced by half, 15 to 20 minutes. Add the stock. Bring to a simmer, then cook until reduced by half, 40 minutes to 1 hour, skimming off the foam. Pour through a fine-mesh strainer and season with the salt and black pepper. The red wine sauce can be prepared up to 3 days in advance and refrigerated. It can be frozen for up to 3 months. Reheat gently before serving.

Veal Stock

makes 8 cups

2 tablespoons grapeseed oil

5 pounds veal knuckle bones, split or cut into 2-inch pieces

1 medium yellow onion, cut into 1-inch pieces

1 medium carrot, cut into 1-inch pieces

1 celery stalk, cut into 1-inch pieces

1 head garlic, cut in half horizontally

1 plum tomato, seeded and quartered

1 tablespoon tomato paste

1 cup red wine

Preheat the oven to 425°F.

Lightly oil a roasting pan large enough to hold the veal bones in a single layer. Place the empty roasting pan in the oven until it is very hot, about 8 minutes. Spread the bones in the

pan in a single layer and roast them until dark golden brown, about 2½ hours, turning throughout to brown all sides.

Transfer the bones to an 8-quart stockpot. Pour off any fat from the roasting pan and add the onion, carrot, celery, and garlic. Return to the oven and roast the vegetables until they are browned, about 25 minutes. Add the tomato and tomato paste to the pan, stir, and continue roasting for 10 minutes. Add the red wine, stir, and allow to simmer in the oven for 10 minutes.

Remove the pan from the oven and add the contents to the stockpot. Add 1 cup of water to the roasting pan, scraping up any browned bits from the bottom of the pan. Add to the stockpot with enough water to cover the bones by 3 inches (about 4 quarts). Bring the water to a boil, reduce the heat, and simmer, uncovered, for 8 hours, skimming off the foam. Add water as needed to keep the bones and vegetables covered throughout.

Pour the liquid through a fine-mesh strainer into a large saucepan without pressing, but tapping, to extract all of the juices. Skim off any fat or refrigerate overnight and remove the congealed fat. Use as needed and freeze any leftover stock for other uses.

Braised Lamb Ribs and Shoulder with Hominy

Lamb ribs are not unusual—all lambs have ribs—but they are not a part of the animal that Americans often eat, so they are not sold at most grocery stores; ask your butcher to order rib racks for you. Just as satisfying to gnaw on as pork and beef ribs, these are especially so, with their hint of Southwestern spice.

makes 4 servings

2 tablespoons extra virgin olive oil

1 pound boneless lamb shoulder,
    cut into 1-inch cubes

2 racks (about 4 pounds total) of lamb ribs,
    cut into 4 pieces

1½ teaspoons sea salt

½ teaspoon freshly ground black pepper

1 small yellow onion, cut into medium dice

1 carrot, cut into 3 x ¼-inch sticks

1 celery stalk, cut into 3-inch lengths

4 garlic cloves, peeled

4 plum tomatoes, chopped

1 dried guajillo chile or other medium-heat chile,
    halved, seeded, and stemmed

1 dried ancho chile, halved, seeded, and
    stemmed

3 cups low-sodium canned chicken stock

3 cups Veal Stock (page 28)

1 cinnamon stick

3 tablespoons sugar

2 tablespoons rice wine vinegar

1½ cups cooked hominy (see Resources)

1 tablespoon unsalted butter

Preheat the oven to 300°F.

Heat 2 medium ovenproof straight-sided sauté pans over high heat and add 1 tablespoon of the oil to each. Season all of the lamb with 1 teaspoon of the salt and ¼ teaspoon of the black pepper. Sear in the 2 pans on all sides over high heat. Remove the lamb from the pans and add half of the onion, carrot, and celery to each pan. Cook until caramelized, about 7 minutes.

Add the shoulder meat to 1 pan and the ribs to the other. Add half the garlic, tomatoes, guajillo and ancho chiles, chicken broth, veal stock, and cinnamon stick to each pan. Bring to a simmer, then transfer to the oven. Braise, covered, until the meat is fork-tender and comes away from the bone, about 2 hours.

Remove the meat from the liquid. Pour the liquid through a fine-mesh strainer. In a large saucepan, combine the chiles and tomatoes with the strained liquid (discard the carrot, onion, and celery). Add the sugar and vinegar. Set over medium-high heat and simmer the liquid, skimming off the fat occasionally, until reduced to about 2 cups, about 30 minutes. Let cool slightly, then puree the liquid in a blender.

Preheat the grill to high, or the oven to 400°F.

In a serving bowl, shred the shoulder meat. Stir 1 cup of the puree into the shoulder meat. Brush the ribs with the remaining 1 cup of puree. Grill them over high heat, just to heat through, before serving, or reheat in the oven for 10 minutes.

In a small saucepan, warm the hominy with the butter, and the remaining ½ teaspoon of salt, and ¼ teaspoon of black pepper. Divide the hominy among four plates and spoon the shredded shoulder meat on top. Place a half lamb rack on the shoulder meat and serve.

Spice-Roasted Leg of Lamb with Wild Mushrooms

This seasoning blend is similar to a Chinese five-spice combination, with strong notes of star anise and cinnamon. When tying the lamb, don't bind the string too tight, as cramping the meat will force out precious juices as the roast expands during cooking. Still, tie it in a tidy way, which will help you slice it into neat, attractive pieces.

makes 4 servings

1 tablespoon black peppercorns

1 cinnamon stick

1 star anise pod

1 teaspoon coriander seeds

1 teaspoon anise seeds

¼ teaspoon fennel seeds

One 2-pound boneless leg of lamb

2 teaspoons salt

2 tablespoons grapeseed oil

2 cups Wild Mushroom Sauté (recipe follows)

1 cup Red Wine Sauce (page 28)

In a medium heavy-bottomed skillet toast all the spices over low heat, until they start to color and the aroma is released, 2 to 3 minutes. Grind the spices together. Spread out the lamb and rub the spice mix all over it. Roll the lamb into a 2-inch-diameter log and tie it at 1-inch intervals. Let marinate in the refrigerator in a 1-gallon zip-top bag for several hours or overnight.

A half hour before cooking, remove the lamb from the refrigerator and preheat the oven to 350°F.

Preheat a large heavy-bottomed skillet over high heat. Season the lamb with the salt. Add the oil to the skillet and sear the lamb on all sides. Transfer to a roasting pan and roast in the oven until the internal temperature is 130°F, 35 to 45 minutes. Remove from the oven and let rest for 5 to 10 minutes. Divide the sautéed mushrooms among four plates. Cut the lamb into ¼-inch slices on the bias and arrange over the mushrooms. Spoon about 2 tablespoons of the wine sauce over the lamb.

Wild Mushroom Sauté

3 tablespoons grapeseed oil

1 ½ pounds wild mushrooms (see Resources),
   tough stems trimmed

1 shallot, minced

1 garlic clove, minced

½ teaspoon sea salt

¼ teaspoon freshly ground black pepper

1 tablespoon minced parsley

1 tablespoon finely sliced chives

1 teaspoon minced thyme

½ teaspoon minced rosemary

In a large sauté pan, heat the oil. Add the mushrooms, shake the pan to loosen the mushrooms, and let them cook over high heat, stirring, until they are golden, 2 to 3 minutes. Stir in the shallot and garlic and cook 1 minute. Add the salt, black pepper, parsley, chives, thyme, and rosemary and toss to mix.

The Three Lambs, Plated

Slice the grilled rack into single chops. Cut the leg of lamb into ¼-inch slices on the bias. Keep warm loosely covered with foil.

Place 2 tablespoons of the cooked hominy mixture at the top right of the plate and spoon 2 tablespoons of the shredded lamb shoulder on top. Place 2 grilled ribs over the top of the shoulder meat. Place 1 tablespoon of the squash and 1 tablespoon of the chard at the top left of the plate, and 1 tablespoon of the mushrooms at the bottom. Place the rack over the squash and place 3 slices of the leg meat over the mushrooms. Spoon 2 ounces of the wine sauce directly over the rack and leg meat, and spoon any additional rib sauce over the ribs.

HOW TO TASTE WINE

Here is what we think about when we wine-taste:

Look: Each wine color will vary tremendously, even when made from the same grape variety. For example, a given grape's white wines may appear green, yellow, or even brown. More color in white wine usually indicates more intense flavors and age, although brown may indicate that the wine is bad. Red wines range in color from a pale red to a deep brown-red or purple, and normally become lighter in color as they age.

Smell: Everyone knows that taste and smell go hand in hand. Before smelling the wine, you should swirl the glass to release molecules in the wine that allow you to smell the aroma, also referred to as the bouquet or nose. There are two techniques for smelling wine:

1. Take a quick whiff and formulate an initial impression, then take a second whiff, or:

2. Take only one deep whiff.

After smelling the wine, sit back and think about the aroma.

Taste: One of the most important qualities of a wine is its balance between sweetness and acidity. There are three steps to fully tasting a wine:

1. Initial Taste: Referred to as your "first impression," this taste will awaken your senses and taste buds.

2. Taste: Slosh the wine around in your mouth and draw in some air. Examine the body and texture of the wine: Is it light or rich? Smooth or harsh?

3. Aftertaste: This refers to the taste lingering in your mouth after you've swallowed the wine. How long did the taste last? Was it pleasant?

When you are finished tasting, take a moment to think about the wine's overall flavor and balance. Was the taste appropriate for that specific wine? Don't worry if you lack the words to describe your tasting—that is what the five-point system abbreviates for you (see page 176 for more on blind wine tasting); it is much harder to communicate a wine's sensations than to appreciate it. And remember, the more you drink, the more difficult communication may become!

Point Reyes Blue Cheese with Cherry, Rose, and Crushed Tellicherry Peppercorns

Each of the three distinct flavors that accompany the cheese—the cherry, rose, and peppercorns—are notes that are echoed in the wine. This course is adult finger food: Run your finger through the jam, or the peppercorns, or the rose syrup—or all three—and then pick up a piece of cheese with that goopy finger, and lick your fingertips as you eat the cheese. Not only delicious, but sensual, and fun.

makes 12 servings

14 ounces Point Reyes blue cheese (see Resources)

4 tablespoons Fresh Cherry Jam with Thyme (recipe follows)

2 tablespoons rose syrup (see Resources)

1 tablespoon coarsely ground Tellicherry peppercorns

Place about 1 ounce of cheese on each plate. Spoon 1 teaspoon of cherry jam, ½ teaspoon of rose syrup, and ¼ teaspoon of Tellicherry peppercorns onto each plate, keeping them separate.

Fresh Cherry Jam with Thyme

makes ½ cup

This jam is all about a burst of cherry flavor, so there is no pectin added, which would require extra water and sugar.

½ pound (about 24) sweet cherries, such as Bing, pitted and chopped

3 tablespoons sugar

1 thyme sprig

¼ teaspoon sea salt

In a small heavy-bottomed saucepan, combine the cherries, sugar, thyme, salt, and ¼ cup of water. Simmer until most of the juice is evaporated and the cherries are cooked through about 15 minutes. Let cool slightly, then remove the thyme sprig. Puree in a blender. The jam can be prepared 3 days in advance and refrigerated. Bring to room temperature before serving.

Bittersweet Chocolate Cake with Oaxacan Mole Sorbet and Muscovado Ice Cream

Great-quality bittersweet chocolate can hold its own with a big red wine. The sorbet offers a light respite from the dusky muscovado sugar, which tastes a little like molasses. Prepare this early in the day or a day ahead.

makes 12 servings

FOR THE CAKE

12 ounces 70% cacao bittersweet chocolate, chopped

½ teaspoon pure vanilla extract

½ teaspoon ground cinnamon

1 cup (2 sticks) unsalted butter, softened, plus more for greasing the pans

1 cup plus 3 tablespoons sugar

8 large egg yolks

1 cup sourdough starter (see Note)

4 large egg whites

Pinch of salt

Pinch of cream of tartar

FOR THE CHOCOLATE SAUCE

2 ounces 70% cacao bittersweet chocolate, chopped

¼ cup heavy cream

1 tablespoon unsalted butter

1 tablespoon light corn syrup

Oaxacan Mole Sorbet (recipe follows)

Muscovado Ice Cream (recipe follows)

NOTE: To make a faux sourdough starter, in a medium bowl combine 1 teaspoon active dry yeast with 1 cup water and 1 cup all-purpose flour and let ferment at room temperature for several hours or overnight.

MAKE THE CAKE: In a small bowl, combine 4 ounces of the chocolate with the vanilla, cinnamon, and 3 tablespoons of water. Set the bowl over a saucepan of simmering water and stir until melted. Let cool, then refrigerate this ganache.

Preheat the oven to 350°F. Butter four 3¼ x 6 x 2-inch loaf pans, or two 8½ x 4½ x 2½-inch loaf pans. Sprinkle with the 3 tablespoons of sugar, shaking out the excess.

In a small bowl set over a saucepan of simmering water, melt the remaining 8 ounces of chocolate, stirring until melted. Remove from the heat. In a medium bowl combine the remaining 1 cup of butter and 1 cup of sugar and beat with an electric beater until creamy and the sugar is dissolved, about 3 minutes. One at a time, beat in the egg yolks. Fold the yolk mixture into the chocolate, and then fold in the starter.

In a medium bowl, whip the egg whites with the salt and cream of tartar until soft peaks form. Fold a third of the beaten whites into the chocolate mixture, then gently fold in the rest.

Divide half of the batter between each of the prepared pans. Divide the ganache between the pans, spooning or scooping it into the center of the pans. Pour the remaining batter over the top of each. Bake until a toothpick comes out clean, about 20 minutes whether using the 4 small pans or the 2 large pans.

MAKE THE CHOCOLATE SAUCE: In a small saucepan, combine the chocolate, cream, butter, corn syrup, and 1 tablespoon water. Bring to a simmer, stir to melt the chocolate, then remove from the heat. This can be made ahead of time and gently warmed to serve.

Cut the cake into 1-inch slices. Place 1 slice of the warm cake on each plate. Spoon a line of chocolate sauce in front of the cake. Place 1 small scoop each of the sorbet and ice cream on top of the sauce. Serve immediately.

Oaxacan Mole Sorbet

makes 3 cups

1 ¼ cups granulated sugar

¼ cup muscovado sugar

¼ cup light corn syrup

1 dried ancho chile, stemmed and seeded

½ dried guajillo chile or other medium-heat chile, stemmed and seeded

½ dried chihuacle negro chile, stemmed and seeded (see Resources)

¼ teaspoon chipotle chile powder

¾ cup dark cocoa powder, such as Green & Black's organic fair trade cocoa or Valrhona

½ teaspoon sugarcane vinegar or rice wine vinegar

Pinch of salt

In a small saucepan, stir together the sugars, corn syrup, chiles, chili powder, cocoa powder, and 2 cups of water. Simmer for 10 minutes, then let cool.

Add the sugarcane vinegar and a pinch of salt.

Blend on high speed for 1 to 2 minutes. Pour through a fine-mesh strainer. Freeze according to your ice-cream maker's directions. Leftover sorbet will keep for 2 weeks in the freezer.

Muscovado Ice Cream

makes 3 cups

1 cup whole milk

½ cup half-and-half

½ cup heavy cream

6 tablespoons muscovado sugar (see Resources)

3 large egg yolks

¼ teaspoon salt

1 tablespoon nonfat dry milk

1 teaspoon pure vanilla extract

Fill a 4-quart bowl halfway with ice and 2 cups of water. Place a 2-quart metal bowl inside the 4-quart bowl. In a medium heavy-bottomed saucepan, combine the milk, half-and-half, and cream. Sprinkle 3 tablespoons of the sugar over the milks; do not stir. Bring to a boil over medium-high heat.

Meanwhile, in a medium bowl, whisk the egg yolks with the remaining 3 tablespoons of sugar, the salt, and nonfat dry milk. Gradually whisk the hot cream into the yolk mixture. Return this mixture to the saucepan and place over medium heat. Cook, stirring constantly with a wooden spoon against the bottom of the pan, until the mixture starts to steam and becomes slightly thickened, about 5 minutes. (Note that since this ice cream does not use a large amount of egg yolks, the mixture will not thicken as much as a custard or traditional ice-cream base.)

Pour immediately into the bowl sitting in the ice bath. Stir in the vanilla extract. Stir often until completely cooled, then pour through a fine-mesh strainer. The base can be prepared a day in advance and refrigerated. At least 2 hours before serving, pour the ice-cream base into an ice-cream maker. Freeze according to your ice-cream maker's instructions, then store in the freezer until serving.

WINE NOTES

Sauvignon Blanc, Oak Savanna, 2004 (Santa Ynez, California)

"Naked" Chardonnay, Oak Savanna, 2004 (Santa Ynez, California)

One Thousand Hills, Oak Savanna, 2003 (Santa Ynez, California)

Recioto della Valpolicella, Classico, "BG," Tommaso Bussola, 2004 (Veneto, Italy)

Vintage Fortified Shiraz, d'Arenberg, 2004 (McLaren Vale, Australia)

With the rich Crayfish Risotto, the Oak Savanna whites offer both complementary and contrasting elements: The herbal aromas of the sauvignon blanc play up the olive/herb flavors in the dish, and the touch of oak aging on this wine lends it added depth to match the richness of the crayfish and bacon. Follow a bite with a sip: There's a mingling of flavors, then the sharp sauvignon acidity to clean everything up and ready you for the next bite.

The luscious crayfish also brings chardonnay to mind, although given chardonnay's bigger structure we went with the unoaked "Naked" Chardonnay, as its acidity is crisper and its fruit more pronounced than it would be in a riper, oakier style. There are fewer aromatic fireworks here, but you'll find a similar combination of richness up front and cleansing acidity on the finish.

Lamb always triggers thoughts of syrah and other spicy, gamey, Rhône-style wines. And the side dishes for the main course—braised chard, wild mushrooms—add earthy tones. The savory elements in the syrah-based One Thousand Hills work together with those in the lamb, and there's plenty of heft in this wine to stand up to the powerful flavors.

For the cheese course, we made a classic contrast: a salty, pungent blue cheese with an unctuous sweet wine as the counterpunch. Here, you have the addition of tart cherries and peppercorns, lending a darker shade to the flavors, and the sweet-yet-bitter red called *recioto*, from the Veneto region of Italy, is an exotic choice. Tommaso Bussola's Recioto della Valpolicella gets its sappy texture and port-like sweetness from *appassimento*, the process by which grapes are dried after harvest to create a dense, sweet wine. It has some tart cherry flavors of its own, but texturally, it envelops the salty cheese like a sweet blanket.

In fact, there are times when the wine becomes more of a condiment than a drink, as in the case of the Bittersweet Chocolate Cake and the tawny port–style shiraz from Australia. This viscous red is like syrup. Tawny is a wood-aged style of port, and this wine's dark red fruit characteristics are complemented by some vanilla and maple elements from the oak, which play off nuances in the dish.

OAK SAVANNA VINEYARD

Oak Savanna Vineyard contains some of the oldest grapevines in Santa Barbara County. Originally part of the Zaca Mesa Vineyards, planted in 1972, our twenty-five hilly acres, along with the steeper and unplantable ranch property surrounding them, were sold off in the late 1980s.

When we started Oak Savanna, the vineyards were all planted with chardonnay vines spaced seven feet apart, and most of the fruit was sold under contract to other wineries. Two years before those contracts ran out, our vineyard manager, Felipe Hernandez, interplanted slightly less than half of the acreage with syrah, as modern viticulture now accepts denser plantings. After our last contracted grapes were harvested, we cut down the chardonnay plants, leaving the roots intact and two feet of each trunk exposed. We grafted more syrah onto those trunks. By doing this, we never missed a harvest, managed to convert half of the vineyard to red grapes, and at the same time doubled the number of plants in those blocks.

Today, the vineyard is comprised of six acres of chardonnay, twelve acres of syrah, and several acres each of viognier, sangiovese, and tempranillo vines. Most of our syrah is taken by our winemaker, Andrew Murray; under his eponymous label, he specializes in Rhône varietals and syrah. The viognier, sangiovese, and tempranillo grapes are used for blending with the small amount of syrah reserved for our premium wine, One Thousand Hills, a meritage-style super-red. The chardonnay is bottled under the estate label Oak Savanna Vineyard.

Because it is so hilly, everything at Oak Savanna Vineyard is worked by hand: caning, dropping fruit, leafing, and harvest. Also, thanks to the hills, we find subtle differences in the flavors of the grapes from block to block. The fruit, and the wine made from it, is more nuanced because of our varied topography.

Under the Oak Savanna Cellars label, Andrew crafts wines from other grape varieties that are contract-grown in climates better suited to nurturing their excellence, like riesling from down valley, pinot noir from the Santa Rita Hills, and cabernet sauvignon from Paso Robles. All of the Oak Savanna wines are made at Andrew Murray's winery, located several miles south of our vineyard, on the Firestone Family Estates property.

Our wines are available for sale in the tasting room we share with Andrew Murray Vineyards on Grand Street, in Los Olivos, as well as on the Web, at www.oaksavannawine.com. And they may be found on the wine lists of at least two restaurants: Brothers at Mattei's Tavern in Los Olivos and Le Bernardin in New York City.

FANDANGO:
A FIESTA LUNCHEON

White Sangria

Heirloom Tomato Gazpacho

Fried Goat Cheese with Honey

Spanish Chorizo Salad

Watermelon Pyramid

Garbanzo Beans with Fried Onion and Blood Sausage

Tortilla de España

Catalonian Pork Tenderloin

Spicy Seared Scallops

Galician Almond Tart

Churros with Peaches and Olive Oil Ice Cream

IT IS SAID TO BE THE LARGEST EQUESTRIAN PARADE IN THE UNITED STATES, WITH ITS origins in the 1920s, when a group of enterprising citizens wished to conjure up the romance of colonial Santa Barbara. To some of our more cynical friends, longtime residents of the county, it is a tourist event. And they are right, if you are a spectator. But for locals, the whole idea is to ride in the Fiesta de Santa Barbara.

For us, it started with the kids: our neighbors David and Polly Walker's three preteen girls wanted an excuse to play dress-up and to ride horses with flowers in their mane through the center of town. Who wouldn't want to be a witness to that? A dozen friends came to that first ride.

It is now an enormous undertaking that begins the week before the annual event. The horses get taken into our small town of Los Olivos for a day to become reacquainted with the noises of cars and horns, and with the sensation of walking on pavement, before their annual performance in Santa Barbara. Tack needs repair and polishing. Costumes, the theme for which is decided by the girls, need to be found and fitted. Flowers need to be ordered and made into clusters that can be easily and securely fastened to manes and tails. The horses need to be washed and clipped, and their trailers cleaned and laid with straw.

On parade day we all meet in the parking lot by the beach. The trailers become communal dressing rooms, with flounces and ribbons flying about as we truss up one another. At last, we fling open the trailer doors just as the marshall is calling our number. Mounted up, it is the first time we see ourselves outfitted as a group.

It was the Walker girls' idea to dress like Spanish gypsies, and I think it was so they would be allowed to wear dangling coin earrings, something they are ordinarily not allowed to do. Our group gets applause from the judges, and the girls are filmed for local TV. We are quickly swept into the excitement of riding through the center of town. But to anyone who asks, I say that we ride in the parade because it is historic and an expression of our civic pride.

The parade is over for us at about 1:00 P.M., but it would be such a letdown to end the day so soon. So we use it as another occasion to get together with family and friends in the cool shade of a friend's backyard.

White Sangria

makes 30 servings

10 bottles Spanish white wine, such as albariño

⅔ cup sugar

1 Bosc pear, cored and cut into ¼-inch dice

1 Granny Smith apple, cored and cut into
  ¼-inch dice

1 Valencia orange, cut into ¼-inch slices

2 peaches, cut into ¼-inch dice

1 pint strawberries, halved

1 pint raspberries

1 cup Grand Marnier

2 liters sparkling water

Combine the wine, sugar, pear, apple, orange, peaches, strawberries, raspberries, and Grand Marnier 24 hours in advance of serving and refrigerate. Just before serving, pour in the sparkling water. Serve over ice.

Heirloom Tomato Gazpacho

This is a very traditional gazpacho with bread blended into it as a thickener. The marinating of the cucumbers and garlic overnight is an important step in blending the flavors. Serve with the traditional Spanish accompaniment of croutons, or *migas*, which add a savory crunch.

makes 6 cups; serves 16 as part of a buffet

FOR THE SOUP

1 medium red bell pepper, cut into ½-inch dice

2 medium cucumbers, cut into ½-inch slices

1 garlic clove, crushed

½ medium red onion, cut into ½-inch dice

2 tablespoons good-quality sherry vinegar

2 tablespoons extra virgin olive oil, preferably
  Spanish

2 teaspoons sea salt

½ teaspoon freshly ground black pepper

2 oregano sprigs, leaves only

3 basil leaves

2½ pounds heirloom tomatoes, coarsely
  chopped

1 slice day-old white bread, torn into chunks

3 tarragon sprigs

FOR THE GARNISH

1 medium tomato, seeded and cut into
  ½-inch dice

½ cucumber, seeded and cut into ½-inch dice

½ medium red bell pepper, cut into ½-inch dice

2 scallions, finely sliced

Migas (recipe follows)

MAKE THE SOUP: The day before, in a large bowl, combine the red pepper, cucumbers, garlic, red onion, sherry vinegar, olive oil, 1 teaspoon of the salt, the black pepper, oregano, and basil. Marinate in the refrigerator overnight.

Early the next day, combine the marinated ingredients with the tomatoes, bread, tarragon, and remaining 1 teaspoon of salt. In a blender puree the ingredients in batches until smooth, about 2 minutes. Pour through a medium-mesh strainer and chill thoroughly. Transfer the gazpacho to a serving bowl and garnish with the chopped tomato, cucumber, red pepper, scallions, and migas.

Migas

½ loaf artisanal sourdough bread, crust removed, cut into ¼-inch cubes (about 2 cups)

2 bacon slices, finely minced

3 tablespoons extra virgin olive oil, preferably Spanish

1 garlic clove

¼ teaspoon ground cumin

½ teaspoon Spanish smoked hot paprika (see Resources)

½ teaspoon sea salt

¼ teaspoon freshly ground black pepper

1 small shallot, minced

2 tablespoons minced Serrano ham

1 tablespoon chopped parsley

Lightly dampen the bread pieces by wetting your hands and shaking them over the bread. Repeat several times. Place the dampened bread cubes on a paper towel and wrap in foil. Let sit several hours or overnight.

In a large sauté pan, heat the bacon slowly over low heat until it renders its fat. Remove and reserve the bacon pieces. Add 2 tablespoons of the olive oil and the garlic to the bacon fat. Cook the garlic over medium-low heat until golden brown, then discard. Add the bread pieces to the skillet along with the cumin, paprika, salt, and black pepper, and stir to coat. Cook, stirring, until the moisture is gone from the bread cubes and they are evenly toasted.

In a small pan, sauté the shallot in the remaining 1 tablespoon of olive oil over medium heat until translucent. Add the ham, reserved bacon, and parsley. Toss this mixture into the toasted bread cubes.

Fried Goat Cheese with Honey

This tapa is a startling combination: The sweet honey melts into the warm goat cheese, and the salty, briny black olives and sharp onions conspire for incredible layers of flavor that unfold as each bite sits on your palate. Try to find white honey, which is more solid—almost chewy—than regular honey.

makes 16 servings as part of a buffet

Two 8-ounce logs fresh goat cheese

4 tablespoons extra virgin olive oil

3 small red onions, halved lengthwise then cut lengthwise into ⅛-inch slices

2 tablespoons unsalted butter

2 teaspoons sherry vinegar

½ teaspoon sugar

2 tablespoons homemade chicken stock, or substitute boxed or canned

2 teaspoons sea salt

1 cup pitted kalamata olives with 2 tablespoons of their brine

1 large egg

½ cup water

1 cup plain dry bread crumbs

¼ cup chopped herbs, such as parsley, chives, and thyme

1 teaspoon freshly ground black pepper

1 cup grapeseed oil, for frying

¼ cup white Hawaiian honey (see Resources)

Cut the goat cheese into 1-ounce pieces and form into disks roughly 1 inch in diameter. Cover and refrigerate.

Heat a large, heavy-bottomed sauté pan over medium-high heat. Add 2 tablespoons of olive oil and the red onions. Reduce the heat to medium and cook, stirring 2 or 3 times, for 15 minutes. Add the butter and reduce the heat to the lowest possible setting. Continue to cook, stirring every so often, until the onions are browned evenly and have lost two-thirds of their moisture, about 1 hour. Stir in the sherry vinegar, sugar, stock, and 1 teaspoon of the salt. Remove from the heat and keep warm.

LEFT: Heirloom Tomato Gazpacho garnished with traditional Spanish *migas*

In a blender, puree the olives and their brine with the remaining 2 tablespoons of olive oil at high speed for 1 minute, scraping down the sides once, until smooth. The recipe can be prepared to this point a day or two in advance and the onions and olive puree refrigerated separately. Reheat the onions gently and bring the olive puree to room temperature before serving.

In a shallow dish, whisk the egg with the water. In another shallow dish, combine the bread crumbs with the remaining 1 teaspoon of salt, the herbs, and black pepper. Working in batches, place 3 or 4 cheese disks in the egg wash. Then place them in the bread crumbs and coat evenly, shaking off any excess. Transfer to a platter. Refrigerate until ready to cook.

In a large heavy-bottomed sauté pan, heat the grapeseed oil over medium-high heat. The amount of oil should reach half the height of the goat cheese in the pan. Add the cheese disks, leaving an inch of space around each piece. Fry until golden brown, about 2 minutes per side. Remove and drain on a paper towel–lined platter. Keep warm to serve.

Dot a platter with eight ½ tablespoons of honey and flatten slightly. Place 2 warm goat cheese disks on top of each smear of honey. Top each piece of cheese with 2 teaspoons of the caramelized red onion and ½ teaspoon of the olive puree.

Fried Goat Cheese topped with caramelized onions and olive puree, served with white honey

Spanish Chorizo Salad

Spanish chorizo is more of a cured sausage than fresh, crumbly Mexican chorizo. Either one could be used in this salad.

makes 16 servings as part of a buffet

6 tablespoons extra virgin olive oil

3 garlic cloves, peeled and thinly sliced

2½ tablespoons white wine vinegar

1¼ teaspoons sea salt

½ teaspoon freshly ground black pepper

4 heads escarole, coarse outer leaves removed, green parts cut away

3 medium heirloom tomatoes, each cut into 8 wedges

9 ounces Spanish chorizo, thinly sliced

3 ounces Idiazábal cheese, thinly sliced with a vegetable peeler

20 basil leaves, torn

One day ahead, preheat a small skillet over high heat and add 2 tablespoons of the olive oil. Add the garlic and sauté until golden brown, about 2 minutes. Remove from the heat and add the vinegar and the remaining 4 tablespoons of olive oil. Season with 1 teaspoon of the salt and the black pepper. Refrigerate for up to 24 hours.

Place the escarole in a bowl with the tomatoes. In a medium sauté pan, bring the vinaigrette to a simmer. Add the chorizo and warm through. Add the vinaigrette, Idiazábal cheese, basil, and the remaining ¼ teaspoon salt to the escarole and toss to mix. Serve immediately.

Watermelon Pyramid

This dish is composed of delightful layers of watermelon, Serrano ham, and Manchego cheese. It is simple, dressed with olive oil and lemon juice and highlighted with a fennel-scented salt.

makes 16 servings as part of a buffet

1½ tablespoons fennel seeds

½ teaspoon white peppercorns

1 tablespoon coarse gray sea salt

1 bunch watercress, large stems removed

One 3½-pound seedless yellow watermelon, rind removed, fruit cut into 1½-inch cubes

One 3½-pound seedless red watermelon, rind removed, fruit cut into 1½-inch cubes

8 ounces Serrano ham, thinly sliced

4 ounces Manchego cheese, thinly sliced with a vegetable peeler

1 tablespoon fresh lemon juice

3 tablespoons extra virgin olive oil, preferably Spanish

In a small saucepan, toast the fennel seeds and peppercorns over medium heat, until fragrant, about 4 minutes. Let cool slightly, then crush in a mortar until the consistency of a fine powder. Add the sea salt and crush a bit more.

Spread the watercress on a large platter. On top of the watercress, make one layer with a quarter of the red and yellow watermelon pieces. Sprinkle the watermelon with ¼ to ½ teaspoon of the fennel salt. Layer a quarter of the Serrano ham and a quarter of the Manchego cheese, and drizzle with a quarter of the lemon juice and olive oil. Follow these steps to make a total of four layers in a pyramid shape.

Garbanzo Beans with Fried Onion and Blood Sausage

Blood sausage is not something most Americans are used to, but because it is crumbled into the dish alongside the beans, it is not threatening. In fact, your guests will not even know what it is, other than delicious, unless you tell them.

makes 16 servings as part of a buffet

5 tablespoons extra virgin olive oil

1 medium yellow onion, halved lengthwise then cut lengthwise into ⅛-inch slices

2 garlic cloves, finely chopped

8 ounces blood sausage (see Resources), removed from the casing and chopped

½ cup golden raisins, soaked in hot water for 30 minutes

½ cup pine nuts, toasted

3 cups cooked garbanzo beans (chickpeas)

3 tablespoons chopped parsley

1 tablespoon fresh lemon juice

2½ teaspoons sea salt

½ teaspoon freshly ground black pepper

In a medium sauté pan, heat 2 tablespoons of the olive oil over medium-high heat. Add the onion and sauté, stirring constantly, until golden brown but still moist, about 5 minutes. Add the garlic and sauté for 30 seconds, then add the blood sausage and heat through. Stir in the plumped raisins, toasted pine nuts, and garbanzos. Cook until heated through, about 3 to 5 minutes, then remove from the heat. Stir in the parsley, lemon juice, salt, and black pepper. Drizzle with the remaining 3 tablespoons of olive oil and serve.

Tortilla de España

The classic Spanish *tortilla* is something of a cross between an omelet, a frittata, and a potato gratin. This one is spread with a garlicky herb mayonnaise and comes with caramelized artichoke salad.

makes 16 servings as part of a buffet

FOR THE GARLIC-HERB MAYONNAISE

2 garlic cloves, minced

1 large egg yolk

1 tablespoon fresh lemon juice

½ teaspoon Dijon mustard

¾ cup extra virgin olive oil

3 tablespoons mixed chopped herbs, such as parsley, chives, thyme, and basil

¾ teaspoon sea salt

¼ teaspoon freshly ground black pepper

FOR THE TORTILLA

3 cups extra virgin olive oil

4 large Idaho potatoes, thinly sliced, preferably using a mandoline

1 large yellow onion, halved lengthwise then cut lengthwise into ⅛-inch slices

4 large eggs

1½ teaspoons sea salt

¼ teaspoon freshly ground black pepper

Caramelized Artichoke Salad (recipe follows)

MAKE THE GARLIC-HERB MAYONNAISE: In a medium bowl, combine the garlic, egg yolk, 1 teaspoon of the lemon juice, and the mustard. Slowly drizzle in the olive oil while constantly whisking to form a thick emulsion. Stir in the remaining 2 teaspoons of lemon juice, 1 tablespoon of water, and the herbs, salt, and black pepper. The mayonnaise can be prepared 1 day in advance and refrigerated.

OPPOSITE: Garbanzo Beans with Fried Onion and Blood Sausage, golden raisins and pine nuts

MAKE THE TORTILLA: In a 12-inch skillet over medium heat, warm the oil. Begin by adding half of the potato slices, one at a time, to prevent them from sticking together. Alternate a few potato layers with some of the onions, using half of the potatoes and onions. Cook slowly over medium heat, lifting and turning the potatoes occasionally until they are tender but not brown, 8 to 12 minutes. Keep the potatoes separated; they should not form a cake. Drain the potatoes and onions in a colander, reserving the olive oil. Strain the olive oil back into the skillet. Cook the remaining potatoes and onions in the same manner, draining them and reserving the oil.

In a large bowl, beat the eggs until they are foamy. Season with the salt and pepper. Add all the potatoes and onions, pressing them down until they are covered. Allow to sit for 15 minutes.

Wipe the skillet clean, then heat 3 tablespoons of the reserved olive oil until very hot. Add the potato and egg mixture and spread it out to form a cake. Reduce the heat to medium and shake the skillet often to prevent sticking. Cook the tortilla until the bottom is golden brown, 8 to 10 minutes. Invert a 12-inch plate over the skillet and turn the tortilla onto the plate. Heat an additional 2 tablespoons of the reserved olive oil in the skillet and slide the tortilla back into the pan to continue cooking on the other side. Reduce the heat to medium-low and cook until golden brown on the bottom, 8 to 10 minutes. Invert the tortilla onto a platter. To serve, spread the tortilla with 1 cup of garlic-herb mayonnaise and top with the caramelized artichoke salad. The tortilla may be cooked early in the day and held at room temperature until you serve it.

Caramelized Artichoke Salad

makes about 1 1/2 cups

1 bacon slice

6 tablespoons extra virgin olive oil

1/2 medium yellow onion, finely diced

1/2 carrot, finely diced

1/2 celery stalk, finely diced

5 large artichokes, leaves and stems removed,
  and artichokes placed in water mixed with the
  juice of 1 lemon

3/4 teaspoon sea salt

2 garlic cloves, minced

3 tablespoons mixed chopped herbs,
  such as parsley, chives, thyme, and basil

1/2 teaspoon freshly ground black pepper

In a large saucepan over medium heat, render the bacon in 2 tablespoons of the olive oil. Add the onion, carrot, and celery and brown slightly, about 5 minutes. Add the artichokes and 1/4 teaspoon of the salt and cover with water. Cover the artichokes with a paper towel or clean kitchen towel to keep them submerged. Bring to a simmer, reduce the heat to low, and simmer until cooked through, 15 to 20 minutes. Remove the artichokes from the liquid and allow them to cool. Remove the choke from the artichokes and cut each heart into 8 wedges.

Heat the remaining 4 tablespoons of oil in a large sauté pan until very hot. Add the artichoke hearts and allow them to caramelize on both sides, taking care not to let them burn, 3 to 5 minutes. Stir in the garlic, herbs, the remaining 1/2 teaspoon of salt, and the black pepper at the last minute, then remove from the heat.

LEFT: Tortilla de España with Garlic-Herb Mayonnaise and Caramelized Artichoke Salad

BELOW: Catalonian Pork Tenderloin with a relish of roasted figs, Cabrales cheese, and marcona almonds

Catalonian Pork Tenderloin

This is a take on a traditional dish from Catalonia, the only region in Spain where fruit is cooked; everywhere else, fruit is served raw.

makes 16 servings as part of a buffet

Four 1-pound pork tenderloins, patted dry and trimmed

4 garlic cloves, chopped

4 oregano sprigs

2 rosemary sprigs

2 teaspoons black peppercorns

1 tablespoon coriander seeds

1 tablespoon Spanish sweet smoked paprika (see Resources)

1 tablespoon Spanish bittersweet smoked paprika (see Resources)

6 tablespoons extra virgin olive oil

2 pints figs, stemmed and quartered

1 teaspoon plus 1 tablespoon sea salt

1 cup pourable honey

2 tablespoons sherry vinegar

1 cup homemade chicken stock, or substitute boxed or canned

4 ounces Cabrales cheese, crumbled

1 cup marcona almonds

One day ahead, place the pork tenderloins in a shallow baking dish. Place the garlic, oregano, rosemary, peppercorns, and coriander seeds in a mortar and pestle. Pound the herbs and spices to release their aromas and the oils. Add the paprikas and olive oil and stir to mix. Pour over the pork tenderloins, making sure they are coated evenly. Cover and refrigerate.

Preheat the oven to 400°F. Place the figs in an even layer in a roasting pan, sprinkle them with 1 teaspoon of the salt, and drizzle with the honey and sherry vinegar. Roast until the figs soften slightly but still have shape and the honey starts to caramelize, about 25 minutes. Gently remove the figs from the pan. Pour the chicken stock into the pan, scraping up the browned bits. Set the pan over high heat and reduce slightly for 1 to 2 minutes, then pour over the figs.

About 45 minutes before cooking, remove the tenderloin from the refrigerator. Preheat a grill or large sauté pan to very hot. Season the pork tenderloins with the remaining 1 table-spoon of salt. Grill or sear on all sides, about 4 minutes per side. Place in the preheated oven to finish cooking, 6 to 10 minutes for medium. Slice the pork tenderloins on a slight bias. Stir the cheese and almonds into the fig mixture and spoon over the pork.

Spicy Seared Scallops

These scallops are seared and then covered in a marinade of wine, chiles, vinegar, and garlic, very similar to a ceviche mixture, but cooked. This is best if made in the morning, then allowed to sit at room temperature all day, infusing the sweet scallop meat with the smoky, garlicky flavors of the marinade—which itself is delicious sopped up with bread.

makes 16 servings as part of a buffet

2 pounds large (about 20) diver scallops, muscle removed

1¾ teaspoons sea salt

¾ teaspoon freshly ground black pepper

½ cup extra virgin olive oil

2 dried red chile peppers, minced

8 garlic cloves, thinly sliced

1 tablespoon sweet smoked paprika (see Resources)

3 bay leaves

½ cup white wine vinegar

½ cup dry white wine

Start this recipe at least 2½ hours before serving. Pat the scallops dry and season on both sides with 1 teaspoon of the salt and ½ teaspoon of the black pepper. In a large sauté pan, heat the olive oil over medium-high heat. Sear the scallops until golden brown on both sides, about 2 minutes per side. Using a slotted spoon, transfer the scallops to a shallow earthenware dish. Strain the cooking oil, wipe the skillet clean, and return the oil to the skillet. Add the chile peppers and garlic and cook until the garlic is golden and fragrant, 3 to 5 minutes. Remove from the heat and stir in the paprika, bay leaves, vinegar, wine, and ½ cup of water. Return the skillet to the heat and bring to a boil for 1 minute. Add the remaining ¾ teaspoon of salt and ¼ teaspoon of black pepper, stir, then pour the liquid over the scallops. Leave the scallops and mixture to marinate at least 2½ hours at room temperature.

Galician Almond Tart

This cake is best if completed a few hours before serving, so that the cream moistens the cake. It is adapted from a recipe in *The Foods and Wine of Spain* by Penelope Casas.

makes 12 to 16 servings

Butter, for greasing the pans

All-purpose flour, for dusting the pans

1 cup plus 1 tablespoon sugar

¼ teaspoon grated lemon zest

7 large eggs, separated

1½ cups whole raw almonds, finely ground

¼ teaspoon ground cinnamon

1 cup heavy cream

2 tablespoons very strong coffee or espresso

1 cup finely chopped almonds, toasted

Preheat the oven to 350°F. Line two 9-inch round cake pans with parchment paper, then butter and flour the pans.

In a large bowl, use an electric mixer to beat 1 cup of the sugar with the lemon zest and egg yolks until the mixture is light and fluffy, about 3 minutes. Stir in the ground almonds and cinnamon.

In a clean bowl, beat the egg whites until they are stiff but not dry, 4 to 6 minutes. Fold a quarter of the beaten whites into the yolk mixture, then very gently fold in the remaining whites.

Divide the batter evenly between the two prepared pans and bake until the cakes are well browned and set, about 45 minutes. Let cool for 5 minutes in the pans, then remove from the pans to cool completely on a wire rack.

For the topping, whip the cream with the remaining 1 tablespoon of sugar and the coffee until medium stiff peaks form, about 4 minutes.

Spread half of the whipped cream on top of one of the cakes. Cover with the second cake. Frost the top and sides of the cake with the remaining whipped cream. Garnish the sides of the cake with the chopped almonds.

Churros with Peaches and Olive Oil Ice Cream

Fine olive oils reflect the expression of a single olive, and the Pons Arbequina olive oil works really well as an ice cream flavor. The churros add a fun, crunchy accent to the silkiness of the ice cream.

makes 16 servings

3 ripe peaches, peeled and cut into ½-inch dice	Juice of ½ medium lemon
¼ cup sugar	32 Churros (recipe follows)
¼ vanilla bean, split and scraped	3 cups Olive Oil Ice Cream (recipe follows)
¼ teaspoon sea salt, plus more for garnish	Single-varietal olive oil, for garnish

In a medium bowl combine the peaches with the sugar, vanilla bean pod and seeds, salt, and the ¼ teaspoon of the lemon juice. Let marinate at room temperature for up to 6 hours.

Remove the vanilla bean pod from the peaches and reserve for another use. Place one freshly fried churro on a plate and spoon 2 tablespoons of the peaches on top of it. Top with a scoop of ice cream. Drizzle with the olive oil and sprinkle a pinch of salt on top.

Churros

makes 30 to 40 2-inch churros

½ cup sugar	⅓ cup all-purpose flour
1 teaspoon ground cinnamon	1 large egg
3 tablespoons unsalted butter	Vegetable oil, for deep-frying
¼ teaspoon sea salt	

In a medium bowl, combine the sugar and cinnamon.

In a small saucepan, combine the butter, salt, and ⅔ cup of water. Bring to a boil. Remove from the heat and vigorously stir in the flour until the dough forms a ball. Beat in the egg, until combined and the dough is shiny.

Preheat at least 2 inches of vegetable oil in a deep-fat fryer or deep, heavy pot over medium-high heat to 375°F on a candy thermometer. Place the dough in a piping bag fitted with a ¼-inch star tip. Pipe the churro batter directly into the hot oil in 1-inch-long segments, being careful not to splatter the oil. Fry until golden brown, 2 to 3 minutes. Using a slotted spoon transfer to a paper towel. Sprinkle with the cinnamon-sugar mixture and serve as soon as possible.

Olive Oil Ice Cream

makes 3 cups

1 cup whole milk

½ cup half-and-half

½ cup heavy cream

¼ vanilla bean, split

6 tablespoons sugar

3 large egg yolks

1 tablespoon nonfat dry milk

6 tablespoons Arbequina extra virgin olive oil, such as Pons Spanish olive oil, or other single-varietal olive oil (see Resources)

1 teaspoon high-quality sea salt

Fill a 4-quart bowl halfway with ice and 2 cups of water. Place a 2-quart metal bowl inside the 4-quart bowl. In a medium saucepan, place the milk, half-and-half, and cream. Scrape the vanilla bean and place the seeds and the pod in the cream mixture. Sprinkle in 3 tablespoons of the sugar; do not stir. Bring to a boil.

Meanwhile, in a medium bowl, whisk the remaining 3 tablespoons of sugar with the egg yolks and nonfat dry milk. Gradually whisk the hot cream into the yolk mixture and return to the saucepan. Continue cooking, stirring constantly with a wooden spoon against the bottom of the pan, until the mixture thickens and starts to steam.

Pour into the bowl sitting in the ice bath. Stir often until completely cooled. The base can be prepared a day in advance and refrigerated. At least 2 hours before serving, pour the ice-cream base into an ice-cream maker with the olive oil and salt. Freeze according to your ice-cream maker's instructions, then store in the freezer until serving.

WINE NOTES

White Sangria (page 45)

Albariño, Bodegas Nora, 2006 (Rias Baixas, Spain)

Rioja Reserva, Bodegas Muga, 2002 (Rioja, Spain)

The white sangria described in this chapter is a refreshing and traditional accompaniment to a Spanish-themed lunch. But if you'd like to serve bottled wine during the meal, as we did, try an albariño, the crisply acidic white from Galicia in the northwest corner of Spain. With its razor-sharp texture and light, citrusy flavors, it is a great choice for the oily, garlicky *tapas*. Anchovies and artichokes, for example, are two foods that can destroy the taste of wine; with albariño there is plenty of acidity to stand up to the food, but not the tropical fruitiness or overt oakiness to start an all-out war. What you want with this assertive menu is something clean and crisp, and albariño surely fits that bill.

On the red wine side, we decided to go a little bolder, but still Spanish. The Reserva from Bodegas Muga is a rich yet versatile red made from the tempranillo grape (which is also grown along California's Central Coast). What characterizes this wine is a robust mix of fruitiness and savor; its black cherry flavors are seasoned with notes of herbs and spice. For some of the meatier items, be they blood sausages or paprika-scented, Cabrales-funky pork tenderloin, here's a meaty red with a mix of muscle and finesse to make a match.

Churros with Peaches and Olive Oil Ice Cream

THE FANDANGO

House parties are part of a historic tradition in Santa Ynez. The valley is geographically isolated between the Coastal Mountain Range to the south, the San Rafael Range to the north and east, and the Pacific Ocean to the west. Even today, it is accessible only by two narrow passes, and these may be more dangerous to cross in a car at 75 mph than they were in mission times, at the speed of a trotting horse. But while the valley is and was isolated, it was never desolate. In fact, the resident population was larger in the late 1800s than it is today. Back then, the isolation, coupled with the relative proximity of other large ranches, forced the *haciendados* to create their own entertainment.

For the big Mexican ranchers, descendants of those who had followed the Spanish missionaries north from Mexico, daily life was not terribly strenuous. The weather is mostly mild and pleasant all year long, so the ranchers and their livestock were seldom threatened by the conditions that ranchers and farmers elsewhere in the world commonly battle. Thatch and adobe shelters were simple to build here, but for the most part, theirs was a life lived outdoors. Grazing land was abundant, and the slaughter (typically the dirty business of cattle ranching) was relatively simple and clean since it could be done seaside, where the valuable hides were loaded directly onto ships that carried them to shoe factories in England, New England, or South America. Most of the meat was considered worthless, and the remains were devoured by grizzly bears and vultures, rotted by the sun, or washed away by the tide. It was a culture given to much idleness, but one with a passion for pomp and circumstance and riotous social occasions.

There were no fences between neighbors here, just great distances. (Ownership of cattle in Alta California was marked with a brand; ownership of the land the cattle grazed on mattered less.) The nearest hacienda might be a few pleasant hours away by horseback. Unannounced visitors were always expected, and when they came, there was no limit to how long they might stay. And nothing has changed: I just received a phone call from my step-son, who informed me that he will be arriving in two hours, with five friends, for dinner. *Mi casa es su casa,* no problem.

These impromptu gatherings were called *fandangos.* They might last for an afternoon or a week, but they were a regular part of life on the *ranchos* in Alta California, so common that they were the principal social activity. By day, a party might begin with some macho horseback riding competitions: an impromptu rodeo. Some of these events, such as steer roping, cattle penning, and bronc riding, still provide an afternoon of entertainment for our guests today. Other spectacles, such as bull and bear fights and the *carrera del gallo* (without falling off his horse, a rider must pull the head off a live rooster that has been buried in sand up to its neck), have been abandoned.

For drinks, they consumed a watery hot cocoa, and because they also grew wine grapes, they made wine and grappa. Meals were casual, and people, like the animals, mainly grazed, consuming their food from clay pots filled with meats and bean or maize mashes that simmered all afternoon on an oak-log fire.

In the evening, the ranch hands formed a small ragtag orchestra. Most *vaqueros* knew how to play a musical instrument; while sitting under the shade of an oak tree watching their cattle graze, they had plenty of time to practice. And when they weren't idling away the workday playing musical instruments, they might be fiddling with any number of other western arts like braiding rawhide, knotting horsehair, tooling silver, or embellishing the leather on a saddle. (Today this is called "pimping your ride.") The California vaquero's daily life was one long break, allowing him plenty of time to primp and preen for the next fandango.

When the dancing began at night, gleaming silver *conchas* on the men's clothing caught the light of the fire, and the jangle-bobs on oversized spurs sounded like castanets for the feet. The clothing the wives of ranch owners wore was made from linen and silk, and was adorned with lace and jewelry imported from Europe by ship captains who had traded these luxuries for the cowhides of the Alta Californios. Even today, few goods are actually manufactured in the Santa Ynez Valley; with the exception of wine, most of our luxuries need to be imported.

Unlike the lonesome Texas cowboy portrayed in the movies, the vaquero in Alta California enjoyed a rich and lively social life surrounded by family, friends, and neighbors. The next fandango could be today.

The Fandango, 1873, Charles Christian Nahl
(Crocker Art Museum, E. B. Crocker Collection)

BACHELOR PARTY

Spicy Watermelon Margarita

Pico de Gallo (page 234)

Guacamole (page 234)

Corte Carne de Buffalo

Grilled Ancho-Orange Quail with Wheatberries

Handmade Flour Tortillas

Fresh Corn Tamales

Jicama and Purslane Salad

Smashed Black Beans

Mexican Fruit Cup

party, I was honored. But I immediately panicked: All the "usual" bachelor-party ideas were out of the question, since Chris would soon be my step-daughter's husband. So instead of calling someone listed under "Adult Entertainment" in the Yellow Pages, I called the police! Specifically, the Santa Barbara County Sheriff's Department and its Special Weapons and Tactics (SWAT team), who have been our friends for some time, since they occasionally use our gun range and the hilly ranch property to simulate tactical field maneuvers. Thankfully, the members of this elite force are only occasionally called into action, so, with permission from the sheriff himself, they were able to spend a portion of a spring morning at Rancho La Zaca.

Their entrance was impressive: an "insertion" by helicopter, during which they slid down ropes suspended from the hovering aircraft. Six officers dropped in wearing full body armor, and two more had driven from headquarters with a sampling of the many different weapons the county department owns, including various models of submachine guns, carbine assault rifles, tasers, flash-bang grenades, and handguns. The guests were awestruck. For two hours, they learned about these modern weapons; then each man had a chance to fire some (under the officers' close supervision, of course).

It seemed to me a breach of bachelor-party etiquette for the mother of the bride to hover around the party, even if the groom did ask her to throw it. So I just checked in when the SWAT team was leaving and the guests were starting at the luncheon buffet. The officers seemed happy for the chance to show off their skills in a relaxed setting.

"This sure beats what we did at my bachelor party," I overheard one newlywed say as he served himself a grilled quail and scooped up some guacamole with a chip. But I deliberately drifted out of range of his voice, lest he go into more detail about these occasions than I wanted to know.

Spicy Watermelon Margarita

This drink was invented on the spot one afternoon in Alamos, Mexico, when we needed a festive cocktail to commemorate a special occasion on a moment's notice. The most notable ingredient we had on hand was a watermelon, distinguished by nothing more than its large size, resting on the countertop. Add to that a little salt, smoky chipotle chile, and jalapeño, and this is no ordinary margarita. You can also make a spicy mixture for the rim of the glass by mixing coarse salt with chipotle chile powder.

makes 12 to 15 servings

One 12-pound seedless watermelon,
  rind removed, fruit cut into 1-inch chunks

2 to 3 chipotle chiles in adobo

½ to 1 jalapeño

¾ cup fresh lime juice (from 6 limes)

1 ½ teaspoons salt

6 tablespoons Grand Marnier

1 to 1 ½ cups Don Julio Añejo Tequila or
  other good-quality tequila

Working in batches in a blender, puree the watermelon with the chipotles, jalapeño, lime juice, and salt. Pour the puree through a medium-mesh strainer into a pitcher and chill. Stir the Grand Marnier and tequila into the watermelon juice. Serve over ice in salt-rimmed glasses.

Corte Carne de Buffalo

Buffalo is returning to American tables partly because it is a leaner alternative to beef. But the rest of the story has everything to do with how it tastes: free of any gaminess, but sublimely perfumed by the grasslands where it is raised. Since buffalo meat is so lean, it is important not to overcook it or it will taste ferrous—not what you had in mind.

makes 12 servings as part of a buffet

4 ears corn, husked

8 tablespoons extra virgin olive oil

2 teaspoons sea salt

1 ¼ cups sliced stuffed olives
   (preferably chipotle chile–stuffed olives)

½ small red onion, minced

Juice of 1 lime

½ cup chopped cilantro

¼ cup chopped basil

1 ¼ teaspoons freshly ground black pepper

Six 8-ounce buffalo steaks (see Resources)

½ cup crumbled cotija cheese
   (Mexican white cheese)

Cilantro sprigs, for garnish

Preheat the grill to high.

Rub the corn with 2 tablespoons of the olive oil and season it with ¼ teaspoon of the salt. Grill over high heat for 6 minutes, turning every 2 minutes. Slice the grilled corn kernels off of the cob. In a medium bowl toss the corn with the olives, onion, lime juice, 3 tablespoons of the olive oil, the cilantro, and basil. Season with another ¼ teaspoon of salt and ¼ teaspoon of the black pepper.

Rub the buffalo steaks with the remaining 3 tablespoons of olive oil and season liberally with the remaining 1½ teaspoons of salt and 1 teaspoon of the black pepper. Grill over high heat until medium-rare, 3 to 6 minutes per side. Remove to a cutting board and let sit for 5 minutes.

Mound the olive salsa in the center of a platter. Slice the buffalo steaks on the bias and place around the salsa. Garnish with crumbled cotija cheese and cilantro sprigs.

Grilled Ancho-Orange Quail with Wheatberries

You don't often come across quail seasoned with Mexican flavors, but the bold spicy tastes are actually a great treatment for the rich dark meat.

makes 12 servings as part of a buffet

FOR THE BBQ SPICE MIX

¼ cup chili powder

¼ cup sea salt

½ cup brown sugar

FOR THE ANCHO-ORANGE GLAZE

2 dried ancho chiles, seeded and stemmed

1 dried New Mexican red chile, seeded and stemmed

½ medium yellow onion, chopped

1 garlic clove, minced

2 tablespoons extra virgin olive oil

¼ teaspoon ground coriander

½ teaspoon ground cumin

½ bay leaf

1 large plum tomato, seeded and chopped

1 cup low-sodium canned chicken stock

½ cup fresh orange juice

1 tablespoon honey

¼ teaspoon sea salt

¼ teaspoon freshly ground black pepper

12 partially deboned quails (see Resources)

Chili-Lime Wheatberries (recipe follows)

MAKE THE SPICE MIX: In a small bowl, mix together the chili powder, salt, and brown sugar. Store in an airtight container.

MAKE THE ANCHO-ORANGE GLAZE: Soak the ancho and New Mexican red chiles in hot water for 30 minutes.

In a medium saucepan over medium-high heat, sauté the onion and garlic in the olive oil until translucent, about 3 minutes. Add the coriander, cumin, and bay leaf and sauté for 1 minute to release the aroma of the spices. Add the tomato, chicken stock, orange juice, drained soaked chiles, and honey. Bring to a simmer and reduce the heat to low. Continue to simmer until reduced by a third, about 15 minutes. Remove the bay leaf and let cool. In a blender, puree the mixture until it is as smooth as possible. Pour the glaze through a fine-mesh strainer and season with the salt and black pepper. Season the quails with the reserved spice mix. Grill over medium-high heat for about 5 minutes on each side, brushing with the glaze as you grill. Serve with the wheatberries and additional glaze on the side.

Chili-Lime Wheatberries

makes 2½ cups

Wheatberries have a nice, chewy texture and are a more interesting alternative to the usual suspect, white rice.

¾ cup wheatberries	½ medium red onion, cut into ⅛-inch dice
½ small yellow onion, halved	¼ cup chopped cilantro
1 oregano sprig	1 teaspoon honey
Juice of 1½ limes	½ teaspoon sea salt
¼ cup extra virgin olive oil	⅛ teaspoon freshly ground black pepper
1 teaspoon chili powder	

In a medium heavy-bottomed saucepan, combine the wheatberries, yellow onion, and oregano. Cover with 2 inches of water and bring to a boil. Reduce the heat and simmer gently until the wheatberries are tender but still a little chewy, about 3 hours. Add more hot water as needed throughout cooking to keep the berries submerged. Drain the berries and remove the yellow onion and oregano. The wheatberries can be prepared to this point 2 days in advance and refrigerated. Bring to room temperature before continuing. Let cool slightly and stir in the lime juice, olive oil, chili powder, red onion, cilantro, honey, salt, and black pepper.

TOP RIGHT: Corte Carne de Buffalo topped with a corn salad and cotija cheese

RIGHT: Fresh Corn Tamales

Handmade Flour Tortillas

Many of the vineyard workers come to the fields each morning carrying a hunk of floury dough in their pockets. At lunchtime, around 11:00 A.M. for them, they'll separate the dough into a few smaller pieces, and roll them by hand, one by one, first into a ball, then flattened into a disk. These are cooked quickly over a little improvised griddle that sits on the tailgate of a pickup truck. Homemade tortillas are fatter and chewier than the kind you'll find in the grocery store, and well worth the small amount of effort.

makes 25 small tortillas

2¼ cups all-purpose flour

½ cup whole wheat flour

½ teaspoon baking powder

½ teaspoon sea salt

3 tablespoons lard

In a large bowl, combine the flours, baking powder, and salt. Work in the lard with your fingertips until it is combined. Make a well in the center of the mixture. Pour ¾ cup water into the well and blend in the flour, using your fingertips, until smooth. On a lightly floured surface, knead the dough until smooth but not overworked, about 2 minutes. Wrap the dough in plastic and let it rest for 30 minutes.

Preheat a griddle on medium. Pinch off walnut-size portions of the dough and form them into balls. On a floured surface, roll out each ball into a disk until it is as thin as possible and the edges almost begin to curl up. Cook on the griddle, turning once, 1 to 2 minutes per side. If the tortillas start to brown as you cook, reduce the heat slightly. As you cook them, stack the tortillas and cover them with a kitchen towel. They should be made just prior to serving.

Fresh Corn Tamales

These are a refined, uptown version of a tamale: masa with a bit of fresh corn, herbs, and cotija cheese wrapped and tied into adorable little packets. (You may make larger tamales, which would work as well as these petite ones.) Because the masa dough is such a wonderful part of the tamale, these side-dish tamales aren't filled with anything. The trick to making your masa light and airy is to actually whip the shortening and add the masa dough in spoonfuls. When a bit of the dough floats in water, you know it has enough fat in it.

makes 35 small tamales

½ small yellow onion, chopped

1 garlic clove, minced

2 tablespoons extra virgin olive oil

2 ears corn, husked and kernels removed

3 tablespoons chopped cilantro

1 tablespoon chopped oregano

1 jalapeño, seeded and minced

1 cup crumbled cotija cheese
  (Mexican white cheese)

Juice of 1½ limes

2 teaspoons sea salt

2½ cups Maseca brand masa harina

1 cup lard or nonhydrogenated vegetable
  shortening

50 corn husks, soaked in warm water until
  pliable

In a medium saucepan, sauté the onion and garlic in the olive oil over medium heat until translucent, about 2 minutes. Add the corn, cilantro, oregano, and jalapeño. Continue to cook, stirring, until the corn is cooked through, about 5 minutes. Stir in the cotija cheese, lime juice, and ½ teaspoon of the salt.

In a large bowl, stir 2 cups of warm water into the masa to form a soft dough and season with the remaining 1½ teaspoons of salt. Place the lard in the bowl of a standing mixer and whip at high speed. Slowly incorporate pieces of the masa dough as you whip the fat, until all of the dough is added. Stir the corn mixture into the dough.

Pat the soaked corn husks dry and lay flat. Form 2 tablespoons of dough into a small ball and place in the center of a corn husk. Roll the long edges up and over the dough, and then fold over the top and bottom to create a neat package. Take a small strip of corn husk and tie a knot around the package to secure it. Repeat with the remaining dough and husks.

Steam the tamales until firm, 20 to 25 minutes. The tamales can be prepared up to 3 days in advance and refrigerated. Steam the refrigerated tamales for 8 to 10 minutes before serving.

Jicama and Purslane Salad

Purslane is in the category called "succulent herb" and it grows wild all over the place here in California; it is sold by local farmers at the markets in Santa Barbara and San Francisco. But it's also native to Mexico, where it's called *berdolaga* and served as a salad or made into a soup or a sauté.

makes 12 servings as part of a buffet

FOR THE CHILI PINE NUTS
½ cup pine nuts

1½ teaspoons chili powder

¼ teaspoon red chile flakes

1½ teaspoons maple sugar or light brown sugar

¼ teaspoon sea salt

½ teaspoon grapeseed oil

FOR THE SALAD
1 bunch (½ pound) purslane, large stems removed

1 bunch (½ pound) watercress, large stems removed

2 ripe avocados, pitted, peeled, and cut into wedges

2 oranges, sectioned

1 small jicama, peeled and cut into ¼-inch sticks

½ small red onion, halved lengthwise then cut lengthwise into ⅛-inch slices

Juice of 1 lime

2 tablespoons extra virgin olive oil

¾ teaspoon sea salt

¼ teaspoon freshly ground black pepper

MAKE THE CHILI PINE NUTS: Preheat the oven to 300°F. In a small bowl, mix the pine nuts with the chile powder, chili flakes, maple sugar, salt, oil, and ¼ teaspoon of water. Spread the nuts on a baking sheet and bake until browned and toasted, 10 to 12 minutes.

MAKE THE SALAD: On a large serving platter, make seven layers using half of the purslane, watercress, avocados, orange sections, jicama, red onion, and pine nuts. Repeat with the remaining half. In a small bowl, combine the lime juice, olive oil, salt, and black pepper, and drizzle over the layered ingredients.

Smashed Black Beans

With just honey and chipotle chiles stirred into the beans, this is delicious; with the addition of little crispy shallots, queso fresco, and cilantro on top, it's true comfort food, Mexican style.

makes 12 servings as part of a buffet

1 pound dried black beans, soaked overnight

½ head garlic

1 thyme sprig

1 oregano sprig

¼ cup lard

3 tablespoons honey

2 chipotle chiles in adobo, chopped, or more to taste

1 ¼ teaspoons plus ⅛ teaspoon sea salt

5 shallots, thinly sliced into rings, preferably on a mandoline

Grapeseed oil, for frying

¼ cup crumbled queso fresco or farmer's cheese

6 cilantro sprigs, for garnish

Drain the black beans and place them in a large pot with the garlic, thyme, and oregano. Cover with water and bring to a simmer. Reduce the heat to low and simmer until the beans are very tender, about 3 hours. Add water as needed to keep the beans submerged throughout cooking. Remove the garlic, thyme, and oregano sprigs. Drain the beans, reserving ⅔ cup of the cooking liquid.

Place the lard in a large sauté pan and heat until it is shimmering. Carefully transfer the beans and their reserved liquid to the pan. With a potato masher or a large fork, smash the beans to the degree you desire. Stir in the honey, chipotles, and 1 ¼ teaspoons of the salt. The beans can be prepared to this point 2 or 3 days in advance and refrigerated. Reheat over medium-low heat, adding water if necessary to loosen the beans.

Place the shallots in a 9-inch sauté pan. Cover with oil and place over medium-high heat. Watch carefully and stir constantly once the oil heats up. Reduce the heat to medium and cook the shallots until they are golden brown, about 5 minutes. Use a slotted spoon to remove them to drain on a paper towel. Season the shallots with the remaining ⅛ teaspoon of salt.

Place the beans in a serving bowl and top with the queso fresco, fried shallots, and cilantro sprigs.

TARANTULAS

Whenever visitors come to Rancho La Zaca in the fall, they remark on the black objects in the middle of the roads that look like tarantulas but couldn't possibly be the big, furry spiders. In fact, they are observing tarantula migration at its height.

Tarantulas are the largest spiders on the ranch. They usually hunt at night and are not considered dangerous, despite a reputation to the contrary, which originally spun out of the scary parts they got in horror movies due to their appearance. In fact, tarantulas make very good pets, even if they are not defanged, and they have some extraordinary characteristics: They have been known to jump distances greater than a foot, and females can live up to twenty years. In August and September, the males migrate across the roads in large numbers, looking for mates. But their ecstasy is short-lived: The females often consume their mates following insemination.

Mexican Fruit Cup

This dish was inspired by the pushcart fruit vendors in Mexico, who cut fresh, local fruits into big chunks and serve them in a sandwich-sized plastic bag. Customers add condiments of chili, lime, and salt to taste, and eat this delicious snack right from the bag. This fancier version has coconut sorbet and pineapple ice. The chili powder blend, or pico de gallo, can be purchased at a local Mexican market.

makes 12 servings

FOR THE PINEAPPLE ICE
½ medium pineapple, peeled, cored, and cut into 1-inch chunks

¼ cup sugar

Juice of 1 lime

Pinch of sea salt

FOR THE COCONUT SORBET
One 14-ounce can unsweetened coconut milk

5 tablespoons sugar

Juice of 2 Mexican limes or 1 regular lime

⅛ teaspoon sea salt

FOR THE FRESH FRUIT
¼ medium pineapple

1 large ripe mango

½ medium papaya

¼ seedless red watermelon

3 young Thai coconuts (also called young coconuts; see Resources)

Juice of 2 Mexican limes or 1 regular lime

Mexican pico de gallo seasoning

Sea salt, for sprinkling

MAKE THE PINEAPPLE ICE: In a blender, puree all of the ingredients until smooth, 2 to 3 minutes. Pour through a fine-mesh strainer and freeze according to your ice-cream maker's instructions.

MAKE THE COCONUT SORBET: In a blender, puree all of the ingredients until combined, about 1 minute. Freeze according to your ice-cream maker's instructions.

PREPARE THE FRUIT AND SERVE: Core and peel the pineapple and cut into 12 wedges. Peel the mango, slice the fruit off the flat pit, and cut the fruit into chunks. Peel and seed the papaya and cut it into chunks. Remove the watermelon rind and cut the fruit into wedges. Using a cleaver, crack the coconuts in half. Reserve the juice for drinking. Scoop out the coconut flesh; use a paring knife to scrape off any tough fiber. Cut the coconut flesh into strips.

In each of 12 serving dishes place 1 or 2 pieces of each fruit. Top with one scoop each of the pineapple ice and coconut sorbet. Squeeze a bit of fresh lime juice onto each and sprinkle with pico de gallo seasoning and salt.

WINE NOTES

Firestone, Walker's Reserve (beer)
Spicy Watermelon Margarita (page 67)

This event could have incorporated some wine—we could have tracked down some Mexican wine, such as L.A. Cetto's Italian-inspired Nebbiolo, for the bison steaks—but we decided to match traditional drinks with Mexican cuisine. Plus, in a group of guys shooting guns, who's going to ask for a glass of pinot grigio?

Given all the chile heat in this menu, beer can be your best friend: Its carbonation cleanses the palate and its cool temperature and lower alcohol tame the spice rather than fanning its flames. Positioned in style somewhere between a porter and a stout, the Walker's Reserve offers up a deep, rich profile that allows it to stand up and go toe-to-toe with the quail and bison on the menu. Produced in small batches, this beer is a real treat, offering sweet coffee and bittersweet aromas that add to its overall complexity and food friendliness.

The attraction of the Spicy Watermelon Margarita, on the other hand, is the addition of some savor to a sweet base, in the same way that the food plays sweet and salty/spicy off one another. This drink transcends the cocktail hour and actually finds harmony with the foods on the table.

ABOVE: Mexican Fruit Cup topped with pineapple ice and coconut sorbet

BEACH RIDE

Guava Cooler

Little Gem Salad

California Coastal Chowder

S'mores with Homemade Marshmallows
and Vosges Chocolate

RIDING A HORSE ON THE BEACH IN CALIFORNIA, SPLASHING THROUGH THE SURF, is one of life's great thrills. A beach where both horses and bonfires are allowed is about an hour's drive from Rancho La Zaca, so we always make a special occasion of it.

The urge to take a beach ride usually hits me in the summer, during an occasional heat wave in the Santa Ynez Valley. (More often than not, when it is especially hot here, the beach is socked in with fog and cold.) The invitations are strictly word of mouth: I·call a friend or two, and they each call a friend or two, and pretty soon we have a group. We rendezvous in the beach parking lot about two hours before dark. This way, we have an hour to ride before we settle around the fire to watch the sunset.

Since the horses get to the beach so infrequently, they always need a little time to become reacquainted with it. As I spur my horse, Gunsmoke, closer to the water, he starts walking sideways and turns his head toward terra firma. But after he hears that some of the other horses have waded in (they almost always heave a loud sigh of relief when they feel the cool water on their bellies), he will skip merrily over the little lapping waves at the shore and boldly make his way to the head of the pack.

With everyone now feeling wet and wild, it is time to lope through the very shallow water. This is the most fun of all, for both the horses and the riders. At the ranch, we rarely run the horses in a full-out gallop because dry hard roads and varmint holes make it too dangerous. But at the shore, the footing is kind and the setting just begs for it. So off we go, with manes and tails flying, sand and saltwater splashing, and each of us wearing a grin from ear to ear. After fifteen delicious minutes, it is time to turn around and walk three miles back to the trailers.

After the horses are put away, we warm up by the campfire, eyeing the pot of chowder bubbling at the center. Since the logistics of getting horses to the beach are complicated enough, we try to keep the food and beverages simple—either edible or disposable. Refreshing Guava Coolers are served at sunset in plastic bags with a straw spout, like Mexican street vendors use. The hearty chowder is ladled into sourdough bread bowls, so the whole dish is edible. Grown-up s'mores, made with exotic chocolate, are the perfect dessert, and all the wrappings get tossed into the fire afterward. With the moon in the sky, we eventually decide it is time to go, and leave behind nothing but hoofprints.

Guava Cooler

In Mexico, street vendors sell tropical fruit juices served in to-go bags: clear plastic gathered at the neck and tied around a plastic drink straw. It looks like the same packaging they use when you buy a goldfish in a pet store, so we added little Murano glass fishes to swim inside each drink, which made whimsical mementos for everyone who joined us on the beach ride.

makes twelve 7-ounce servings

1 quart sweetened guava puree

Juice of 8 limes

2 cups light rum

1 liter sparkling water

1 cup Midori (melon liqueur)

In a large pitcher, combine the guava puree, lime juice, rum, water, and Midori and stir well. Serve over ice with a straw.

Little Gem Salad

Little gem lettuce is a cross between romaine and butter lettuce, with a perfectly sweet crunch—and each head is a perfect serving size. If you can't find it, you may substitute hearts of romaine. Dried seaweeds are available at most upscale supermarkets and health food stores.

makes 12 servings

FOR THE DRESSING

½ cup tahini

3 tablespoons apple cider vinegar

½ cup extra virgin olive oil

3 tablespoons dulse seaweed

2 teaspoons soy sauce

Juice of 1 large lemon

1 teaspoon grated lemon zest

1 garlic clove, minced

1½ teaspoons sea salt

1 tablespoon sliced chives

1 tablespoon chopped parsley

FOR THE SALAD

3 heads little gem lettuce, tough outer leaves discarded and leaves removed from core

1 small head butter lettuce, tough outer leaves discarded and leaves removed from core

1 head curly baby red leaf lettuce, tough outer leaves discarded and leaves removed from core

1 head frisée lettuce, tough outer leaves discarded and leaves removed from core

2 tablespoons hijiki seaweed, rehydrated in water for 10 minutes, then drained

3 tablespoons wakame seaweed, rehydrated in water for 10 minutes, then drained

1 cup dulse seaweed, broken into small pieces

1 small cucumber, peeled, halved lengthwise, and sliced into ⅛-inch half-moons

½ small red onion, halved lengthwise then cut lengthwise into ⅛-inch slices

½ cup cherry tomatoes, halved

24 small nasturtium petals or other edible flower petals

MAKE THE DRESSING: In a blender, combine the tahini, vinegar, olive oil, dulse, soy sauce, lemon juice and zest, garlic, salt, and ½ cup plus 2 tablespoons of water. Blend for 2 minutes. Add the chives and parsley and pulse for 5 seconds. This will keep for several days, refrigerated.

MAKE THE SALAD: In a large bowl, toss the lettuces together and place 1 cup on each plate. Garnish with the seaweeds, vegetables, and nasturtium petals. Drizzle each serving with 1 to 2 tablespoons of dressing and serve.

California Coastal Chowder

Santa Barbara's Channel Islands are a major source of the world's sea urchin or "uni," a delicacy especially prized in Asia. Uni have a rich, buttery flavor that sings with the mignonette sauce on this chowder. If you cannot find live sea urchins at your market, call your favorite sushi bar and ask them to help you find them. If you live near the coast, ask for locally caught fish at your market. You can make this chowder from any combination of fish and shellfish—the most important thing is that whatever you use, make sure it is the freshest you can find. If you are daunted by shellfish shucking, most fishmongers will do it for you, but make sure to ask to retain the "liquor" (you don't need the shells).

makes 10 servings

FOR THE MUSSELS
2 tablespoons extra virgin olive oil

2 medium shallots, sliced

2 large garlic cloves, sliced

½ lime, sliced

2 oregano sprigs

4 thyme sprigs

6 cilantro sprigs

¼ teaspoon red chile flakes

¼ teaspoon fennel seeds

¼ teaspoon coriander seeds

1 cup chardonnay

1 cup low-sodium canned chicken stock

¾ teaspoon sea salt

4 dozen mussels, rinsed under cold water and beards removed

10 small (6-inch) round sourdough bread loaves (optional)

FOR THE CHOWDER
½ cup (1 stick) unsalted butter

1 yellow onion, diced

2 garlic cloves, minced

3 celery stalks, diced

½ teaspoon coriander seeds, toasted and ground

½ teaspoon fennel seeds, toasted and ground

1 thyme sprig

½ cup all-purpose flour

1 cup low-sodium canned chicken stock, hot

6 cups whole milk, hot

2 cups heavy cream, hot

2 Idaho potatoes, peeled and diced

8 ounces linguiça-style sausage (see Resources), thinly sliced

1½ teaspoons sea salt

2 dozen ridgeback shrimp or 21 to 25 count medium shrimp, shelled and deveined

2 dozen oysters, shucked (reserve any liquor) and halved

3 small lobster tails, meat removed from the shell and chopped into ½-inch chunks (about 8 ounces lobster meat)

½ teaspoon freshly ground black pepper

Sea Urchin Butter (recipe follows)

Herb Mignonette (recipe follows)

COOK THE MUSSELS: In a large stockpot, heat the olive oil. Add the shallots, garlic, and lime slices, and sauté over the heat until the shallots are translucent, about 1 minute. Add the oregano, thyme, cilantro, chile flakes, fennel seeds, coriander seeds, chardonnay, chicken stock, and salt. Bring to a boil.

Add the mussels, cover, and reduce the heat to low. Simmer until the mussels have opened, about 5 minutes. Discard any mussels that have not opened. Remove the opened mussels from their shells, and discard the shells. Pour the cooking liquid through a fine-mesh strainer and reserve.

MAKE THE BREAD BOWLS: If using bread bowls rather than standard bowls, make a horizontal slice to remove ½ inch from the top of each sourdough loaf. Discard the "lid" or reserve for another use. Hollow out the interior of each, making sure to leave ½ inch of bread on the sides and bottom so the bowl doesn't leak.

MAKE THE CHOWDER: In a large stockpot, melt the butter over medium heat. Add the onion, garlic, celery, coriander seeds, fennel seeds, and thyme. Sauté until the onion is translucent, about 4 minutes. Add the flour, stir well, and cook for 6 to 8 minutes. Slowly add the hot stock, milk, and cream while stirring to keep the flour from clumping. Add the potatoes, sausage, and 1 teaspoon of the salt. Bring to a boil and simmer, stirring constantly, until the potatoes are tender, about 20 minutes. Add the shrimp, oysters, and lobster and cook until just done, about 5 minutes. Add the mussels and heat through. Season with the remaining ½ teaspoon of salt and the black pepper. The chowder can be made up to 3 days ahead if cooled in an ice bath and refrigerated. It freezes well, but take care not to overcook the seafood when you reheat it.

Ladle the piping hot soup into the bread bowls, top with 1 to 2 teaspoons of sea urchin butter and 1 teaspoon herb mignonette, and serve immediately.

Sea Urchin Butter

makes 1 cup

2 live sea urchins or 10 roe sections of prepared
  sea urchin (see Resources)

3 tablespoons unsalted butter

¼ teaspoon red chili flakes

½ teaspoon soy sauce

½ teaspoon mirin

1 teaspoon minced cilantro

1½ teaspoons fresh lime juice

½ teaspoon sea salt

CLEAN THE SEA URCHINS: Cut out the beak of the live sea urchin with a paring knife. Using the tip of a heavy chef's knife, cut 1 inch into the body of the shell. Break the shell in half by twisting the knife against the shell and using the shell for leverage. Be careful not to damage the roe. Scoop out the roe with a spoon and rinse it under cold running water. Pat dry with a paper towel.

In a blender, combine the urchin roe with the butter, chili flakes, soy sauce, mirin, cilantro, lime juice, and salt. Blend until smooth, about 2 minutes. Refrigerate until completely chilled, about 2 hours.

Herb Mignonette

makes about ¼ cup

3 small shallots, minced

1½ teaspoons freshly cracked black pepper

2 tablespoons chopped thyme leaves

1 teaspoon chopped oregano leaves

¾ teaspoon sea salt

1 tablespoon thinly sliced chives

1 plum tomato, seeded and cut into ⅛-inch dice

3½ tablespoons red wine vinegar

Combine all the ingredients. The mignonette can be prepared 12 hours in advance and refrigerated.

S'mores with Homemade Marshmallows and Vosges Chocolate

Of the millions of s'mores eaten each year in the United States, you may not come across many with homemade marshmallows. But store-bought marshmallows are gummy—any food that has a shelf life of eternity must have some downside—while the homemade versions are softer and airier. And when they are toasted, they make a subtle sound when you bite into them.

makes 1 serving

1 square Vosges exotic chocolate bar
(see Resources)

1 or 2 Homemade Graham Crackers
(recipe follows)

1 Homemade Marshmallow (recipe follows)

1 stick, for toasting

Place the chocolate on a graham cracker. Place the marshmallow on a stick and toast it over an open fire. Place the marshmallow on the chocolate and top with the second graham cracker unless you would like to eat it open-faced. Let the s'more sit for 30 seconds—if you can—so the chocolate can begin to melt.

Homemade Marshmallows

makes 4 dozen

Butter, for greasing the pan

1 cup confectioners' sugar, plus more for
dusting the pan

2 tablespoons plus 2½ teaspoons unflavored
gelatin

2 cups granulated sugar

½ cup light corn syrup

½ vanilla bean, split and scraped

½ teaspoon sea salt

2 large egg whites (if egg safety is a concern,
substitute pasteurized egg whites)

Butter the bottom and sides of a 13 x 9-inch pan and dust with ¼ cup of the confectioners' sugar.

In the bowl of a standing mixer or a large mixing bowl, sprinkle the gelatin over ½ cup of cold water and let bloom, or soften.

In a 3-quart heavy-bottomed saucepan, combine ⅔ cup of hot water with the granulated sugar, corn syrup, vanilla bean seeds, and salt. Set over low heat, stirring with a wooden spoon, until the sugar is dissolved. Increase the heat to medium-high and boil, without stirring, until the syrup reaches 240°F on a candy thermometer. Remove from the heat and add to the gelatin, stirring until the gelatin is dissolved.

Using the standing or handheld electric mixer, beat the gelatin and syrup at high speed until white, thick, and nearly tripled in volume, 6 to 10 minutes. If you are using a standing mixer, drape a kitchen towel over the top of the mixer to catch any splatter.

In a large bowl with clean beaters, beat the egg whites until they just hold stiff peaks. Beat the whites with the sugar mixture until just combined. Quickly spread the mixture evenly into the prepared pan and sift ⅓ cup of the confectioners' sugar over the top. Refrigerate, uncovered, until firm, at least 3 hours and up to 1 day.

Run a thin knife around the edge of the pan and invert onto a large cutting board. (Make sure it is a cutting board that has never been used for onions or garlic.) Lift up one corner of the inverted pan and loosen the giant marshmallow with your fingers or a small spatula, letting it drop onto the cutting board. Using a large knife dusted with confectioners' sugar, trim the marshmallow into 2 x 1-inch rectangles. Sift the remaining ⅔ cup of confectioners' sugar into a large bowl and dredge the marshmallows in batches, tossing evenly to coat and shaking off the excess. (These will keep in an airtight container for 3 days.)

Homemade Graham Crackers

1 cup all-purpose flour, plus more for dusting

½ teaspoon sea salt

½ teaspoon baking soda

1 teaspoon ground cinnamon

1½ cups graham flour

¾ cup (1½ sticks) unsalted butter, softened

½ cup packed brown sugar

2 tablespoons honey, preferably local and raw

2 tablespoons unsulfured molasses

In a medium bowl, sift together the all-purpose flour, salt, baking soda, and cinnamon. Stir in the graham flour.

In a large bowl, use an electric mixer to cream the butter with the brown sugar, honey, and molasses until light and fluffy. Add the flour mixture and mix at low speed until just combined and the mixture forms a ball. Knead the dough until well combined, about 30 seconds. On a piece of parchment paper, divide the dough into thirds and shape into three 1-inch-thick rectangles. Refrigerate for 30 minutes.

Preheat the oven to 350°F. Line 2 cookie sheets with parchment paper. Remove the chilled dough from the refrigerator and roll each piece between two sheets of parchment paper until it is ⅛-inch thick. Return to the refrigerator for 15 minutes. Cut into 2 x 2-inch squares and place on the prepared cookie sheets. Prick the squares with a fork in an even pattern. (Any leftover dough may be combined, rolled, and cut as well.) Refrigerate if the dough becomes too soft to work with.

Bake until the edges begin to darken and the cookies do not look raw, about 10 minutes. Let cool completely on the cookie sheets. The graham crackers can be stored in an airtight container for up to 3 days.

WINE NOTES

Guava Cooler (page 83)
Brut, Gruet, MV (Multi-Vintage) (New Mexico, USA)
Tocai Friulano, Palmina, 2003 (Santa Maria, California)
Muscadet Sèvre et Maine Sur Lie, Domaine de la Pepière, 2005 (Loire, France)

When you're on the beach, you want something light, refreshing, and not too alcoholic. The easy and exotic flavors of the guava and Midori are mouthwatering and fruity on their own, and they work really well together. And if you want a wine-based alternative to the cooler, try this: Add guava puree (or passion fruit puree) to a nice crisp sparkling wine base, such as a prosecco from Italy or a domestic blanc de blanc from Domaine Carneros in Napa, or Domaine Ste. Michelle from Washington state.

Still, as delicious and thematic as the Guava Cooler is for this event, some of your guests might want to move on to wine when the food comes out. With each plate kissed by the sea air and punched up with the likes of seaweed and shellfish, think of pouring vibrant, mineral-rich whites. The seafood chowder would sing with some Champagne, or if you'd like to stay on theme—and stay domestic to boot—you might pop the cork on the well regarded multi-vintage brut from Gruet in New Mexico. This crisp, chardonnay-based

sparkler has plenty of green apple and grapefruit to go with the salad, and a chalky texture to match the briny mussels.

Along this same line, you might opt for the archetypal shellfish white, muscadet, from the north coast of France. This is, quite simply, a bottled expression of the sea. Should you prefer to stay local, the exotic aromas and mineral grip of the Palmina Tocai—made from an Italian grape that appears to be a genetic relative of sauvignon blanc—will highlight the aromatic elements of the chowder while matching its richness.

In the eighteenth century, as the Spanish missionaries moved north into Alta California from Mexico, they were followed by the Sonoran *vaqueros* and their cattle. Accustomed to the harsh desert of Mexico, the vaqueros discovered the grazing land dramatically improved as they rode along the northern border of the Los Angeles basin. The gentle topography of the vast coastal regions north of Santa Barbara is often swaddled in fog blankets and is irrigated by a brief, mild rainy season. The vaqueros found that the grass was indeed greener in Alta California.

Under almost any circumstance, the job of minding livestock is rarely sparked by ambition. And with the spectacular grazing conditions here, the California vaqueros quickly found they could work less and earn more than their counterparts anyplace else in the world. This didn't mean they spent their idle time asleep in the shade of a tree, however. Instead, they whiled their days away riding horses.

Some of their tack was adapted from that of the Andalusian Moors who had occupied southern Spain since the eighth century. Until their skills were surpassed by the California vaquero, who could spend 360 days a year in the saddle, the Moors were considered to be the greatest horsemen in the world.

Typically in cultures with ample leisure time, personal adornment increases in importance and becomes more elaborate. The California vaquero and his horse had a look all their own. The vaquero hat is often made of woven grass, with a flat brim. The size of the crown and its shape went through every permutation, from shallow and flat to tall and elaborately dimpled, but always based on fashion, not practical reasons. In California, a hat gives shade. But temperature, wind, rain, and snow—the elements that commonly shape hats—weren't a problem here. The vaqueros were as proud as peacocks, and their embellished clothing shouted this with embroidery, fringe, trim, silver studs and *conchas,* lace, and color.

It was said that vaqueros never walked more than fifty feet. Instead, they rode. Their spurs are proof of this. While early vaqueros often rode barefoot, they were never without their unique "irons," distinguished by delicate heel bands and rowls as large as saucers. That they were barefoot means that they had no intention of walking, but those spurs would have made it impossible.

Paradoxically, the larger the rowl, the kinder it is to the horse. Spurs with large rowls are mainly for show; the vaqueros controlled their horses by neck-reining them, and contests were held to see who could control his horse with the gentlest touch. To ascertain this, a man would substitute a piece of twine for his horse's metal bit. Evidence of a gentle reining hand was acknowledged when a man returned from a day's herding work with the twine unbroken.

Strapped to the right side of every saddle was a coiled riata, the vaquero's most important tool. Made of braided rawhide, these ropes typically varied in length from sixty to one-hundred feet, depending on the throwing skill of the vaquero who made and owned it. A riata is to a vaquero what monofilament is to a fisherman: With little inherent tensile strength, used masterfully, it is capable of reeling in a greater weight than its delicate diameter might suggest. The vaqueros practiced throwing a riata until they could rope a cow single-handedly, a feat that today would take a pair of cowboys with lesser skills. Just for fun, the vaqueros also roped bulls and grizzly bears.

The horse, an extension of the vaquero, was also decorated. Unique tack included braided reins with complex knot patterns studded in silver; the revolutionary Santa Barbara spade bit with its gentler mouthpiece and signature Moorish crescent moons on the cheek; horned leather saddles embossed with delicate floral patterns; and the *tapadero,* a long tapered swatch of leather that covered the toe of the stirrups.

In the early nineteenth century, as Yankees came west seeking fortunes, first in cattle, then in gold, the Mexican word vaquero began evolving into the American term buckaroo, the anglicized pronunciation. If you carefully examine a California cowboy today, though, you will still see traces of the Spanish and Mexican legacy.

INDIAN FEAST

Tamarind Switch

Naan

Seared Duck Breast with Three Chutneys

Tandoori-Spiced Lobster Tails

Mint and Coconut Rice

Vindaloo Haricots Verts and White Asparagus

Cauliflower Kari

Masala Apple Cake with Cardamom Ice Cream

ON A TRIP TO CAMBODIA TO SEE THE TEMPLE COMPLEX AT ANKOR WAT, I RODE AN elephant for the first time. Tom and I were traveling with Brooks and Kate Firestone, and for the same corny reasons that I cannot resist an occasional hansom cab ride through Central Park, we two couples found ourselves on the backs of a pair of elephants, trudging through bamboo forests to a hilltop outside of Siem Riep to watch the sunset play on the façade of the ancient Khmer ruins.

We traveled in Southeast Asia for almost a month and toured many impressive major sights. But on the flight home, I sheepishly admitted that the touristy elephant ride was one of the high points of the trip. And sadly, I thought it might have been a once-in-a-lifetime experience. Then my imagination went wild. "Wouldn't it be fun to have an elephant at the ranch?" I asked before considering anything remotely practical like the size of the pen, a source of food, vet bills, and the like. But after I got home, I discovered that one of the finest elephant stables in the United States is located near both the ranch and Hollywood, where the giants are almost continually employed. These elephants could be mine for a day.

Have Trunk Will Travel is a well-named business. Gary and Kari Johnson packed the "trunks," into a spotlessly clean semi truck, and they arrived a polite thirty minutes before the guests did. The elephants lumbered down the gangplank and into the vineyard, and Tai, the freckled one, pointed her trunk straight into the nearest tender grape leaves. I thought Felipe, our vineyard manager, would jump out of his skin at the sight of the animal threatening his tender vines. Using a small device shaped like a shepherd's crook, Gary tapped Tai's trunk and said, "Don't touch."

"Right," I said. "She speaks English?" I began to fear that this elephant-in-the-vineyard brainstorm was one I might live to regret.

"Oh, yes," Gary assured me. "She knows about seventy-five words and commands." Kitty, the second elephant, came out of the truck, and all Gary had to say to her was, "No." The grapes were safe.

The guests, all women, soon arrived, each one costumed in a sari. The invitation had made clear this was an Indian party, honoring Ganesh, the Hindu deity with the head of an elephant. But no one imagined there would be any real elephants.

Carrying two or three of us at a time, Tai and Kitty took all the guests on a vineyard tour like no other. And then we sat down to this splendid luncheon.

Tamarind Switch

The flavor of toasted cumin is carried nicely by the bubbly wine or sparkling water. You might not expect your guests to flock to this odd-sounding version of a Bellini—tamarind and cumin, after all, aren't run-of-the-mill cocktail ingredients—but have confidence, and be sure to make a big batch.

makes 16 servings

1½ cups Tamarind Paste (recipe follows)

1⅓ cups sugar

1½ tablespoons toasted cumin seeds, ground and sifted

3 (750 ml) bottles sparkling wine such as prosecco, or sparkling water for a nonalcoholic version

In a medium bowl, stir together the tamarind paste, sugar, cumin, and 1 cup of water. Chill and mix about 2 tablespoons into each glass of sparkling wine or sparkling water.

Tamarind Paste

makes 3 cups

One 14-ounce block tamarind paste (use processed seedless tamarind from

Thailand, which contains nothing but tamarind and saves a lot of time)

Break up the tamarind paste into a medium heavy-bottomed saucepan. Add 6 cups of water and bring to a simmer. Cook until the tamarind is very soft, 20 to 25 minutes. Let cool slightly and then press through a medium-mesh sieve. Discard the pulp. The paste should be the consistency of slightly thin ketchup. The tamarind paste can be prepared up to 3 days in advance and refrigerated, or it can be frozen for up to 3 months.

Naan

For this luncheon, we asked a local Indian restaurant, Taj, to bring over their charcoal fired tandoori oven and make naan bread. But it's possible—and easy—to make your own on a home grill.

makes six 7-inch breads

One ¼-ounce package active dry yeast

¼ cup sugar

3 tablespoons milk

1 large egg, beaten

1 tablespoon sea salt

3 to 3½ cups bread flour

2 teaspoons minced garlic (optional)

Grapeseed oil, for greasing the grill

¼ cup (½ stick) unsalted butter, melted

In a large bowl, dissolve the yeast in 1 cup of warm water. Let stand until frothy, about 10 minutes. Stir in the sugar, milk, egg, salt, and enough flour to make a soft dough. On a lightly floured surface, knead until smooth, 6 to 8 minutes. Place the dough in a well-oiled bowl and cover with a damp cloth. Let the dough rise until it has doubled in volume, about 1 hour.

Punch down the dough and knead in the garlic if using. Divide the dough into 6 equal pieces. Roll into balls and place on a baking sheet. Cover with a towel and allow to rise until doubled in size, about 30 minutes. Preheat the grill to high.

At grill side, roll out one ball of dough into a thin circle 7 to 8 inches across. Lightly oil the grill. Place the dough on the grill and cook until puffy and the bottom is lightly browned, 2 to 3 minutes, turning 90 degrees after 1 minute. Brush the uncooked side with the melted butter and turn over. Brush the cooked side with butter and cook until the bottom is browned, another 2 to 4 minutes, turning 90 degrees after 1 minute. Remove from the grill and continue the process until all of the naan has been prepared. Cut the naan into quarters and serve hot.

Seared Duck Breast with Three Chutneys

Serve this with idlis, the steamed rice and lentil dumplings from southern India. There's no need to make your own batter because store-bought idli mixes such as Gits brand are great; simply cook according to the package directions. And one or all three of the following chutneys—Cilantro and Mint Chutney, Coconut Chutney, and Sweet-and-Sour Tamarind Chutney—is a must.

makes 10 servings

FOR THE DUCK BREASTS
2½ pounds duck breasts

1 teaspoon grated ginger

1 garlic clove, minced

2 tablespoons chopped mint

2 tablespoons chopped cilantro

2 tablespoons garam masala

2 tablespoons muscovado sugar

½ teaspoon sea salt

½ teaspoon freshly cracked black pepper

1 tablespoon grapeseed oil

FOR THE GARNISHES
10 idlis, hot

10 tablespoons Cilantro and Mint Chutney (recipe follows)

10 tablespoons Sweet-and-Sour Tamarind Chutney (recipe follows)

10 tablespoons Coconut Chutney (recipe follows)

1 ounce (about 1 cup) micro basil (see Resources) or coarsely chopped regular basil

1 ounce (about 1 cup) micro mint (see Resources) or coarsely chopped regular mint

1 ounce (about 1 cup) micro cilantro (see Resources) or coarsely chopped regular cilantro

½ teaspoon extra virgin olive oil

¼ teaspoon fresh lemon juice

½ teaspoon sea salt

¼ teaspoon freshly ground black pepper

½ cup chevdo mix, or other crunchy Indian snack mix (see Resources)

MAKE THE DUCK BREASTS: Using a very sharp knife, score the skin of each duck breast ⅛-inch deep in a crosshatch pattern, being careful not to cut all the way to the flesh. In a mortar, combine the ginger, garlic, mint, cilantro, garam masala, sugar, salt, black pepper, and oil and grind to a paste. Spread this paste over both sides of each duck breast. Place in a shallow baking dish, cover tightly with plastic, and refrigerate for 24 hours.

Place the marinated duck breasts in a large sauté pan, skin side down, with ¼-inch of water. Set over medium-high heat and bring the water to a simmer. Reduce the heat to medium-low and allow the water to evaporate. Cook until the skin becomes crispy and golden brown, 12 to 15 minutes. Drain some of the fat from the pan. Turn the breasts over, and continue cooking until medium-rare; about 2 minutes. Let rest for 5 minutes.

Place a steamed idli on each plate. Spoon the cilantro and mint chutney across the right side of the idli and spoon the tamarind chutney across the left side of the idli. Spoon the coconut chutney on top.

Thinly slice the duck breasts crosswise and arrange half of each breast on a plate in front of the idli.

In a medium bowl, toss the micro herbs with the olive oil and lemon juice and season with the salt and black pepper. Place a big pinch of the herbs on top of each idli and sprinkle with the chevdo.

Cilantro and Mint Chutney

makes ½ cup

2 cups cilantro leaves and softer stems

1 cup mint leaves

1 serrano chile, seeded and minced

1 teaspoon minced ginger

1 teaspoon sugar

½ teaspoon sea salt

2½ tablespoons fresh lime juice

2½ tablespoons water

In a blender, combine all of the ingredients and puree until smooth. Scrape down the sides of the blender several times as you go. Cover and refrigerate until chilled thoroughly. (The chutney can be made a day in advance and stored, covered, in the refrigerator.)

Coconut Chutney

makes 1¼ cups

1 cup packed freshly grated coconut
  (see Resources)

½ cup plain yogurt

2 tablespoons chopped cilantro leaves

1 serrano chile, seeded and minced

½ teaspoon sea salt

2 tablespoons ghee (clarified butter)
  (recipe follows)

1 teaspoon black mustard seeds

In a blender, combine the coconut, yogurt, cilantro, chile, salt, and ¼ cup hot water. Puree until smooth, 1 to 2 minutes. Scrape down the sides of the blender several times. The chutney can be prepared to this point 2 days in advance and refrigerated.

Just before serving, in a small skillet, warm the ghee over medium-high heat. Carefully add the mustard seeds. Keep a cover handy as the seeds will pop and splatter. After about 3 minutes, when the seeds stop popping and turn gray, remove the skillet from the heat and pour the mustard seeds over the coconut. Mix thoroughly.

Ghee, or Clarified Butter

makes ¾ cup

1 cup (2 sticks) unsalted butter

In a small saucepan over low heat, slowly melt the butter, about 10 minutes. Remove from the heat and let stand for 5 minutes. Use a spoon to skim off the foam. Spoon or ladle the clear butter fat into a container and discard the milky liquid and solids that remain. The clarified butter willl keep for 1 month in the refrigerator.

Sweet-and-Sour Tamarind Chutney

makes 1½ cups

¾ cup Tamarind Paste (page 97)

½ cup brown sugar

¼ cup golden raisins, chopped

¼ cup finely chopped pitted dates

1½ teaspoons cumin seeds, toasted and ground

1 teaspoon garam masala

2 teaspoons minced ginger

¼ teaspoon ground Kashmir red pepper or
  cayenne pepper

½ teaspoon sea salt

Place the tamarind paste in a medium bowl and stir in 2 tablespoons of water, the brown sugar, raisins, dates, cumin, garam masala, ginger, red pepper, and salt. Cover and let stand at least 4 hours or refrigerate overnight to let the flavors blend together. (This can be made up to 3 days in advance and stored, covered, in the refrigerator.)

Tandoori-Spiced Lobster Tails

This lobster is marinated overnight in a robust tandoori spice mixture, grilled, and then paired with a caramelized onion and tamarind sauce in the eastern Bengalese style. Serve this "thali" style, with the side dishes that follow: Mint and Coconut Rice, Vindaloo Haricots Verts and White Asparagus, and Cauliflower Kari.

makes 10 servings

3 tablespoons coriander seeds

3 tablespoons fennel seeds

1½ tablespoons Indian red chile powder or cayenne

2½ teaspoons turmeric

¾ cup plus 1 tablespoon grapeseed oil

6 tablespoons Tamarind Paste (page 97)

3 teaspoons sea salt

Ten 8- to 10-ounce lobster tails, in the shell

¾ teaspoon freshly ground black pepper

Caramelized Onion and Tamarind Sauce (recipe follows)

2 tablespoons Sweet-and-Sour Tamarind Chutney (page 100)

1 tablespoon fresh lime juice

20 cilantro sprigs, for garnish

In a small sauté pan, toast the coriander seeds and fennel seeds over medium heat until fragrant, about 4 minutes. Let cool. Grind in a mortar with the chile powder, turmeric, ¾ cup of the oil, the tamarind paste, and 1 teaspoon of the salt.

Using kitchen shears, cut through the bottom side of the lobster shell, being careful not to cut into the meat. Remove the lobster meat from the shell, keeping the shells intact. Rub the lobster tails all over with the spice and tamarind mixture. Place back in the shells and place the shells in a glass baking dish. Marinate in the refrigerator 12 hours or overnight.

Preheat the grill to medium. Season the lobster meat with the remaining 2 teaspoons of salt and the black pepper. Place the lobster in the shell on the grill and cook until done, about 12 minutes total, turning twice. During the last 2 minutes, work the lobster tail out of the shell to put the meat directly on the grill.

In a small bowl, combine the tamarind chutney, lime juice, and the remaining 1 tablespoon of grapeseed oil to make a vinaigrette. Whisk to combine. Spoon some Caramelized Onion and Tamarind Sauce onto the center of each plate. Add a lobster tail, spoon the vinaigrette over, and garnish with a few cilantro sprigs.

Caramelized Onion and Tamarind Sauce

makes 3 cups

¼ cup grapeseed oil

3 medium yellow onions, halved lengthwise then cut lengthwise into ⅛-inch slices

2 garlic cloves, finely minced

1 tablespoon finely minced ginger (about a 1-inch knob)

1 tablespoon ground coriander

½ teaspoon turmeric

¼ teaspoon fennel seeds

¼ teaspoon red chili flakes

1½ teaspoons sweet paprika

4 medium plum tomatoes, peeled, seeded, and chopped

3 cups low-sodium canned chicken stock

5 tablespoons Tamarind Paste (page 97)

1½ teaspoons sea salt

In a large skillet, heat the oil over high heat. Add the onions, reduce the heat to medium, and cook, turning often, until dark brown, about 8 minutes. Add the garlic, ginger, and spices. Cook for 1 minute to release the fragrance of the spices. Add the tomatoes, stock, tamarind paste, and salt. Simmer the sauce until it is slightly thickened and has a pulpy, thin ketchup consistency, 4 to 8 minutes. The sauce can be prepared up to 2 days in advance and refrigerated. Reheat before serving.

Mint and Coconut Rice

This is much more substantial than the typical side of basmati rice. Infused with the flavors of mint, coconut, chile, and spices, plus the addition of chewy chunks of potato, it's really a dish unto itself— and a wonderful accompaniment to any Indian entrée.

makes 4 cups; serves 10 as a side dish

¾ cup packed freshly grated coconut
  (see Resources)

¾ cup mint leaves

1 serrano chile, seeded and minced

¼ teaspoon ground cloves

¼ teaspoon ground cinnamon

6 tablespoons clarified butter (page 100)

2 medium Yukon Gold potatoes, peeled and
  cut into ¼-inch dice

1½ cups basmati rice

1¾ teaspoons sea salt

In a blender, combine ¾ cup of water with the coconut, mint, chile, cloves, and cinnamon and puree until smooth, 2 to 4 minutes.

Heat the clarified butter in a medium saucepan over medium heat. Add the potatoes and fry, stirring constantly, until golden brown on all sides, about 6 minutes. Remove the potatoes from the pan. Add the mint mixture to the pan and fry until the fat begins to separate, about 2 minutes. Add the rice and fry, stirring, until all of the grains are coated with the mint mixture, about 1 minute. Add 1¾ cups plus 2 tablespoons of water to the pan along with the fried potatoes and salt. Bring to a simmer. Cover, reduce the heat to low, and let cook for 15 minutes. Turn off the heat and allow to stand, covered, for an additional 10 minutes. Stir gently just before serving.

Vindaloo Haricots Verts and White Asparagus

Baby white asparagus is a luxury. You can substitute regular white asparagus, often available at upscale grocers; just make sure to quarter them lengthwise before proceeding with the recipe.

makes 10 side-dish servings

3 tablespoons grapeseed oil

4 serrano chiles, halved

1 tablespoon minced ginger
  (about a 1-inch knob)

6 fresh curry leaves (see Resources)

1 teaspoon black mustard seeds

¾ teaspoon turmeric

½ teaspoon ground cinnamon

½ teaspoon Indian red chile powder,
  such as Kashmir red pepper

⅛ teaspoon ground cloves

1 medium yellow onion, halved lengthwise then
  cut lengthwise into ⅛-inch slices

8 ounces haricots verts, stemmed

16 ounces pencil-thin baby white asparagus,
  tough ends removed

2 plum tomatoes, peeled, seeded, and chopped

2 tablespoons freshly grated coconut
  (see Resources)

1 tablespoon chopped peanuts

¾ teaspoon sea salt

¼ teaspoon freshly ground black pepper

In a large saucepan, heat the oil over medium heat. Add the chiles, ginger, curry leaves, mustard seeds, turmeric, cinnamon, chile powder, and cloves. Cook, stirring, for 1 minute to release the flavors. Add the onion and continue cooking until lightly browned, 4 to 5 minutes.

Stir in the haricots verts, white asparagus, tomatoes, and 4 tablespoons of water. Cover and cook over low heat, stirring occasionally, until the vegetables are tender and the liquid has evaporated, about 8 minutes. Stir in the coconut and peanuts, season with the salt and black pepper, and serve.

Cauliflower Kari

Cauliflower can be a tough sell. As with most often-maligned ingredients, the way to overcome resistance is to pack the dish with intriguing flavors and color. Here, the spicy mustard seeds and chile combine with the color contrasts between the bright green scallion and the yellow imparted by the turmeric to create a beautiful, flavor-packed side dish. The Kari leaves—also known as curry leaves—are worth seeking out for their delicate but noticeable background flavor.

makes 10 side-dish servings

4 tablespoons grapeseed oil

½ teaspoon black mustard seeds

1 teaspoon white split gram beans
  (see Resources)

½ teaspoon turmeric

1 serrano chile, seeded and minced (optional)

2 bunches scallions (about 12), sliced into
  ½-inch pieces

½ teaspoon sea salt

1 small head cauliflower, separated into large
  florets with stems trimmed

8 fresh curry leaves (see Resources)

Heat 3 tablespoons of the oil over high heat in a large skillet with a lid. Add the mustard seeds; they will pop and splatter. As they are popping, add the split gram beans and cook until the beans are light brown and the mustard seeds are gray, about 4 minutes. Add the turmeric, chile, if using, and scallions, season with the salt and sauté for 15 seconds. Add the cauliflower florets and stir to distribute the spices.

Stir in ⅓ cup of water and reduce the heat to medium-low. Cover and cook until the cauliflower is tender, about 15 minutes. Uncover and raise the heat to medium-high to evaporate any moisture in the pan. Stir in the remaining 1 tablespoon of oil and the curry leaves and allow the cauliflower to brown, 5 to 8 minutes.

Masala Apple Cake with Cardamom Ice Cream

The fragrance of the masala spice blend is the very essence of India in this incredibly easy, deliciously moist cake.

makes 12 servings

FOR THE CAKE

1 cup walnut halves

4 unpeeled Fuji apples, cored and cubed

2 large eggs

½ cup extra virgin olive oil

2 cups sugar

½ teaspoon ground cinnamon

1 tablespoon ground and sifted tea masala
  (see Resources)

2 cups all-purpose flour, plus more for the pan

¾ teaspoon salt

2 teaspoons baking soda

Butter, for greasing the pan

FOR THE FROSTING

½ cup (1 stick) unsalted butter,
  at room temperature

4 ounces cream cheese, at room temperature

1 cup confectioners' sugar, sifted

1 teaspoon pure vanilla extract

Caramel Sauce (recipe follows)

2 cups Cardamom Ice Cream (recipe follows)

Preheat the oven to 300°F. Butter and flour a 13 x 9-inch pan.

MAKE THE CAKE: Spread the walnuts on a rimmed baking sheet and toast them in the oven until golden brown all the way through, 20 to 30 minutes. Let cool and chop. Raise the oven temperature to 350°F.

Place the cubed apples in a large bowl. Break the eggs over them, then add the olive oil, sugar, cinnamon, ground tea spice, and toasted walnuts. Mix with a fork. Sift the flour, salt, and baking soda over the apple mixture and stir with a fork to combine.

Pour the batter into the prepared pan and bake until the top is well browned and the center of the cake springs back when lightly touched, about 55 minutes. Let cool slightly. The cake can be prepared up to 2 days in advance and kept well wrapped at room temperature.

MAKE THE FROSTING: Cream together the butter, cream cheese, confectioners' sugar, and vanilla. Spread over the warm cake.

Place a square of cake on each plate and spoon some of the Caramel Sauce around it. Spoon a scoop of Cardamom Ice Cream on top and serve.

Caramel Sauce

makes ¾ cup

½ cup sugar

¼ teaspoon fresh lemon juice

½ cup heavy cream

2 tablespoons unsalted butter

⅛ teaspoon sea salt

In a small saucepan, combine the sugar and lemon juice with 2 tablespoons of water. Stir over medium heat until the sugar has dissolved, then raise the heat to medium-high and bring to a boil. Do not stir while the mixture is bubbling, but wash down the sides of the pan with a wet pastry brush to prevent crystallization. Cook the sugar until it reaches an even, deep brown color, about 12 minutes. Carefully whisk in the cream, butter, and salt, and simmer for 1 more minute. The caramel sauce can be prepared 2 to 3 days in advance and refrigerated. Reheat gently on the stovetop, or use a microwave.

Cardamom Ice Cream
makes about 3 cups

1 cup whole milk

½ cup heavy cream

½ cup half-and-half

6 tablespoons sugar

6 crushed green cardamom pods

3 large egg yolks

1 tablespoon nonfat dry milk

Pinch of salt

Fill a 4-quart bowl halfway with ice and 2 cups of water. Place a 2-quart metal bowl inside the 4-quart bowl. In a medium heavy-bottomed saucepan, combine the milk, cream, and half-and-half. Sprinkle 3 tablespoons of the sugar on top, (do not stir) and add the crushed cardamom pods. Bring to a boil over medium-high heat.

Meanwhile, in a medium bowl, whisk the remaining 3 tablespoons of sugar with the egg yolks, dry milk, and salt. Gradually whisk the hot milk into the yolk mixture. Return this mixture to the saucepan and place over medium-low heat. Cook, stirring constantly with a wooden spoon against the bottom of the pan, until the mixture thickens and starts to steam. Pour into the bowl sitting in the ice bath. Stir often until completely cooled. Pour through a fine-mesh sieve. The base can be prepared a day in advance and refrigerated. At least 2 hours before serving, pour the ice-cream base into an ice-cream maker. Freeze according to your ice-cream maker's instructions, then store in the freezer until serving.

WINE NOTES

Tamarind Switch (page 97)
Riesling, Oberhäuser Brücke, Spätlese, Dönnhoff, 2005 (Nahe, Germany)
Pinot Gris, Late Harvest, Willakenzie Estate, 2003 (Willamette Valley, Oregon)

Once again there's a savory element in our cocktail, making the Tamarind Switch not only a tangy, refreshing starter but also a potential accompaniment to the food. This drink, like its inspiration, the Bellini, is a true aperitif: Rather than dulling the palate with excessive alcohol, it enlivens the appetite with its crispness and spice. We chose prosecco not only because it is light in alcohol but also because it can always be found at a great price—something to keep in mind when serving bubbly to a crowd.

Wine pairings, meanwhile, can be tricky with Indian cuisine. The spices here are often more intense than those in Mexican dishes, and there's also the counterbalancing sweetness of the assorted chutneys. In a sense, you need the wine to do double duty, and here's where the versatility of German riesling comes in handy. Not only is it typically low in alcohol (so as not to exacerbate spiciness), but there is also a bit of sweetness to contrast (and complement) what's happening on the plate.

German riesling's sweetness varies according to the style in which it is made. A wine labeled as kabinett has enough residual sugar to be just off-dry; a spätlese is the next step up from there; and an auslese is often unctuous enough for dessert. You will want to raise the sweet-ness level in accordance with the heat of the dish.

For this menu, aim for a spätlese-level wine. The sweetness here will not only counterbalance the spice but will complement sweet elements like the coconut rice. You'll also love the luscious texture of a spätlese with the rich lobster tails.

You could continue on to dessert with the same wine, as a good spätlese has plenty of honeyed, appley notes. Should you prefer to go a click sweeter with the Masala Apple Cake, check out the late-harvest pinot gris from Willakenzie Estate. It is sweet without being cloying, and is a great value.

TRUFFLE DINNER

Braised Rabbit with Tagliatta and White Truffles

Lobster with Braised Pork Belly and Black Truffle Salad

Pear Tarts with White Truffle Whipped Cream and Raw Honey

ABOUT THIRTY YEARS AGO, I WAS A YOUNG MAGAZINE EDITOR IN MILAN ON MY first European business trip. I had always been interested in exotic foods and their specialized table accessories, and I discovered a small cutlery shop on the Via Montenapoleone called G. Lorenzi. Amid escargot forks, asparagus tongs, fruit cutlery, sewing kits encased in tortoiseshell bobbins, shoe button hooks, cigar cutters, miniature pocketknives, and other curious sharp metal items I'd never imagined, I found a little truffle shaving set: a pretty hardwood plank on which sits a stainless steel shaver, a fine dust brush made of horsehair, and a blown glass bell-jar cover to protect the precious commodity. It suggested to me the most simple yet decadent entertaining idea: a shave-it-yourself truffle dinner. The salesman at Lorenzi told me where to buy the best truffles in Milan (I had never even tasted one before) and advised me to serve it over hot buttered pasta. Even with the little truffle smothered inside a box filled with arborio rice and bound by three layers of plastic wrap, the smell of it still filled the plane as I carefully carried the tuber and its set back to my fifth-floor walk-up apartment in New York.

Ever since, it has been my tradition to put a whole truffle—the largest my budget would allow—beneath the bell jar and pass it around the table, the implication being that everyone can have "as much as they want." Of course, most guests are far too polite and sensible to take more than a little, which is a good thing because with Stephanie's recipes—much evolved since my days of pasta al dente—we have to make the truffle last all the way through to dessert.

There are few foods more special than a truffle: expensive, rare, and volatile. Stephanie usually manages to get just one truffle each season (calling upon her professional connections, as most of the best ones go directly to restaurants and bypass the retail market entirely). The arrival of our annual truffle always warrants a special occasion at Rancho La Zaca. And it's not difficult to get friends to drop everything and come to dinner: The allure of the fragrant tuber is universal.

Braised Rabbit with Tagliatta and White Truffles

White truffles, although rare and expensive, are increasingly available to the home chef from specialty markets and online. With a top-quality white truffle, as soon as you open the package the aroma should slowly fill the room and linger; if the aroma hits you up front and then dissipates, you may have gotten an inferior product.

makes 4 servings

2 fresh rabbit legs (see Resources)

1 ½ teaspoons sea salt, plus more for salting the water

¼ teaspoon freshly ground black pepper

2 tablespoons grapeseed oil

1 small yellow onion, cut into eighths

1 small carrot, cut into ¼-inch dice

1 celery stalk, cut into ¼-inch dice

1 teaspoon tomato paste

½ cup syrah

1 rosemary sprig

1 oregano sprig

1 summer savory sprig

3 thyme sprigs

2 sage leaves

2 cups low-sodium canned chicken stock

1 ½ ounces fresh white truffle, plus more for serving (see Resources)

3 tablespoons unsalted butter

2 tablespoons sliced chives

2 tablespoons chopped parsley

½ bunch (about 4 ounces) arugula, stems removed and leaves coarsely chopped

1 ounce young Pecorino Romano cheese, cut into ⅛-inch dice (¼ cup)

Roast Butternut Squash (recipe follows)

2 tablespoons white truffle oil

½ pound Chickpea Pasta (recipe follows)

Caramelized Fennel (recipe follows)

Preheat the oven to 300°F.

Pat the rabbit dry with a paper towel. Season with ½ teaspoon of the salt and the black pepper. In a large ovenproof sauté pan, heat the grapeseed oil over medium-high heat and arrange the rabbit legs in the pan without crowding them. Sear on each side until golden brown, 3 to 4 minutes. Remove the legs from the pan, reduce the heat to medium-low, and add the onion, carrot, and celery. Caramelize for about 8 minutes, stirring occasionally. Add the tomato paste and cook, stirring, for 1 minute. Off the heat, add the red wine, herbs, and stock. Bring to a simmer, then return the rabbit legs to the pan.

Cover the pan and place in the preheated oven. Cook for 1 hour and 45 minutes, turning after 1 hour. Remove the legs from the braising liquid and set aside. Pour the reserved liquid into a small saucepan and reduce over medium-high heat by about half, about 20 minutes. When cooled, shred the rabbit meat and discard any sinew or bone, keeping only the meat and skin. Stir the rabbit and the reduced stock together. The recipe can be made to this point one day in advance. Cover the rabbit and stock and refrigerate. Bring to room temperature before continuing.

Bring a large pot of salted water to a boil.

In a large bowl, thinly shave the fresh white truffle. In a large sauté pan, heat the butter, then add the shredded rabbit, chives, parsley, and the remaining 1 teaspoon of salt. Cook until the rabbit is heated through, about 5 minutes. Add this to the bowl of truffles, then add the arugula, cheese, butternut squash, and truffle oil. Add the chickpea pasta to the boiling water and cook for 1 minute. Drain well. If you are cooking it ahead of time, toss lightly with some olive oil and a pinch of salt. Add the drained pasta to the truffle bowl and toss gently together to combine.

Place 1 tablespoon of the warm fennel in the center of each plate. Pile about 1 cup of the pasta and rabbit mixture on top of the fennel. Let guests shave additional truffle on top!

Caramelized Fennel

makes ¾ cup

1 tablespoon grapeseed oil

1 small yellow onion, halved lengthwise then
   cut lengthwise into ⅛-inch slices

3 small fennel bulbs, trimmed and thinly sliced,
   preferably with a mandoline

1 tablespoon unsalted butter

¼ teaspoon sea salt

Heat a medium sauté pan over high heat and add the oil. Add the onion and fennel and reduce the heat to low. Add the butter and caramelize for 30 minutes, stirring occasionally, until dark brown. Season with the salt. The fennel can be prepared 2 days in advance and refrigerated. Reheat gently before serving.

Roast Butternut Squash

makes 1 cup

7 ounces butternut squash

1 small shallot, minced

1 garlic clove, minced

1 ½ tablespoons extra virgin olive oil

½ teaspoon sea salt

⅛ teaspoon freshly ground black pepper

Preheat the oven to 450°F.

Cut the squash in half lengthwise, scoop out all of the seeds, and peel. Cut into ¼-inch-square pieces. Toss with the shallot, garlic, olive oil, salt, and black pepper. Roast on a rimmed baking sheet, stirring halfway through, until the edges are brown and the squash is tender, 20 to 30 minutes.

Chickpea Pasta

makes 1 pound

Use half of this versatile pasta dough for the Braised Rabbit with Tagliatta and freeze the rest, tightly wrapped, for another use.

¾ cup chickpea flour (see Resources)

1 cup all-purpose flour, plus more for sprinkling

1 ¼ teaspoons sea salt

1 tablespoon whole milk

1 ½ teaspoons extra virgin olive oil

6 large egg yolks

1 large whole egg

In a small bowl, mix the flours and salt, then empty into a pile on a clean countertop or wooden cutting board. Make a well in the flour and add the milk, olive oil, egg yolks, and egg. Using your fingers, begin turning the liquid in a clockwise motion, keeping it within the well. Keep moving the liquid while slowly incorporating the flour until all the flour is incorporated and the dough forms a ball. Sprinkle the dough with an additional 1 to 2 tablespoons of flour, as needed, and knead for 5 to 8 minutes. Form the dough into 2 rectangles. Wrap tightly and let the dough rest in the refrigerator. The pasta can be made to this point a day or two ahead and refrigerated. Cut one of the dough rectangles in half. Keeping one half covered, use a pasta machine to roll the dough on the largest setting. Fold the rolled rectangle into thirds like a letter and roll again. Repeat this process five times to help knead the dough. Roll down to the #8 setting and hand-cut the pasta into 1 x 8-inch ribbons. The pasta can be prepared to this point one day in advance and hung to dry.

Lobster with Braised Pork Belly and Black Truffle Salad

Every few years, an ingredient catches the fancy of chefs across the United States. Pork belly, long the backbone of many Asian dishes, recently burst on the American culinary scene, cropping up on four-star menus everywhere. And what's more four-star than combining the ultimate luxuries—truffles and lobster—with a classic peasant ingredient? This is a complicated recipe, with a lot of elements, but the result is truly a showstopper—both on the plate and on the palate. Serve it with the White Sweet Potato Puree, following the sculptural plating instructions here.

makes 4 servings

½ pound Slow-Roasted Asian-Style Pork Belly (recipe follows)

Lobster Sauce (recipe follows)

Lobster Tail and Claws (recipe follows)

1 tablespoon unsalted butter

1 small shallot, finely diced

1 large bunch spinach, large stems removed

Sea salt, for seasoning, plus ¼ teaspoon

2 teaspoons black truffle oil (see Resources)

1 ounce fresh black truffle, chopped (see Resources)

1 teaspoon red wine vinegar

⅛ teaspoon freshly ground black pepper

3 ounces micro lettuce blend (see Resources)

½ cup micro celery or small yellow celery leaves

Sweet Potato and Shallot Chips (recipe follows)

White Sweet Potato Puree (recipe follows)

Roast Cipollini Onions (recipe follows)

Preheat the oven to 275°F.

Slice the pork belly into ¼-inch-thick slices and place in a small baking dish with about 3 tablespoons of the lobster sauce. Place in the oven until heated through, about 8 minutes. Remove the lobster tail and claws from the refrigerator. Add 2 tablespoons of water to the baking dish and reheat in the oven for 30 minutes.

In a large sauté pan, melt the butter and sauté the shallot until translucent, about 2 minutes. Add the spinach with some of the water left over from washing and cook until done, about 5 minutes. Season with salt and set aside.

In a small saucepan over low heat, warm the black truffle oil with the chopped black truffle, red wine vinegar, ¼ teaspoon of salt, and the black pepper. Cool slightly and toss gently with the tiny lettuce blend, the micro celery, and the sweet potato and shallot chips.

Place 2 tablespoons of sautéed spinach on each plate. Top this with ¼ cup of sweet potato puree and 2 or 3 slices of pork belly. Next to this, place 1 lobster claw, half of a lobster tail, 1 roasted onion, and 3 tablespoons of lobster sauce. Garnish the lobster and pork belly with ¼ cup of the salad mixture.

Slow-Roasted Asian-Style Pork Belly

makes 1 pound; 4 to 6 servings

4 garlic cloves, minced

1 teaspoon red chili flakes

¼ cup light brown sugar

3 tablespoons Yokoi's brown rice and malt vinegar (see Resources)

3 tablespoons high-quality soy sauce or tamari

2 tablespoons grapeseed oil

1 tablespoon minced ginger

3 scallions, sliced

Juice of ½ lime

1 pound pork belly

Combine all of the ingredients and marinate the pork belly in a 1-gallon zip-top bag overnight.

Preheat the oven to 225°F.

Place the pork belly on a rack above a foil-lined rimmed baking sheet and slow roast in the oven for 3 hours. Reserve the marinade. In a small saucepan over high heat, simmer the marinade for 1 minute. Reserve for the lobster sauce. The pork belly and marinade can be prepared 2 to 3 days in advance and refrigerated separately.

Sweet Potato and Shallot Chips

makes 1 cup

Vegetable oil, for deep-frying

1 small white sweet potato, 2 to 4 inches long, peeled

¼ cup all-purpose flour

2 large shallots

½ teaspoon sea salt

Fill a medium straight-sided sauté pan with oil to a depth of 2 inches. Heat the oil to 375°F. Cut long strips of sweet potato with a vegetable peeler and dust with flour, shaking off the excess. Fry the sweet potato strips in batches until golden brown, about 3 minutes. Drain on a paper towel and sprinkle with half the salt. Thinly slice the shallots into rounds and dust with flour, shaking off the excess. Fry the shallots in batches until golden brown, about 1 minute. Drain on a paper towel and sprinkle with the remaining salt. The chips can be prepared 2 hours in advance and stored in an airtight container at room temperature.

White Sweet Potato Puree

makes 2 cups

2 large white sweet potatoes, peeled and cut into 1-inch cubes

1 teaspoon sea salt, plus a large pinch for seasoning

1 tablespoon unsalted butter

⅛ teaspoon freshly ground white pepper

Place the sweet potatoes and the 1 teaspoon of salt in a medium saucepan and cover with water. Bring to a boil and cook until tender, about 12 minutes. Drain completely and press through a food mill or blend in a food processor until smooth. Stir in the butter and season with salt and the white pepper. The potato puree can be prepared a few hours in advance and refrigerated. Reheat in the microwave before serving.

Lobster Tail and Claws

3 teaspoons sea salt

1½ cups white distilled vinegar

2 live 1½-pound lobsters

½ cup (1 stick) unsalted butter, softened

Bring 3 gallons of water, the salt, and vinegar to a boil in a large pot and add the lobsters. Boil for 2 minutes and remove. Using rubber gloves and a dish towel, hold the hot lobster by the tail. Twist and pull to detach the tail. Twist and pull off the claws and return to the water for 5 minutes. Remove the lobster body from the shell and discard the shell. Pull the featherlike lungs from the body and discard the lungs. Refrigerate the body until needed for the sauce.

To remove the tail meat, hold each tail flat and twist the fan to one side. Pull off and discard. Use your fingers to gently push the meat through the tail end, pulling the meat out through the large opening at the other end. Discard the shells. Cut the tail in half lengthwise and remove any veins. For the claw meat, twist off the small pincer by twisting gently and pulling it off with the claw cartilage attached. Then gently crack both sides of the shell with the back side of a French knife and carefully remove the claw meat in one piece. Rub the tails and claws with butter and place on a parchment-lined baking sheet. Cover with additional parchment and refrigerate. The tails and claws can be prepared a day in advance.

Roast Cipollini Onions

4 medium cipollini onions

2 teaspoons grapeseed oil

1 tablespoon unsalted butter

½ teaspoon sugar

¼ cup homemade chicken stock, or substitute boxed or canned

1 thyme sprig

1 sage leaf

¼ teaspoon sea salt

Preheat the oven to 225°F.

Trim the onions by cutting out the root end and peeling off the tough outer layer. Cut a circle of parchment paper slightly smaller than the top of a small, ovenproof sauté pan and set aside. Heat the pan over high heat and add the oil. Place the onions in the pan, reduce the heat to medium-low, and cook until nice and brown, about 1 minute per side. Add the butter and cook for 2 minutes, then add the sugar, stock, thyme, sage, and salt. Bring to a simmer, then press the circle of parchment paper onto the top of the onions and place the pan in the oven for 2 hours. Remove the onions from the pan and transfer the roasting liquid to a small saucepan. Reduce over medium heat until it forms a thick glaze, about 5 minutes. Pour the glaze through a fine-mesh strainer and stir it back into the onions. The onions can be prepared 2 days in advance and refrigerated. Reheat before serving.

Lobster Sauce

3 tablespoons grapeseed oil

Reserved and cleaned lobster bodies

½ medium yellow onion, diced

1 carrot, diced

1 celery stalk, diced

1½ tablespoons tomato paste

½ cup pork belly marinade (see page 116)

Heat a large stockpot over high heat and add the oil and lobster bodies. Cook for 3 minutes. Reduce heat to medium and add the onion, carrot, and celery. Caramelize, about 8 minutes. Add the tomato paste and cook for 1 minute more. Add 3 quarts of water to cover and simmer, skimming off the foam. Simmer for 1 hour, then pour through a fine-mesh strainer. Reduce by half, or until 1½ cups of liquid remain. Strain again. Add ½ cup of the reserved pork belly marinade to the lobster sauce and mix. The sauce can be prepared 2 days in advance and refrigerated. Reheat gently before serving.

Pear Tarts with White Truffle Whipped Cream and Raw Honey

We end the truffle menu on a whimsical truffle note. The truffle oil in the whipped cream really captures the essence of the oil. Having the guests drizzle the honey over the tarts as the scent of truffle wafts through the air adds to the sensory experience.

makes 4 servings

Flour, for dusting

1 pound Puff Pastry Dough (recipe follows) or store-bought

4 tablespoons (½ stick) unsalted butter, cut into pieces

3 D'Anjou pears, peeled, cored, and sliced ⅛-inch thick

¼ cup honey, plus more for drizzling

¼ teaspoon plus ⅛ teaspoon sea salt

1 cup heavy cream

1 ¼ teaspoons truffle oil

1 tablespoon sugar

¼ cup chopped almond nougat (see Resources)

On a lightly floured surface, roll out the pastry dough to about ⅛-inch thick. Dust off the excess flour from the top and bottom and cut the dough into four 6-inch circles. Place the circles on a parchment-lined baking sheet and refrigerate for 20 minutes.

Preheat the oven to 450°F.

Heat a large sauté pan over high heat. Add the butter and pears, cook for 30 seconds, then add the ¼ cup of honey and the ¼ teaspoon of salt. Caramelize until brown, 3 to 4 minutes, then let cool slightly. Arrange the pear slices in a thin layer on the puff pastry circles, allowing the slices to overlap slightly. Bake until the edges begin to brown a bit, 8 to 10 minutes.

In a medium bowl, whip the heavy cream, truffle oil, sugar, and the ⅛ teaspoon salt to soft peaks, about 4 minutes. Fold the nougat gently into the whipped cream.

Serve each tart on a plate and the whipped cream in a bowl on the side. Let each guest scoop a dollop of the truffle cream and drizzle their tart with additional honey before eating.

Puff Pastry Dough

makes 1 ½ pounds

Use two-thirds of this versatile pastry dough for the pear tart and freeze the rest, tightly wrapped, for another use.

1 ¼ cups plus 2 tablespoons plus 3½ tablespoons all-purpose flour

7 tablespoons whole wheat pastry flour

1 ½ teaspoons sea salt

1 ½ teaspoons sugar

4 tablespoons plus 1 cup (2 sticks) unsalted butter, cold and cut into ¼-inch dice, measures kept separate

1 ½ teaspoons rice wine vinegar

In a medium bowl, sift together the 1¼ cups plus 2 tablespoons of all-purpose flour with the pastry flour, salt, and sugar. Rub in the 4 tablespoons of diced butter until the flour resembles small peas. Stir in ½ cup of water and the vinegar and knead the dough until combined. Form into a 6-inch square, wrap in plastic, and refrigerate.

Place the 1 cup of diced butter on a cold surface and pound it with a rolling pin to make it malleable. Fold it over onto itself and pound again. Repeat. Sprinkle the remaining 3½ tablespoons of all-purpose flour over the butter. With a bench scraper or metal spatula, cut the flour into the butter until combined. Knead the butter dough, until it is the same consistency as the flour dough, about 30 seconds. Form this dough into a 4-inch square.

Remove the flour dough from the refrigerator and place it on a lightly floured surface. Mark a diamond in the center of the dough with its tips at the midpoint of each side of the dough square. Roll out the triangle-shaped edges about 4 inches from the side of the diamond. You will have a square in the middle with 4 petals surrounding it. Place the butter dough in the diamond and bring the edges over the butter, one at a time, like an envelope. Now you will have a 4-inch or so square mass of dough. Gently roll the dough into a 6 x 8-inch rectangle. Refrigerate the dough for 30 minutes.

Remove the dough from the refrigerator and place on a lightly floured surface with the short side facing you. Roll it into an 8 x 16-inch rectangle. Fold the rolled rectangle into thirds like a letter. Turn the dough by 90 degrees and repeat the rolling and folding process. Refrigerate the dough for 30 minutes, and do the rolling and turning two more times for a total of three double turns. (Make an indentation in the dough before refrigerating to indicate the number of turns you have made so you don't lose track during the process.)

Cut the dough into three equal portions and refrigerate or freeze. The dough can be prepared 3 days in advance and refrigerated, or frozen for up to 3 weeks.

WINE NOTES

Barolo, La Mora, Elio Altare, 2001 (Piedmont, Italy)

Anas-cetta, Elvio Cogno, 2005 (Piedmont, Italy)

Grüner Veltliner, Beerenauslese, Weingut Knoll, 1998 (Wachau, Austria)

White truffles are one of the many treasures of the earth to be found in Piedmont, Italy, along with porcini mushrooms, hazelnuts, and, of course, wines made from the legendary nebbiolo grape. Barolo and Barbaresco are the most famous nebbiolo-based wines, but there are many others from elsewhere in Piedmont, including Gattinara, Roero, and Carema. Should you not wish to shell out for the sometimes expensive Barolo or Barbaresco, all of these producers make less expensive varietal nebbiolos (usually called either Langhe Nebbiolo or Nebbiolo d'Alba) as simpler alternatives to their top-tier wines.

With its heady aromas of tobacco, spice, and, yes, truffles, nebbiolo—in any of its forms—is the ultimate accompaniment to a white truffle dish. What distinguishes nebbiolo is its assertive, perfumy aroma, which will remind you of great Burgundy or California pinot, yet with an earthier, more masculine edge. This menu is all about your sense of smell, so engage it with one of the world's most aromatically complex reds.

This nebbiolo has a slightly rustic quality that plays nicely off the earthy notes in the dish. Elio Altare is one of the top nebbiolo producers in Piedmont, and his wines are atypical with their layers of fruit and complex aromatics from the famed La Mora vineyard.

For a white wine, we looked for something that would not only be from Piedmont, the home of the world's greatest white truffles, but would offer flavors and aromas rooted in the earth. The anas-cetta grape is nearly extinct, yet it remains a specialty of Novello, a village on the southwest edge of the Barolo wine zone in Piedmont. Think of a hypothetical mix of viognier, sauvignon blanc, and chenin, and you've got an idea of anas-cetta, which combines an oily quality on the palate with earthy, mineral tones. It has the weight to work with the lobster and pork belly, along with the aromatic complexity to play up the truffles. It is a rare treat, as only about five hundred cases are made, but should you manage to track it down you'll only pay about twenty dollars for a bottle of something truly unique.

For the pear tart, treat yourself to an Austrian beerenauslese, a sweet treasure that is one of the best dessert wines in the world. The classification beerenauslese refers to the wine's very high degree of residual sugar, but since these grapes grow in cooler regions with longer ripening, they maintain an exceptionally high level of acidity. The magic of these wines is the way their rich sweetness is balanced by this refreshing acidity, and this balance is what makes them such wonderful partners for desserts—too much sweet-on-sweet is no good for anyone.

JACKIE'S BESPOKE HERBS

At Rancho La Zaca, we keep our best flower arrangements hidden in the fridge. Open the stainless steel door and a riot of color and scent tumbles forth: nasturtiums and pansies, amaranth, fennel, thyme, oregano, and sometimes a dozen or two other edible flowers and fragrant herbs. These are all supplied to Stephanie and other chefs-in-the-know by local gardener Jackie Rosa.

Jackie has lived in the Santa Ynez Valley since 1976, and though she has moved locally several times over the years, she simply picks up her mother plants and pops them in the ground at the new place; wherever she goes, her gardens go with her. Jackie started growing herbs, and some fruits and vegetables, at first because she didn't want to pay the steep prices at the grocery store, and later because she loved the varieties she could grow herself and never could have found in a store.

Jackie sees an aesthetic to growing and picking. "Herbs love to be handled, picked, and touched," she says. "They don't need a lot of TLC." Her garden has more than fifty types of herb, which meander around her yard seemingly at random. "I can't do rows," she announces. "I just plant 'em wherever they'll get along with the others." She offers to "taste tour" a visitor through her garden, but only as long as they arrive early in the morning. Jackie picks right after the dew dries and before the morning sun, so the herbs will look their best when she delivers them to customers.

Stephanie doesn't always remember the name of each herb in Jackie's weekly bouquet, so she picks and nibbles as she cooks to determine how she wants to use the herbs. Sometimes she knows well in advance that she's going to need something for a special dish, so she calls Jackie to make sure that Jackie puts some seeds in the ground. No matter what Jackie grows for us, it is always put to good use, even if just to add another sensory dimension to the kitchen fridge.

While we like to joke that Stephanie took up beekeeping because she liked the outfit, that's in fact not the whole story. While she was working at Roxanne's in Marin County, she encountered several hives that were kept on the restaurant's three-acre farm. The hives were managed by a local beekeeper who had bees all over the county, and Stephanie was deathly afraid of them.

She reasoned that the only way to confront her fear was to educate herself and get some hives of her own. She started going to beekeeping meetings in Northern California, and when she came to Rancho La Zaca, she immediately recognized the property as an optimal place for beekeeping. She joined the local beekeepers' club and was set up with a mentor; beekeepers are eager to pass down the trade, since it has started to die out due to urbanization. In Marin County, for instance, it's not even legal to keep bees, deemed "wild and dangerous animals," unless your yard has a certain amount of space.

The day after she went to her first meeting in the Santa Ynez Valley, Stephanie had her first hive, thanks to Dave, her mentor and a local beekeeper who sells his honey at the farmers' market. Stephanie set up the hive with frames, the bees built the honeycombs, and then they filled it with honey. Out of her very first harvest, Stephanie reaped forty pounds of honey. At Rancho La Zaca, we enjoy the honey over sumptuous desserts, but also every morning with blueberries, roasted almonds, and yogurt. It's the only sweetener Stephanie uses in her home.

After a season of beekeeping, Stephanie is no longer afraid of the busy little creatures. She explains that though it's a little scary when they get angry, she's learned that they attack only when you bother their hive. The bees have different jobs: Some leave the hive and pollinate, some circle and guard the hive, and then, of course, there's the queen, who is a bit larger than the others and lives up to five years. When Stephanie gets within a certain distance of the hive, the guard bees collide with her bee suit and try to chase her away from the hive. Because it's not fun to upset the guard bees, and also because the bees work to keep the hives at a constant temperature and moisture level, Stephanie opens the hive only if she has something specific to do.

And, let's be honest, she loves wearing that white suit.

FATHER'S DAY

Aphrodite's Tea

Foie Gras and Kumquat Terrine

Panfried Soft-Shell Crabs with Licorice Cream

Green Explosion

BARNABY CONRAD IS THE AUTHOR OF MORE THAN THIRTY-FIVE BOOKS, INCLUDING the thrilling novel set in the last days of World War II, *Last Boat to Cadiz*; *Matador*, a classic bullfighting novel; and a biography of the greatest bullfighter who ever lived, *Manolete*. He is also a refined painter, a clever sculptor, a university professor, a former vice-consul to Spain, and somewhat improbably (given his proper Yale education and reputation for glamorous hobnobbing with the denizens of *Who's Who* during the 1950s and 1960s), the first American matador to debut in a bullring in Spain. He was a friend of Ernest Hemingway, and many parallels have been drawn between the two bon vivants, the obvious difference between them being that—no doubt about it—Barnaby loves life. He is a legendary Californian, having been the toast of the town in San Francisco, and for the last thirty-five years considered a living treasure in Santa Barbara. But to Luisa, Fanny, and Helen, he is just "Opa" (Grandpa), and to my dear friends Tani and Kendall, he is "Dad."

I decided that a father as special and esteemed as Barnaby needed to know how much he was loved by the ones who love him most. Since he has always had a reputation for being a ladies' man—and even at eighty-four he hasn't lost a bit of his flirtatious charm—it seemed only fitting to invite exclusively female admirers, including his daughters, granddaughters, his gorgeous and admirably confident wife, Mary, and a handful of other beautiful women, for a very special Father's Day luncheon in his honor. And to commemorate the occasion, I commissioned a special drinking cup, jewel encrusted with Barnaby's name. Never mind that such a goblet is commonly known as a pimp cup (a fact that seemed unknown to him). He raised his full glass. "Hmmm," he said, looking at the baker's dozen of beauties gathered within the enclosure of exuberant red roses, "thirteen to one: The ratio is just about right for me!"

Aphrodite's Tea

All of the floral ingredients for this refreshing and beautifully colored tea are available in the bulk section of most health food stores.

makes 8 cups dried tea, enough to brew 4 dozen cups

2½ cups dried hibiscus leaves

1 cup jasmine-scented green tea

1 cup dried calendula leaves

1 cup dried raspberry leaves

1 cup dried red clover

⅔ cup dried pink rosebuds

⅔ cup dried nettle leaves

½ cup sugar

Mix all of the ingredients except the sugar together and store in an airtight container.

To make the tea, steep 1 cup of tea in 6 cups of boiling water in a medium saucepan for 10 minutes. Strain, then stir in the sugar. Chill and serve over ice.

Foie Gras and Kumquat Terrine

This is a once-a-year, pull-out-the-stops luncheon. Don't let the seemingly complicated dishes scare you off serving them at midday. Most of the work can be done the day before. After slicing the terrine, let each piece sit out for a few minutes so it softens slightly. The terrine freezes well, and the recipe can also be cut in half; if you do that, block the empty side of the terrine mold with an apple or potato that has been cut in the shape of the mold.

makes 15 servings

¾ pound kumquats

½ cup plus 3 tablespoons sugar

3 thyme sprigs

3 bunches (about 18) scallions, trimmed

2½ tablespoons extra virgin olive oil

Sea salt and freshly ground black pepper to taste

One 2 to 2½ pound grade A foie gras
  (see Resources)

Vegetable oil, for greasing the mold

1 bunch large spinach leaves, large stems
  removed (3 cups loosely packed)

2 cups loosely packed micro lettuces

2 tablespoons fresh lemon juice

Basil Oil (recipe follows)

Slice the kumquats $\frac{1}{16}$-inch thick, preferably with a mandoline. Pick out and discard any large seeds. Place the sliced kumquats, sugar, and thyme in a medium saucepan with ¾ cup of water. Bring to a simmer over medium heat. Remove from the heat and allow the kumquats to cool. The kumquats can be prepared 1 or 2 days in advance and stored in the refrigerator. Before using, drain, reserve the juices, and remove the thyme sprigs.

Preheat the grill to medium. In a dish, toss the scallions with the olive oil and season with salt and black pepper. Grill until the scallions are softened and cooked through, about 5 minutes. Turn two or three times during grilling to prevent the green parts from blackening, although a bit of black on the edges is okay. Once cooled, trim off ¾ inch from the white end and reserve greens and white ends separately.

Remove the foie gras from the refrigerator and let it soften at room temperature for 30 minutes. Separate the 2 lobes and clean away any visible membrane. Dip a sharp knife in hot water and cut ½-inch slices, wiping the knife clean after each slice and redipping in the hot water. Using needle-nose pliers dipped in a cup of hot water, pull out any visible veins from the sliced foie gras, being careful not to break the slices apart. After cleaning all of the slices, cover and refrigerate for at least 30 minutes.

COOK THE FOIE GRAS: Preheat 2 large heavy-bottomed sauté pans over high heat until very hot. Liberally season both sides of the foie gras slices with salt and black pepper. Place half of the slices in 1 hot pan with at least 1 inch between the slices; do not overcrowd. Sear until dark brown, about 30 seconds. Then turn, being careful not to splatter the grease. Cook the second side for 1 minute. Turn once more and cook the first side for an additional 30 seconds. Remove from the pan and place on a rack with a sheet pan underneath to catch the grease. Tent with foil. Sear the remaining slices in the other pan. Hold all the seared foie gras at room temperature. Strain and refrigerate the fat drippings.

PREPARE THE TERRINE MOLD: Place a few drops of oil inside a 12 x 1¼ x 2¼-inch mold and brush to coat the inside completely. Line the mold with plastic wrap, making sure to push the wrap into all of the corners. Leave 1 inch of excess plastic wrap on either side.

Make a layer using one-third of the warm foie gras, 4 to 4½ slices, on the bottom of the terrine mold. Cut small pieces to completely fill in the layer. Next, layer half of the grilled scallion greens, flattening with your fingers to make an even layer. Then, layer ½ cup of the drained kumquats. Press lightly after each layer to evenly spread each ingredient. Repeat with more foie gras, the remaining grilled scallions, another ½ cup of the kumquats, and finish with the remaining foie gras. The final layer should be just above the top edge of the mold. Pull the excess plastic wrap up and over the foie gras to cover it completely. Place an 11 x 1½ x ½-inch wood block on plastic-covered foie gras (you can use any firm object that fits the top of the terrine mold; I used my microplane). Using a long length of plastic wrap, gently tie the block to the foie gras terrine in three places: once at each end and also in the middle. This will hold the terrine together as it cools. Place the terrine on a tray to catch any fat and refrigerate overnight.

Prepare an ice-water bath by filling a 4-quart bowl halfway with ice and 2 cups of water. Place a 2-quart metal bowl inside the 4-quart bowl. Bring a medium pot of water to a boil. Add the spinach to the pot and blanch for 30 seconds. Remove with a slotted spoon to the ice bath. Put the bowl on a dish towel and pick the individual leaves out of the bowl, draping them over the edge of the bowl to dry. Continue until all of the leaves are hanging from the edge of the bowl. (This sounds a bit odd, but it is the easiest way to do this.) Spread out a 12-inch-square sheet of plastic wrap. Take the spinach leaves from the edge of the bowl and lay flat side down or face down, slightly overlapping, to form an 11-inch-square sheet. Cover with another sheet of plastic wrap, fold into quarters, and refrigerate. The spinach can be prepared 1 day in advance.

Remove the terrine and the spinach wrap from the refrigerator. In a small saucepan, warm the reserved foie gras fat slightly. Carefully lay out the spinach and brush lightly with the fat, being careful not to create any holes. Remove the terrine from the mold and remove the plastic wrap. Place horizontally on the bottom of the spinach sheet, leaving a 1-inch border of spinach. Wrap the terrine by pulling the bottom of the plastic wrap upward and slowly rotating until the terrine is covered completely, similar to rolling sushi. Rewrap the terrine tightly in plastic wrap and chill for at least 10 minutes or up to 2 days.

Using a serrated knife, cut ½-inch-thick slices of terrine, leaving the plastic wrap on to help hold the terrine together. Watch the tip of the knife to ensure your cut remains straight. Remove the plastic wrap from each slice and brush the top side with the reserved fat.

Place 1 slice of the terrine slightly off the center of each plate. Place 1 teaspoon of the remaining preserved kumquat next to the slice of terrine. Lightly toss the micro lettuces with the lemon juice, 2 tablespoons of basil oil, and salt and black pepper. Place 2 tablespoons of the greens on top of the kumquats. Top each with the reserved white parts of the grilled scallions. Drizzle the plate with 1 teaspoon of kumquat juice and ½ teaspoon of basil oil.

Basil Oil

3½ ounces (about 3 loosely packed cups) basil,
  large stems removed

1 cup grapeseed oil

Bring a medium saucepan of water to a boil. Fill a 2-quart metal bowl halfway with ice and 2 cups of water and set a small strainer in the water. Blanch the basil until the color changes to a bright green, about 30 seconds. Remove with a slotted spoon to the strainer. Once chilled, wring out the excess water by hand. Place the basil in a dish towel, roll up, and wring out all the water. Roughly chop the basil and add to a blender with the oil. Process until well blended and smooth, about 3 minutes. Spoon the basil mixture into a small bowl. Cover and refrigerate 24 to 48 hours.

Place a fine-mesh sieve over a container large enough to hold the oil. Place the basil-oil mixture in the sieve to strain. Do not press it; merely let the oil drip out, to prevent water and other impurities from clouding the oil. Let this drip for 1 hour minimum, then discard the basil pulp. Leftover oil will freeze nicely for another use.

Panfried Soft-Shell Crabs with Licorice Cream

This luncheon fell perfectly in the middle of soft-shell crab season, which made it easy to pick a winner for the entrée—simply dredged in seasoned flour and sautéed. The crabs are served over a warm salad that has several different layers of flavor, from fresh corn to earthy mushroom to light sweetness from the candied parsnip. This was all finished with freshly squeezed lemon juice and extra virgin olive oil.

makes 15 servings

FOR THE LICORICE CREAM

One 7-inch stick dried licorice

One ½-inch piece dried ginger

1 small sliver cinnamon stick

4 cardamom pods

1 piece mace

½ star anise pod

¼ teaspoon fennel seeds

¼ teaspoon ground coriander

½ bay leaf

7 black peppercorns

2 cups low-sodium canned chicken stock

3 cups half-and-half

1 cup heavy cream

¾ teaspoon sea salt

FOR THE CANDIED PARSNIPS

5 medium parsnips

1½ tablespoons grapeseed oil

Sea salt and freshly ground black pepper to
  taste

3 tablespoons unsalted butter, cut into chunks

2½ tablespoons sugar

2 tablespoons sliced chives

2 teaspoons chopped thyme

1 tablespoon chopped flat-leaf parsley

FOR THE SALAD

3 tablespoons extra virgin olive oil

Three 8-ounce packages hon-shemiji
  mushrooms, trimmed

Sea salt and freshly ground black pepper to taste

1 garlic clove, minced

1 medium shallot, minced

4 ears corn, shucked, kernels cut off cobs

3 bunches watercress, large stems removed

2 heads frisée lettuce, outer edges and bitter
  green cut away

2 tablespoons fresh lemon juice

1 tablespoon unsalted butter, at room temperature

FOR THE CRABS

3 cups all-purpose flour

2½ teaspoons sea salt

1 teaspoon freshly ground black pepper

15 jumbo soft-shell crabs
  Grapeseed oil, for frying

MAKE THE LICORICE CREAM: In a mortar, pound together the licorice, ginger, cinnamon, and cardamom pods. Place these pounded spices in a 2-quart heavy-bottomed saucepan and add the mace, star anise, fennel, coriander, bay leaf, and peppercorns. Toast over medium heat for 2 minutes, stirring constantly. Add the chicken stock and reduce over medium heat to approximately ¼ cup, about 30 minutes. Add the half-and-half and heavy cream, bring to a simmer, and reduce to approximately 3½ cups, about 10 minutes. Finish with the salt. Pour the cream through a fine-mesh sieve. The cream can be prepared 1 day in advance and refrigerated.

MAKE THE CANDIED PARSNIPS: Cut the parsnips into ¼-inch pieces using an oblique cut: Place the parsnip on a diagonal, cut, then roll 180 degrees and cut on the same diagonal. Continue rolling and cutting until finished.

In a large sauté pan, heat the oil until very hot. Add the parsnips, season with salt and black pepper, and cook over medium-high heat until just beginning to caramelize, about 5 minutes. Shake the pan occasionally. Add the butter and sugar and reduce the heat to medium-low. Cook until cooked through, stirring or shaking occasionally to keep the sugar from burning, about 10 minutes. Remove from the heat and stir in the chives, thyme, and parsley.

MAKE THE SALAD: Heat a large sauté pan over high heat. Add 2 tablespoons of the olive oil, then the mushrooms. Season with salt and black pepper and sear for 30 seconds. Add the garlic and shallot and cook 2 more minutes. Add the corn kernels and cook until tender, about 5 minutes. Add the reserved parsnips and stir, then remove from the heat. Stir in the watercress, frisée, lemon juice, butter, and the remaining 1 tablespoon of olive oil.

MAKE THE CRABS: In a wide, shallow bowl, combine the flour, salt, and black pepper. Using kitchen shears, trim away the face of each crab. Remove the lungs by lifting the top flap of the shell and pulling away.

Heat 2 large sauté pans over high heat until very hot and add ¼ inch of oil to each pan. Lightly dredge the crabs in the flour and shake off the excess. Put half the crabs in each pan, top down, and fry until nicely browned, 1 to 2 minutes. Turn and fry until cooked through, 3 minutes more. Use caution: The crabs will pop and splatter while frying.

Reheat the licorice cream. Place 1 to 1½ cups of the warm salad in the center of each plate. Top with a fried crab and ladle hot licorice cream onto the plate. If possible, this should be done tableside.

Green Explosion

This dessert is a play on the color green and contrasting flavors—salty, sweet, and bitter—that are intense and vibrant and literally explode in your mouth. As with the terrine, everything for this dessert can be prepared ahead, so it is easier than it looks. Which, on looks alone, is pretty complicated: There are eight separate recipes here. With all of these elements combined, Green Explosion is a spectacular dish. But some of the individual elements would make excellent stand-alone desserts, especially the Green Tea Ice Cream and the Almond Cake.

makes 15 servings

Pure Chocolate Sauce (page 136)   Green Tea Fluff (page 138)

Almond Cake (page 136)   Green Tea Ice Cream (page 138)

Almond Garnish (page 136)   Greengage Plum Sorbet (page 139)

Sweet and Salty Grapefruit (page 136)   Green Herb Granité (page 139)

Spoon 1 teaspoon of the chocolate sauce down the middle of each plate. Place a 1-inch square of almond cake to the right of the sauce and place ¼ teaspoon of the almond garnish to the left of the sauce. Spoon 3 or 4 grapefruit segments with 1 teaspoon of their juice over the cake. Top the grapefruit with 1 tablespoon of green tea fluff and lightly brûlée them with a kitchen torch or under the broiler. Place a 1½-ounce scoop each of the ice cream and sorbet next to each other on top of the almonds. Then center a single scoop of the granité on top of the other scoops.

Pure Chocolate Sauce makes 6 tablespoons

2½ ounces 70% cacao bittersweet chocolate, coarsely chopped

Pinch of sea salt

In a small saucepan, bring ½ cup of water to a boil. Coarsely chop the chocolate and place it in a small stainless steel bowl with the salt. Pour 3 tablespoons of the boiling water over the chopped chocolate. Let sit for 1 minute, then stir until smooth.

Almond Cake makes one 9-inch cake

¾ cup all-purpose flour

2 teaspoons baking powder

¾ teaspoon sea salt

½ cup Bob's Red Mill almond meal/flour (see Resources)

¾ cup (1½ sticks) unsalted butter, at room temperature, plus more for greasing the pan

1 cup sugar

2 large eggs

¾ cup whole raw almonds, toasted and finely chopped in a food processor

Preheat the oven to 350°F. Butter a 9-inch-square cake pan and line the bottom with parchment paper. Butter the paper.

In a large bowl, sift together the all-purpose flour, baking powder, and salt. Whisk in the almond flour. In a separate large bowl, using an electric mixer, cream the butter and sugar until light in color and fluffy. Beat in the eggs alternately with the flour mixture. Use a spatula to fold in the chopped almonds. Pour into the prepared cake pan. Bake until the edges are browned and the center is set, 30 to 40 minutes. The cake can be prepared a day in advance and stored at room temperature.

Almond Garnish makes about ¼ cup

¼ cup toasted and coarsely chopped almonds

1 teaspoon coarse gray sea salt

4 teaspoons turbinado sugar

In a mortar, pound the almonds with the salt and sugar. Do not crush to form a paste, just combine.

Sweet and Salty Grapefruit makes about 1 cup

4 medium pink grapefruits, peeled, all white pith removed, and segmented

½ teaspoon sea salt

3 tablespoons sugar

In a medium bowl, mix the grapefruit segments with the salt and sugar.

Green Tea Fluff

makes 2 cups

1 tablespoon gelatin (1 envelope)

2 cups sugar

½ cup light corn syrup

¼ teaspoon sea salt

1 tablespoon powdered green tea (if you do not have powdered green tea, simply grind 2 tablespoons loose green tea in a spice grinder and sift through a fine-mesh sieve)

2 large egg whites (if you are concerned about raw egg safety, pasteurized egg whites can be substituted)

Pour ½ cup of cold water into the bowl of a standing mixer or large bowl if you are using a handheld mixer, and sprinkle the gelatin on top; do not stir.

In a 3-quart, heavy-bottomed saucepan, combine the sugar, corn syrup, and salt with ½ cup hot water. Stir with a wooden spoon over low heat until the mixture comes to a boil and the sugar is dissolved. Increase the heat to medium-high and cook without stirring until the mixture reaches 240°F on a candy thermometer.

Add the green tea powder to the gelatin mixture. Remove the sugar mixture from the heat and pour slowly over the gelatin while beating on low speed (being very careful not to burn yourself with the hot sugar mixture) until the gelatin is dissolved. Raise the speed to high and beat until very fluffy, thick, and tripled in volume, 8 minutes if using a standing mixer or 10 if using a handheld one. Set aside.

In a clean, large bowl with clean beaters, beat the egg whites until stiff peaks form. Scrape the sugar mixture into the beaten whites and beat until just combined, 1 minute. The fluff can be prepared 1 day in advance and stored at room temperature. Refluff by whisking briskly by hand before serving.

Green Tea Ice Cream

makes 3 cups

1 cup whole milk

½ cup heavy cream

½ cup half-and-half

1½ tablespoons loose Matcha or other green tea

6 tablespoons sugar

3 large egg yolks

1 tablespoon nonfat dry milk

Pinch of sea salt

Fill a 4-quart bowl halfway with ice and 2 cups of water. Place a 2-quart metal bowl inside the 4-quart bowl. In a heavy-bottomed saucepan, combine the milk, cream, half-and-half, and green tea. Sprinkle 3 tablespoons of the sugar over the liquid without stirring and bring to a boil over medium-high heat.

Meanwhile, in a bowl, whisk the yolks and the remaining 3 tablespoons of sugar with the nonfat dry milk and salt. Slowly pour the hot cream into the yolk mixture, whisking constantly. Pour back into the saucepan and place over medium heat. Cook, stirring constantly with a wooden spoon against the bottom of the pan, until the mixture thickens and starts to steam. (Note that since this ice cream does not use a large number of egg yolks, the mixture will not thicken as much as a custard or traditional ice-cream base.) Pour immediately into the bowl sitting in the ice bath. Stir often until completely cooled. Pour through a fine-mesh strainer. The base can be prepared a day in advance and refrigerated. At least 2 hours before serving, pour the ice-cream base into an ice-cream maker. Freeze according to your ice-cream maker's instructions, then store in the freezer until serving.

Greengage Plum Sorbet

makes 3 cups

1 pound green or yellow flesh plums,
  such as greengage

¼ cup plus 1 tablespoon sugar

½ teaspoon fresh lemon juice or ½ tablespoon
  verjus

Pinch of sea salt

Several hours before serving, halve the plums and remove the stones. Place the plums, sugar, lemon juice, 2 tablespoons of water, and salt in a blender and blend until smooth. Pour through a fine-mesh strainer. Freeze immediately according to your ice-cream maker's directions.

Green Herb Granité

makes 2 cups

3 cups loosely packed flat-leaf parsley leaves

2 cups loosely packed dill sprigs

2 cups loosely packed basil leaves

2 cups loosely packed mint leaves

1 cup loosely packed tarragon

¼ cup loosely packed thyme

2 tablespoons Sambuca or other anise liqueur

3 tablespoons sugar

1 teaspoon sea salt

Bring a medium pot of water to a boil. Fill a medium bowl with ice water. Blanch the herbs for 20 seconds in the boiling water. Remove with a slotted spoon to the ice-water bath to stop the cooking and set the color. Drain.

Coarsely chop the herbs. Put the herbs in the blender with 1½ cups cold water, the Sambuca, sugar, and salt. Blend until the herbs are as liquefied as possible, about 3 minutes. Pour through a fine-mesh strainer and press out all the liquid, discarding any leftover herbs. Pour the liquid into a 11 x 7-inch pan, cover, and freeze overnight. Scrape with a metal spoon along the surface of the ice until all of the ice has been scraped into crystals. The granité can be prepared up to 2 days in advance and frozen. Scrape again just before serving.

WINE NOTES

Sparkling Ice Wine, Vidal, Inniskillin, 2002 (Niagara Peninsula, Canada)
Brut, Veuve Clicquot, NV (Champagne, France)
Bigaro, Elio Perrone, 2006 (Piedmont, Italy)

With the terrine, there are lots of intense sensations and contrasting elements to consider. You've got the fatty-rich qualities of foie gras nicely offset by the bite and drive of the kumquat. And since this is a first course, it's ideal to have a wine that leaves a clean, mouthwatering finish to lead into the next course.

The challenge of foie gras is finding a wine with enough stuffing to stand up to it. One of the true classics in the world of food-and-wine pairing is the marriage of foie gras and the sweet Sauternes, a complementary pairing of two rich, palate-coating items. We introduced a twist on this classic by using a sparkling ice wine,

which is plenty unctuous up front to mingle with the rich liver, then cleans up nicely on the finish with its bracing acidity and effervescence. The vidal grape offers a terrific mix of exotic, tropical flavors, and the sparkles help lift the rich foie gras flavors off the palate.

As noted previously, Champagne should not be relegated to the cocktail hour. With the delicate, flaky crabmeat, there may be no better choice than a Champagne, with its mineral tang, clean flavors, and finesse. Veuve Clicquot's NV Brut is a fruit-forward style, playing nicely off the slightly pungent licorice cream while complementing the sweetness of the corn.

The Green Explosion is, admittedly, a difficult pairing because of the myriad sweet, salty, and bitter sensations. So we chose to go with something mildly sweet, lightly alcoholic, and ever-so-slightly sparkling. Moscato d'Asti, from Piedmont, Italy, made in a semi-sparkling style dubbed *frizzante*, is really more about freshness and fruitiness than all-out sweetness, making it a subtle, unobtrusive partner for bold desserts. It will insinuate itself into the Green Explosion mix quietly but effectively. Always go for the most recent vintage possible when buying moscato; above all else, what you're looking for in these wines are fresh, primary fruit flavors.

TREASURE HUNT AND FAMILY COOKOUT

Mom's Barbecue Chicken

Grilled Vegetable and Olive Salsa

Braised and Barbecued Pork Spareribs

Cowboy Beans

Creamy Coleslaw

Corn with Herb Butter

Herb Biscuits

Mini Hot Fudge Sundaes

WHEN CHRIS GAUGHAN MARRIED OUR DAUGHTER ALEXIS THIS YEAR, OUR FAMILY grew fourfold: Not only did Chris already have two young daughters, but his four siblings have spouses and young broods of their own. Much to our delight, all but one family member lives no more than a few hours' drive away, and the Gaughans who live in Hawaii come to visit every summer. The idea for a grand treasure hunt began as a way to introduce our newest family members to Rancho La Zaca.

The children used a map of the property I painted on canvas with acrylics, and they followed clues they discovered along the way as they navigated the course. The older ones felt so grown-up, getting to shuttle the little ones around in the gas-powered ranchmobiles. They went from the range to the vegetable garden, snuck into the chicken coops (where they "stole" the clue from some terrified hens), raced on foot through horse pastures and grape rows, climbed into trees, dove to the bottom of the pool, and swam across the pond. When they reached the spot marked X on the map, they dug, at first with shovels, and then with bare hands, to unearth an old chest filled with candy coins and gaudy Mardi Gras jewelry. Then the hot and tired children had a spontaneous cannonball-dive contest which, in addition to a recharging effect, had the added benefit of washing away the grime of the day. After swimming, we all headed up to the campsite at the tepees.

At sunset, we feasted on a dinner of barbecued chicken and ribs, followed by the showstopping entrance of Babalu, the miniature donkey (see page 153), carrying his cart loaded with the fixings for hot fudge sundaes. I'd thought that a few campfire songs and some ghost stories would lull the kids to sleep, leaving us with plenty of grown-up time, but I was wrong about that. We grown-ups sang among ourselves, while the boys, who had discovered the lasso ropes hanging in the horse barn, amused themselves with a newly invented ranch game: girl roping! It was such a success that our neighbor Brooks Firestone was prompted to comment, before tucking into his own sleeping bag for the night, "If I had known it was so easy to catch a giggling girl with a rope, I might have used that trick myself when I was a younger man!"

Mom's Barbecue Chicken

There are hundreds of jarred barbecue sauces on grocery store shelves, and of course you can use them for your cookout. But these sauces are always overly sweet and sticky, and have the homogenized texture that you expect from a jar. This homemade sauce, on the other hand, is chunky with bits of sweet-and-sour onions, and has the perfect balance of bite and sweet. It's ideal for chicken, but also great with pulled pork or spareribs.

makes 15 servings as part of a buffet

1 ½ cups (3 sticks) unsalted butter

2 medium yellow onions, diced

1 tablespoon freshly ground black pepper

1 tablespoon prepared yellow mustard

½ cup plus 2 tablespoons apple cider vinegar

1 teaspoon sea salt

One 24-ounce bottle ketchup

Three 3-pound chickens, each cut into 8 pieces

MAKE THE SAUCE: In a large saucepan, melt the butter. Add the onions, black pepper, mustard, vinegar, and salt, and stir until combined. Bring to a simmer over medium-low heat and cook for 20 minutes. Add the ketchup, stir, and bring to a simmer, then remove from the heat. The sauce can be prepared 3 days in advance and refrigerated.

Preheat the grill to medium.

Brush the chicken with the sauce and place on the grill, skin side down. Continue basting and cooking, turning often, until the chicken is cooked all the way through, about 45 minutes.

Grilled Vegetable and Olive Salsa

This pairs wonderfully with Cowboy Beans (page 147), offering that perfect vinegary olive finish. It also goes really well with the chicken and biscuits, and is great on sandwiches.

makes 4 cups

1 medium red bell pepper, quartered

1 medium orange bell pepper, quartered

1 medium yellow bell pepper, quartered

1 small red onion, sliced into ¼-inch rounds

2 medium zucchini, halved lengthwise

2 medium Japanese eggplants, halved
  lengthwise

6 cremini mushrooms

4 plum tomatoes, halved lengthwise

½ cup plus 1 tablespoon extra virgin olive oil

2 teaspoons sea salt

½ teaspoon freshly ground black pepper

1 cup chopped peperoncini

½ cup chopped pitted green olives

2 tablespoons fresh lemon juice

Preheat the grill to medium-low.

In a large bowl, toss the bell peppers, red onion, zucchini, eggplants, mushrooms, and tomatoes with the ½ cup of oil, 1½ teaspoons of the salt, and the black pepper. Grill the vegetables over medium-low heat until they are just tender and a little blackened, 5 to 8 minutes. Turn all the vegetables and grill for 5 minutes more. Remove from the grill and set aside to cool.

Once the vegetables are cooled, chop all of them into ¼-inch pieces. In a large bowl, toss with the remaining ½ teaspoon of salt and 1 tablespoon of oil, the peperoncini, olives, and lemon juice. The salsa can be prepared 1 day in advance and refrigerated.

Braised and Barbecued Pork Spareribs

There are passionate debates about how to cook pork spareribs, but here's a fantastic method: Cook them at length in an oven, then take the braising liquid, reduce it into a sauce, and put the spareribs onto the grill to finish them. Slow-cooked meats are succulent and tender, but it's difficult to cook this way on an open-fire grill: If you want to grill the whole time, keep the temperature low and even, and keep the ribs covered with some moisture.

makes 15 servings as part of a buffet

3 racks pork spareribs (about 6 pounds)

2 teaspoons sea salt

¾ teaspoon freshly ground black pepper

3 tablespoons grapeseed oil

1 carrot, cut into large dice

1 small yellow onion, diced

3 garlic cloves, minced

3 oregano sprigs

3 thyme sprigs

One 2-inch Ceylon cinnamon stick

Three 1-inch strips orange zest

½ teaspoon ground coriander

1 bay leaf

¼ teaspoon sweet paprika

1 dried ancho chile, soaked in hot water for 30 minutes (see Resources)

1 dried pasilla chile, soaked in hot water for 30 minutes (see Resources)

1 dried New Mexican chile, soaked in hot water for 30 minutes (see Resources)

2 plum tomatoes, halved

½ cup fresh orange juice (from 2 oranges)

1½ cups low-sodium canned chicken stock

6 tablespoons rice wine vinegar

1 cup light brown sugar

Preheat the oven to 250°F.

Season the spareribs with the salt and black pepper. In a large sauté pan, heat the oil over high heat and sear the ribs, 1 rack at a time, until nicely browned, about 5 minutes. Repeat with the remaining racks and transfer all 3 racks to a large roasting pan.

In the same sauté pan over medium heat, add the carrot, onion, garlic, oregano, thyme, cinnamon stick, orange zest, coriander, bay leaf, and paprika. Cook until softened, about 5 minutes. Add the rehydrated chiles, the tomatoes, orange juice, chicken stock, vinegar, and brown sugar and bring to a simmer. Pour the braising mixture over the spareribs and cover the roasting pan with a tight-fitting lid or aluminum foil. Place in the oven and braise until the meat is fork-tender, about 2 hours. Remove the ribs from the pan. Remove the carrot and the herb sprigs and discard, then pour the braising liquid into a saucepan. Bring to a boil, reduce the heat to low, and simmer for 20 minutes, skimming the fat off the surface. Remove from the heat, let cool slightly, then blend to a smooth puree. Pour through a fine-mesh strainer. The ribs and sauce can be prepared to this point 2 days in advance and refrigerated separately. Preheat a grill to medium-high. Place the rib racks on the grill and continuously brush with sauce until they are heated through and a nice sticky crust forms from the sauce, about 20 minutes. Cut into 2- or 3-rib sections and serve.

TOP LEFT: Braised and Barbecued Pork Spareribs

TOP RIGHT: Grilled Vegetable and Olive Salsa

ABOVE: Mom's Barbecue Chicken

Cowboy Beans

Smoked ham and lots of savory herbs make these almost a meal in themselves.

makes 15 servings as part of a buffet

1 ½ pounds dried small red beans

1 head garlic, halved

½ medium yellow onion

One 2-pound smoked ham hock, halved

4 oregano sprigs

8 thyme sprigs

¼ cup (½ stick) unsalted butter

In a large bowl, cover the beans with water and soak overnight.

Drain the beans, then place in a large stockpot and cover by 2 inches with water. Add the garlic, onion, ham hock, 2 oregano sprigs, 6 thyme sprigs, and the butter. Bring to a boil, then reduce to a simmer and cook until the beans are tender, about 2 hours.

Remove the ham hock from the beans and let cool, then shred the meat and discard the bones. Drain the beans and reserve half of the cooking liquid. Remove the garlic, onion, and herb sprigs. Chop the leaves of the remaining 2 oregano sprigs and 2 thyme sprigs. Stir the chopped herbs into the beans with the shredded pork, heat through, and serve. The beans can be prepared 2 days in advance and refrigerated. Reheat over medium heat, stirring, before serving.

Creamy Coleslaw

Some recipes serve a purpose other than being delicious in and of themselves. The classic American slaw is one of them: It's the perfect foil for other things on a barbecue plate. The crisp texture of cabbage offsets the softness of the beans and pork, and the vinegary bite cuts through the sweet barbecue sauce, balancing out the tastes.

makes 15 servings as part of a buffet

½ head (1 ¾ pounds) purple cabbage, finely shredded

½ head (1 ¾ pounds) green cabbage, finely shredded

1 carrot, julienned

1 bunch (about 6) scallions, finely sliced

6 tablespoons apple cider vinegar

3 tablespoons sugar

1 cup mayonnaise

1 ½ teaspoons sea salt

¼ teaspoon freshly ground black pepper

Toss the cabbages, carrots, and scallions together in a large bowl. Stir in the remaining ingredients until well combined. Refrigerate for at least 1 hour and up to 3, then serve.

Corn with Herb Butter

15 ears corn	1 teaspoon plus 2 tablespoons sea salt
1 jalapeño	1 teaspoon freshly ground black pepper
1 cup (2 sticks) unsalted butter	2 teaspoons sugar
4 marjoram sprigs	3 tablespoons thinly sliced chives

Husk the corn and remove the silk.

Roast the jalapeño under a preheated broiler or on a grill until the skin is black and blistered, about 2 minutes per side. Place in a bowl and cover with plastic wrap for 10 minutes. Peel away the skin and remove the seeds. Julienne the flesh.

In a medium saucepan over medium heat, melt the butter with the julienned chile, marjoram, 1 teaspoon of the salt, and the black pepper.

The butter can be prepared 3 days in advance and refrigerated.

Bring a large stockpot of water to a boil with the remaining 2 tablespoons of salt and the sugar. Add the corn and bring to a simmer. When the water returns to a simmer, remove from the heat and drain. Brush the corn with the melted butter and sprinkle with the chives.

Herb Biscuits

The secret to great biscuits is to work the butter into the flour—gently and quickly—with hands that are as cool as possible, to prevent the butter from melting while you mix. If you're making these on a hot day, chill all the ingredients before you work. And on any day, try to time these so they go directly from the oven to the table, piping-hot.

makes about 16 biscuits

2 cups all-purpose flour	¾ cup buttermilk
2 teaspoons baking powder	3 tablespoons thinly sliced chives
½ teaspoon baking soda	1 tablespoon thyme leaves
¾ teaspoon sea salt	¼ cup whole milk
6 tablespoons (¾ stick) cold unsalted butter, cut into pieces	

Preheat the oven to 450°F.

In a large bowl, whisk together the flour, baking powder, baking soda, and salt. Drop in the pieces of cold butter and cut in with 2 knives or a pastry blender, or by rubbing the butter and flour between your hands. Coat and separate the butter pieces as you work. Continue working until the butter/flour pieces resemble the size of peas, but do not allow the butter to melt or form a paste.

Mix in the buttermilk, chives, and thyme with a wooden spoon or a fork just until the dry ingredients are moistened. Gather the dough into a ball and knead it gently against the sides and bottom of the bowl 5 to 10 times, pressing any loose pieces into the dough until the bowl is fairly clean.

On a lightly floured surface, roll or press out the dough into a ½-inch-thick square or rectangle. Trim away some of the rough edges and cut the rest into 1½-inch squares.

Place the biscuits on an ungreased baking sheet at least 1 inch apart. Brush the tops with milk and bake until golden brown on top and deeper golden on the bottom, 10 to 12 minutes.

Mini Hot Fudge Sundaes

This is a build-your-own-sundae affair. We offer little pleated Dixie cups to make them in, which is the perfect size for both kids and adults, and 1-ounce scoops for the ice cream. We have noticed, however, that some guests return to the cart two or three times. But maybe that's just for a visit with Babalu.

serves 15

2 pints vanilla ice cream

2 pints chocolate ice cream

1 cup M&M's, crushed

1 cup toasted walnuts, chopped

6 chocolate-filled Newman-O's cookies, crushed

6 mint-filled Newman-O's cookies, crushed

2 cups Hot Fudge Sauce (recipe follows)

15 maraschino cherries with the stem, drained

1 can whipped cream, such as Reddi-Wip

Hot Fudge Sauce

makes about 2 cups

6 tablespoons sugar

6 tablespoons unsweetened cocoa powder

½ teaspoon sea salt

1 cup heavy cream

½ cup plus 2 tablespoons light corn syrup

¼ teaspoon white wine vinegar

4 ounces bittersweet chocolate, coarsely chopped

1 tablespoon pure vanilla extract

In a large saucepan, whisk together the sugar, cocoa, salt, and 1 cup of water. Bring to a simmer over medium heat. Remove from the heat and add the cream, corn syrup, vinegar, and 2 ounces of the chopped chocolate. Return the pan to medium-high heat and whisk frequently, until the bubbles become small and the syrup reaches about 225°F on a candy thermometer, about 5 minutes. Remove from the heat and whisk in the remaining 2 ounces of chopped chocolate and the vanilla. Whisk until smooth. The hot fudge sauce can be prepared 1 week in advance and refrigerated. Reheat over low heat before serving.

WINE NOTES

Zinfandel, Rafanelli, Dry Creek Valley, 2005 (Sonoma, California)
Zinfandel, Aldo's Vineyard, Robert Biale, 2005 (Napa, California)

Wines for barbecue should be kept simple and should echo the flavors of the food: juicy, bold, and ripe, with more than a touch of spice. California zinfandel has been anointed over the years as the go-to wine for barbecue, thanks to its inimitable blend of juicy black fruitiness and exotic spice. The best zins have an unmistakable woodsiness that makes them great partners for smoky barbecue; there are a number of grenache-based wines that work well also. They, too, have smoky, underbrush-y notes behind a layer of ripe fruit that meld well with barbecue. Whatever you choose, it should be really bold, but only moderately oaked.

BABALU

Tito Puente has lived next door with our neighbors Chuck and Stephanie Roven since he was four months old. Tito is not the Latin bandleader, of course, but rather the name of a miniature Sicilian donkey whom they keep in their stables as a pet. We have always thought he was adorable, and who wouldn't? He stands just slightly larger than a full-grown German shepherd, he is mischievous and playful, and, like most minidonks, he comes at the call of his name.

Last year for my birthday, the neighbors sent me one of my own. Ricky Ricardo arrived in a trailer with a big red bow tied around his neck. The breeder told me that this would be the first night Ricky had ever spent away from his mother, as she handed me a set of care and feeding instructions and a complimentary subscription to *Miniature Donkey Talk* magazine.

I didn't have the heart to leave him alone, so Ricky spent his first two nights in the little enclosed dog run outside our bedroom. On the first night, he slept with his nose pressed against the glass, gazing inside with envy at the three Jack Russells who slept at our feet. Sometime in the middle of the second night, he figured out a way to open the door, and I awoke to him crawling into our bed.

The next morning, I called the breeder. "He's lonely," she told me. "He needs someone to keep him company. And I suggest you get yourself a goat for this purpose," she added, just as I was wondering how I was going to save my marriage.

By the third day, we had fixed him up with a stall of his own and a roommate, a two-year-old billy goat we named Fred Mertz. Happy in his new home, Ricky quickly revealed the sweet disposition of a family pet. He craved attention and adored meeting guests, allowing us to bring him on walks with the dogs and even into the living room on special occasions. There was only one problem: Ricky Ricardo would not come when his name was called. He needed a catchier name, and the first one that came to mind was Babalu, the name of the song Ricky's character was best known for singing on *I Love Lucy.* His ears immediately pricked up.

Now that he heeded his owner's call like a dog, Babalu was ready for more: party tricks! Thumbing through my complimentary magazine, I was inspired by a shot advertising mini donkey carts for carrying children. "How about seeing if we can get a street vendor–style cart made for him so he can carry something useful?" I asked Stephanie.

"Like what?"

"Hot fudge sundaes."

This, like some of my other ideas (see elephants, page 96), was slightly more complicated than it seemed. Getting the cart made was the easy part. But I learned that donkeys need to be trained to pull. I had always thought they were born for such labor.

Six months later, Babalu returned from training and was ready for his debut at Rancho La Zaca. The only problem we didn't anticipate was that the kids can't decide if they're more interested in making sundaes or in kissing Babalu.

THE FIRESTONE FAMILY

They are the kind of American family portrayed in movies and fifties television shows, but that so rarely exists in real life. The patriarch, Brooks Firestone, is a grandson of Firestone Tire and Rubber Company founder Harvey Firestone. Brooks was raised in California, but he went to college in New York, at Columbia. One night while he was still a student, he and some buddies attended a performance by the Royal Ballet, which was visiting from London. Cross-referencing the program during the performance, they noted the names of certain ballerinas whom they were interested in asking on a date.

After the show they slipped the stage doorman a note to take to the girls. All of the ladies accepted, except one who was ill. Another ballerina volunteered to take her place: Kate Boulton, an Anglican vicar's daughter on her first world tour with the company. And Brooks fell head over heels for her.

Over the next two years they corresponded. When the company returned to New York, Brooks proposed marriage. The rumor is that he filled her dressing room with flowers every night until she finally accepted. I have never asked them to confirm this because I wouldn't want to know if it wasn't true.

Kate quit the company and they married, then Brooks was tapped by his family to run a European office of the tire company, so off they went to the Continent. But after a while, Brooks's American roots began tugging him homeward, and he was trasferred back to a company office in Los Angeles. From there, he began to take an interest in a special tract of ranch property with a wildcat vineyard scheme that his father had bought into, about two hours north of L.A. Compared to the sprawl of parking lots and the mostly mundane modern architecture cluttering the increasingly smoggy L.A. basin during the sixties and seventies, cattle grazing on golden grassy hills beneath a clear blue sky appealed to them.

Not long after they resettled here in the early 1970s, Brooks and Kate watched California wines—which were mostly made north of San Francisco—achieve worldwide recognition. Even today, I can imagine the cogs of this unashamed epicure turning: "If they can do it up in Napa, we should be able to do it here. Better." And grapes were soon growing in Santa Barbara County, and wines being bottled with a Firestone label.

Among their many other interests, Brooks and Kate have been prominent in state and county politics. He has consulted for the U.S. Army and taught American history at the high school, and now serves as our county supervisor. For a time, Kate ran her own winery, Curtis, which is contiguous to the Firestone Estate. Now she is retired, but never idle. Together, they sing every Sunday in the church choir and in performance with the Santa Barbara Choral Society, and have a hand in practically every worthy charity in the county. They have won buckles in western riding events at the rodeo, ribbons in the hunt, and trophies at the state fair. But their greatest achievement is their family: four children, three married with children of their own. All of the eleven grandchildren are already well on the way to building their own impressive accomplishments.

The Firestones are as much a part of what makes this valley so exceptional as the way the hills turn purple seconds before sunset almost every day.

DINNER FOR TWO

Spring Rolls with Peanut Sauce and Sweet Chile Sauce

French Fries with Truffle Mayonnaise

Naked Caviar

Stone Crab Claws

Burrata Cheese, Medjool Dates, and Strawberries

a great party every year, since it would give us a chance to bring in friends from all over the country. But he just won't hear of it. I managed to pull it off once, a big surprise bash for his sixtieth. Although he was gracious about it, he made me promise never to do it again.

But I couldn't bear the idea of an "ordinary dinner" at home, pretending there was nothing special about the day, so I figured out something that makes us both happy: dinner for two and a menu comprised of nothing but his favorite foods. Forget about conforming to the FDA food pyramid; it's all about guilty pleasures and eating with our fingers: a mountain of caviar, for which we have toast, but which, in fact, gets eaten on French fry tips, and Joe's Stone Crabs, delivered by FedEx. When we're finished sucking the sweet meat out of the shells, we toss the empties over our shoulders into the pond.

The dinner doesn't require this setting to enjoy it. Once we celebrated with a dinner in bed, and the only item on the menu was birthday cake. We fed each other right off the cake plate using a single fork. But a few years ago, I gave him this little boat as a birthday gift, so we changed the venue to the pond. And last year, the gift was a sun bed, which we put on the dock.

He looks forward to celebrating his birthday now.

Spring Rolls with Peanut Sauce and Sweet Chile Sauce

These are very easy to make and full of fresh, light ingredients. The key is to load the spring rolls with lots of Thai basil, cilantro, and mint. The wrappers and basil are both usually available at Asian markets or farmers' markets.

makes 6 rolls

6 sheets spring roll wrappers

¼ cup chopped mint leaves

¼ cup chopped cilantro leaves

¼ cup chopped Thai basil leaves

6 medium shrimp, cooked, deveined, and halved lengthwise

2 ounces rice vermicelli noodles, cooked according to package directions

½ carrot, julienned

½ red bell pepper, julienned

½ cucumber, seeded and julienned

½ avocado, pitted, peeled, and cut into ¼-inch sticks

Peanut Sauce (recipe follows)

Sweet Chile Sauce (recipe follows)

Soak the spring roll wrappers individually in warm water and lay out 2 at a time. Sprinkle the 2 sheets all over with a third of the herbs. Lay 2 pieces of shrimp in the center of each wrapper. Place some vermicelli noodles on top of the shrimp and lay out a row of each of the vegetables. Curl the bottom edge of the wrapper over the vegetables. Next, bring the sides in and continue to roll tightly.

Peanut Sauce

makes ¾ cup

½ cup smooth peanut butter

1 tablespoon plus 1 teaspoon shoyu or soy sauce

2 tablespoons brown sugar

¼ to ½ teaspoon red chile flakes

1 tablespoon rice wine vinegar

1 teaspoon sesame oil (optional)

Combine all of the ingredients in a blender with ¼ cup of water. Blend until smooth. The peanut sauce can be prepared 2 or 3 days in advance and refrigerated.

Sweet Chile Sauce

makes ¾ cup

¾ cup sugar

½ cup plus 2 tablespoons rice wine vinegar

1 tablespoon minced ginger

1 red jalapeño, seeded and minced, or 1 teaspoon dried red chile, seeded and minced

¼ teaspoon sea salt

In a small saucepan, combine the sugar, the ½ cup of vinegar, the ginger, chile, and salt and bring to a simmer. Simmer until the sauce has slightly thickened, about 15 minutes. Stir in the remaining 2 tablespoons of vinegar. The sauce can be prepared 2 to 3 days in advance and refrigerated.

French Fries with Truffle Mayonnaise

There are two secrets to making a great French fry: One is under your control, the other is not. What you can't control is the spud's history: If the potato was ever refrigerated below 55°, it just won't crisp up properly, although it will still taste just fine. Unfortunately, there's no way to know a given potato's refrigeration history, so you'll just have to chance it. But the thing you can control is the double-frying method: Be sure to monitor your oil temperatures closely, and don't skip the step of letting the fries cool, at least to room temperature, before the second immersion in hot oil.

makes 2 servings

FOR THE MAYONNAISE
1 large egg yolk

1 teaspoon grainy mustard

1 teaspoon fresh lemon juice

¼ teaspoon sea salt

⅛ teaspoon freshly ground black pepper

½ cup grapeseed oil

⅓ cup white truffle oil

1 tablespoon finely sliced chives

1 tablespoon chopped parsley

1 teaspoon chopped thyme leaves

FOR THE POTATOES
2 large Idaho potatoes that have never been refrigerated below 55°F

3 cups grapeseed or canola oil, for deep-frying

Sea salt, for sprinkling

MAKE THE MAYONNAISE: In a medium bowl, whisk together the egg yolk, mustard, lemon juice, salt, and black pepper. Slowly—one drop at a time—whisk in the oils. As the mixture begins to emulsify, you can start adding the oils in a slow, steady stream. When the oil is completely incorporated, stir in the herbs. The mayonnaise can be prepared a day in advance and refrigerated.

MAKE THE POTATOES: Peel the potatoes and cut them into ¼-inch strips. Place the potato strips in a large bowl of water and refrigerate for at least 30 minutes, then drain and pat dry.

In a large, deep, heavy pot, heat the oil to 330°F. Fry the potatoes in batches for about 3 minutes each. Using a slotted spoon, remove them to a baking sheet, then refrigerate, uncovered, until the next frying.

Heat the oil to 365°F. Fry the pre-blanched potatoes until they are golden brown, 2 to 4 minutes. Drain on a paper towel, sprinkle with salt, and serve with the truffle mayonnaise.

Naked Caviar

Caviar is not only finger food, it's also something you can easily feed to someone else—and what could be more romantic than feeding your partner with your fingers? We began eating the caviar on the bread crisps, then discovered that dipping French fries into the bowl of roe was even more delicious and decadent. We used farmed Osetra caviar from Italy, as Caspian Beluga is difficult to get now.

makes 2 servings

½ loaf French bread

4 ounces Caviar de Venise farmed Osetra caviar (see Resources)

Preheat the oven to 350°F.

Slice the French bread into $\frac{1}{16}$-inch slices and place in a single layer on a baking sheet. Place in the oven until very crispy, about 8 minutes.

Place the caviar in a glass bowl over crushed ice and serve with the crisps on the side.

Stone Crab Claws

The beauty of stone crab claws is the big, sweet chunk of meat that you can get at once, without all the tedious work that goes into extracting a few flakes of other crabmeat. The season for stone crabs starts October 15th and lasts until spring. There are many different companies that sell them by mail order, and some even come packed in kits with sauce, mallets, and other accessories. Joe's Stone Crabs is one of the bigger mail-order suppliers.

makes 2 servings

FOR THE HORSERADISH MUSTARD MAYONNAISE
½ cup plus 2 tablespoons mayonnaise

¼ cup grainy mustard

2 tablespoons prepared horseradish

2 pounds jumbo stone crab claws (see Resources)

1 lemon, cut into wedges

MAKE THE HORSERADISH MUSTARD MAYONNAISE: In a small bowl, combine all of the ingredients and stir. The mayonnaise can be prepared 2 days in advance and refrigerated.

Just before serving, crack the stone crab claws with a wooden mallet so that the shell remains intact but is easily removed by hand. To do this, place the claw on a clean kitchen towel set on a cutting board. Hold the large part of the pincer with your hand and whack the body of the claw hard enough to break it but not so hard that it breaks apart. Turn the claw over and repeat. Arrange the claws over crushed ice with a bowl of the sauce in the middle, and garnish with lemon wedges. Serve with an additional bowl for the discarded shells.

LEFT: Spring Rolls with Peanut Sauce and Sweet Chile Sauce; Stone Crab Claws with Horseradish Mustard Mayonnaise

Burrata Cheese, Medjool Dates, and Strawberries

The fruit-cheese combination, with aged balsamic vinegar, is the perfect complement to the rest of the menu, in keeping with the idea of finger food. Simply slice the Burrata, place the strawberries and dates on top, and drizzle them with an extra-aged balsamic.

makes 2 servings

3 ounces Burrata cheese

3 medjool dates, halved

3 ripe strawberries, halved

1 teaspoon extra-vecchio balsamic vinegar

Slice the cheese into 6 slices or chunks. Break the dates in half and remove the pit. Place a half date on each slice of cheese. Place a half strawberry on each date. Drizzle with the aged balsamic vinegar.

WINE NOTES

Sekt Brut, Georg Breuer, 2004 (Rheingau, Germany)
Brut Rosé, Paul Bara, MV (Champagne, France)

A celebratory occasion such as this one calls for something with bubbles, so Champagne or sekt, the German sparkling wine, would both fit the bill. A sekt is basically a sparkling riesling, so you get all the benefits of a riesling (fruity yet focused) in an off-dry, bubbly format. Georg Breuer is a noted producer in Germany's Rheingau region whose sparklers rival any other in quality, including French bubblies.

But there is a reason that Champagne and caviar are so often found together, and it's not just because the combination connotes luxury and decadence. The pungency of caviar presents one of the most assertive challenges to wine imaginable. Once again, Champagne's sleek, clean flavor and chalky texture swoop in to the palate's rescue. Think of the gripping texture of Champagne and how it mimics the brininess of foods such

as shellfish and caviar; follow that with a wave of bright acidity to clean up the lingering fishiness and you've got a match.

We chose a rosé Champagne not just for its romantic color but because it is in essence a pinot noir in sparkling form—a little more intensely flavored than a regular Champagne but, ultimately, one of the most flexible wines around for food.

KANSAS LIMESTONE GRAPE POSTS

The row of limestone grape posts, viewed from across the pond, makes a composition, and examining them one by one reveals their sculptural beauty. Each one is unique—hand hewn and flecked with prehistoric fossils. But it is the recent history of this ancient stone that is most interesting to us.

The stone is native to the plains of Kansas, where early pioneers were faced with an unusual difficulty, a lack of trees. For firewood, they resourcefully substituted bison "patties," but for building they substituted stone. In the east, durable fieldstone boulders were commonly found during field clearing and used as a building material. Midwestern farmers, lacking fieldstones, discovered a nearly uniform layer of sedimentary limestone just a few feet beneath the surface of the soil and only eight to twelve inches thick. Into this rock, which is soft and chalky when first exposed, they drilled rows of holes at regular intervals, and allowed them to fill with water. This froze in winter and naturally fractured the rock into neat building stones or oblong post shapes, which made quarrying this stone surprisingly simple.

Fence posts were more difficult than building blocks to maneuver into place. Each post weighs between 250 and 400 pounds, so a horse could pull a load of no more than six to eight of them at a time. However, the benefits of stone posts outweighed the difficulties in placing them: The hole could be shallower than for a wooden post, they were fireproof (useful in an area prone to grass fires), the drill holes made permanent, wiggle-proof grooves for the horizontal wire, and the stones would last decades longer than wood. At one time, stone post fences were used over forty thousand miles of Kansas farm country.

So what are these historic relics doing at Oak Savanna? We recycled them. A California-based entrepreneur is reclaiming the posts in Kansas as fast as the old fences are being torn down to make way for development there. At first, we considered using just a few for some residential landscape effects, but when we heard the whole history of the Kansas fence post limestone (there is even a museum dedicated to this beautiful material in LaCrosse, Kansas) we decided the posts deserved to be put back into agricultural service and showcased, like functional sculpture, at the same time. There are more than one thousand Kansas limestone grape posts currently in use at Oak Savanna Vineyard.

VINTNERS' POTLUCK

"Santa Maria–Style BBQ" Oakwood Grilled Tri-tip

Venison Tenderloin with Cherry-Olive Chutney

Cheese Board with Kalamata and Kumquat Breadsticks

I SHOULD HAVE KNOWN IT WOULD BE IMPOSSIBLE TO GATHER A ROOMFUL OF SOME of the best winemakers in Santa Barbara County and not expect some rivalry. But it's all friendly in the valley's small and close-knit wine industry. Besides, everyone here has received the highest acclaim from critics and, more important, from customers. On the table, underneath the kraft paper wrapping, there were bottles of Andrew Murray, Au Bon Climat, Calzada Ridge, Consilience, Cold Heaven, Curtis, Firestone, Foxen, Great Oaks, Hitching Post, Koehler, and our own Oak Savanna.

"Why don't we do this every month?" Jenny Doré asked, and she had only been here a few minutes; her Foxen pinot hadn't even been bagged yet. Jim Clendenen, who bottles his Au Bon Climat in extremely heavy glass, was confident that he'd be able to recognize his own wines, even in disguise. "It is not a competition," I teased. "The point of this is to enjoy everyone's wine in a democratic way, without the burden of thinking about who made what."

I have always loved potlucks. While this old-fashioned party idea was originally conceived to take the burdens of hosting a party off a single household, dinner parties in recent times have become a means of expressing the generosity of the host. So the potluck became retro—some would even say passé. But a potluck dinner brings an instant feeling of we're-all-in-this-togetherness that no other party plan can match.

For this evening, I tried something I had never done before: potluck seating. In addition to asking each winemaker to bring four bottles of wine and a dinner dish to pair with it, they also brought their own favorite dinner plates, and put those plates anywhere that was open at the table. Until we all sat down, no one knew who they were sitting next to, only what their neighbor's favorite dishes looked like. The result was a break in conventional boy-girl seating, and gave people some unexpected dinner partners, mostly delightful pairings. (But also including a former boss and an ex-husband. Oops!) In my toast, I confessed the truth: I handpicked all the guests because I knew that not only did they make great wines, but they also knew how to cook!

The evening was dynamic, with people swapping places up and down the long table and circulating the different wines from one end to the other. Everyone did indeed figure out which wine was Jim's (the heavy one!), but mostly there were surprises and congratulations when the bottles were stripped of their wrappers.

Jenny was right: We really should do this more often.

"Santa Maria–Style BBQ" Oakwood Grilled Tri-tip

Santa Maria, the self-proclaimed "Barbecue Capital of the World," is renowned for its distinct style, which consists of a top block sirloin or the triangular bottom sirloin (tri-tip) seasoned with salt, pepper, and garlic and cooked slowly over native red oak coals. This traditional style originated in the nineteenth century, when ranch owners would hold barbecues to thank their workers (these vaqueros were often neighbors, friends, and family) for a hard day's work branding calves. Now, on any Saturday, visitors to the northern half of Santa Barbara County can see the telltale smoke wafting from barbecue pits all over town—even the Santa Ynez gas station, the Los Olivos Grocery store, and the airport have huge outdoor grills, where barbecued tri-tip is sold. Or you can taste a more refined version of this tradition, made with only the best cuts of aged meat, at the Hitching Post II Restaurant, made famous in the film *Sideways*. Frank Ostini, owner of the Hitching Post, kindly provided this recipe.

makes 8 servings

FOR THE BASTING SAUCE
½ cup red wine vinegar
½ cup garlic-infused light olive oil

FOR THE SEASONING SALT
2 teaspoons freshly ground black pepper
2 teaspoons freshly ground white pepper

2 teaspoons cayenne pepper
1 teaspoon onion powder
¼ cup granulated garlic
6 tablespoons sea salt

Three 2-pound tri-tip roasts

Prepare your barbecue fire. Locally, our preferred fuel is live oakwood, which imparts a special flavor to everything grilled over it.

MAKE THE BASTING SAUCE: In a small bowl, combine the vinegar and olive oil.

MAKE THE SEASONING SALT: In a small bowl, combine all of the ingredients.

Baste and season both sides of the tri-tip. Place the roasts on a low-temperature fire. Turn as the first side gets crispy, 6 to 8 minutes. Turn the tri-tips before the heat pushes the juices out of the top (and continue to turn, using this timing method, throughout the cooking). After turning, baste and season lightly, 3 or 4 times per side. Continue turning until the tri-tips are cooked to your preference. Remove from the fire and let rest on a cutting board for 10 minutes before cutting ½-inch slices on an angle against the grain.

Venison Tenderloin
with Cherry-Olive Chutney

Game with fruit is a classic combination, and for venison, the fruit is traditionally cherry—the tart-sweet cherry is a great foil for the mildly gamey, ultra-lean meat. You never want to overcook meat, but that's especially true for venison, which can become tough in just a few minutes. Our venison comes from Broken Arrow Ranch in southern Texas, where the wild animals are free ranging and eat a natural diet of grasses and other vegetation, resulting in meat with a complex, natural flavor. For a potluck dish, it is best to make something that can come to room temperature and still taste great, like this.

makes 30 servings as part of a buffet

6 pounds boneless venison loin or tenderloin (see Resources)

9 tablespoons extra virgin olive oil

3 tablespoons Tellicherry peppercorns, toasted and crushed

1½ tablespoons juniper berries, toasted and crushed

1 tablespoon plus ¼ teaspoon sea salt

1 pound pea shoots or arugula

⅛ teaspoon freshly ground black pepper

2 tablespoons balsamic vinegar

Cherry-Olive Chutney (recipe follows)

3 tablespoons chopped toasted hazelnuts

Preheat the grill to high.

Dry the venison on paper towels. Rub the tenderloins with 6 tablespoons of the olive oil, the crushed peppercorns, juniper berries, and 1 tablespoon of the salt. Place in a large baking dish and let sit at room temperature for 30 minutes before grilling.

Place the tenderloins on the grill and grill until rare to medium-rare, about 2 minutes on each of 3 sides. Remove the tenderloins from the grill and let them rest on a cutting board for at least 5 minutes before slicing.

Place the pea shoots on a platter and sprinkle with the remaining ¼ teaspoon of salt and the black pepper. Drizzle with the balsamic vinegar and the remaining 3 tablespoons of olive oil. Slice the tenderloins on the bias and place them over the pea shoots. Spoon the relish over the top, serving any additional relish on the side, and sprinkle the chopped hazelnuts on top.

Cherry-Olive Chutney

makes 2 cups

Cranberries could be substituted for the cherries. The chutney is also superb as a sandwich condiment.

3 tablespoons extra virgin olive oil

2 small red onions, halved lengthwise, then cut lengthwise into ⅛-inch slices

½ teaspoon sugar

¼ cup niçoise olives, pitted and cut lengthwise into thirds

½ cup dried Michigan tart cherries

¾ cup low-sodium canned chicken stock

4 tablespoons good-quality red wine vinegar

1 tablespoon chopped thyme

¼ teaspoon sea salt

Heat a medium sauté pan over medium-high heat. Add the olive oil and the red onions and cook, stirring occasionally, until the onions are lightly caramelized, about 15 minutes. Add the sugar, olives, and cherries and stir to combine. Add the stock and 3 tablespoons of the vinegar. Bring to a simmer and simmer until most of the liquid is gone, 5 to 8 minutes. Stir in the remaining 1 tablespoon of vinegar, the thyme, and salt. Let cool. The chutney can be prepared up to 3 days in advance and refrigerated. Warm slightly before serving.

Cheese Board with Kalamata and Kumquat Breadsticks

For dessert we brought out a cheese board laden with California cheeses. Pozo Tomme was a particularly big hit, made by Christine McGuire at Rinconada Dairy. It's an aged sheep's milk cheese that everyone went crazy for. The same dough used in the Butter Sandwiches (see Wedding Picnic, page 9) can be made into the Kalamata and Kumquat Breadsticks. To adequately stock a cheese board, make sure that you have no less than 1 ounce of cheese per person. It is okay to present only one cheese if it is very special, but for a crowd, you should have at least four different varieties, such as soft-ripened, cow's milk, goat's milk, blue-veined, and the like. To make a dramatic presentation like ours, buy your cheeses in whole or half rounds or large chunks without rigidly adhering to the 1-ounce rule.

makes 25 servings

FOR THE KALAMATA AND KUMQUAT
BREADSTICKS
½ recipe Kalamata and Kumquat bread dough
 (page 13)

¼ teaspoon sea salt

FOR THE CHEESE BOARD
8 ounces Rinconada Dairy Pozo Tomme
 (see Resources)

1 wheel Cowgirl Creamery Mount Tam
 (see Resources)

8 ounces Point Reyes Blue cheese
 (see Resources)

6 ounces Cypress Grove soft-ripened
 goat cheese (see Resources)

1 bunch grapes

1 pint medjool dates

1 cup toasted walnuts

MAKE THE KALAMATA AND KUMQUAT BREADSTICKS: Preheat the oven to 375°F.

Cut the bread dough into walnut-size pieces and roll into balls; let rest, covered, for 15 minutes. Roll each ball into a long, skinny rope about 10 inches long. Place the ropes on a parchment-lined baking sheet. Let rest, covered, for 30 minutes. Brush very lightly with water and sprinkle with the salt. Bake until golden brown, about 18 minutes.

MAKE THE CHEESE BOARD: Arrange the cheeses on a board with the breadsticks, grapes, dates, and walnuts.

WINE NOTES

One Thousand Hills, Oak Savanna Vineyard, 2003 (Santa Ynez, California)

Venison, like lamb, has a gamey richness and a deep, satisfying color. The same could be said of a good California syrah. We brought our own premium wine, Oak Savanna One Thousand Hills, to this potluck, but there are myriad California syrahs with the kind of rich, robust personality to go with this hearty fare.

Because of the barbecue element in the menu, there is something especially appealing about California syrah as opposed to, say, something from the Rhône Valley in France. Whereas both the Californian and French wines will have those appealing notes of gaminess and spice, the California wine will have a sweeter fruitiness to play off the barbecue sauce.

Don't be confused by the word "sweet" in this context: Technically speaking, a wine can be bone dry yet still be perceived as sweet because of the sheer ripeness of the fruit. This rich, seemingly sweet feel is what you get from warm-climate California syrah, and it's precisely the kind of viscous, sappy red you want with some barbecue.

If you would like to have your own Santa Barbara County wine tasting, try some of our personal favorites, made by our neighbors and friends (see Resources):

Viognier, Calzada Ridge, 2005 (Santa Ynez, California)
Viognier, Deux C, Cold Heaven, 2004 (50% California, 50% France)
Syrah, Hillside Reserve, Andrew Murray Vineyards, 2004 (Santa Ynez, California)
Syrah, Hampton Vineyard, Consilience, 2003 (Santa Barbara, California)
Syrah, Ambassador's Vineyard, Curtis, 2003 (Santa Barbara, California)
Syrah, Williamson Doré, Foxen, 2004 (Santa Ynez, California)
Syrah, Purisima Mountain, Parr Selections, 2004 (Santa Ynez, California)
Pinot Noir, Isabelle Morgan, Au Bon Climat, 2004 (California)
Pinot Noir, Rio Vista, Hitching Post, 2005 (Santa Rita Hills, California)
The Ambassador, Firestone Vineyards, 2003 (Santa Ynez, California)
Windham Hill Cuvée, Great Oaks, 2003 (Santa Ynez, California)
Cabernet Sauvignon, Reserve, Koehler, 2002 (Santa Ynez, California)

BLIND WINE TASTING

Wine is essentially sociable. The greatest pleasure winemaking offers is the opportunity to share it with other people.

Some of the attention paid to wine can be frivolous (like fretting over the shape of its serving glass) and even absurd (automatic corkscrews, wine bottle clothing). The pleasure of the wine-drinking experience is enhanced by a conscious effort to really "taste" it, but never in a stuffy or self-conscious way. And one of my favorite excuses for gathering friends and family is for a tasting.

We begin by gathering a large number of different single bottles—with ten guests, we might taste as many as twenty or thirty wines. It also helps to envision a theme: all wines of the same grape varietal or from a single region, new releases, warm-weather drinking wines, or great buys with a few more-expensive wild cards thrown in for fun.

Each bottle is placed in a brown paper wine bottle bag—ask your wine retailer for these—onto which a number has been written. The number corresponds to a list, which you need to make beforehand and onto which you may divulge as much or as little information as you deem useful (sometimes we just list the numbers, and other times we print everything but the price). The list should have plenty of writing space in the right-hand "score" column. Each guest gets a copy of the list and a pencil. We score using a five-point system: Five points is for the very best and zero is undrinkable.

Empty ice buckets are placed on the table so guests can spit out the wine or dump it from their glass when they are ready to move on to the next taste. Full pitchers of fresh water (no ice) are on the table and each guest gets a linen tea towel. The water is for rinsing the mouth between tastes, and also so every guest can rinse and dry his or her own glass as needed. All guests pour their own glasses—usually just an ounce or two—so portions are self-controlled.

At the end of the tasting, we add up all the scores for each bottle. The wine with the most total points wins Best of Tasting. All the bottles are then revealed, along with any other information the score sheet did not divulge. We usually try to taste wines that are readily available locally so everyone can buy a favorite. (And, by the way, your local wine shop owner may be very helpful in putting together a tasting list, especially since the incentive is great that you and your friends will return for favorites).

INDEPENDENCE DAY BLAST

Red Hot, Pure White, and Justice for All

Planked Salmon with Habanero Pesto

Antelope with Coffee and Chili Crust

Grilled Lobster with Green Mango Butter

Bison Riata

Spicy Blackstrap Chicken

Smoked Mushroom Pinot Salsa

Oak-Smoked Onion Steak Sauce

Grilled Vegetables and Corn with Smoked Tomato Mayonnaise

LaLa Salad

Minted Cucumber Salad

Asaca Salad

Red, White, and Blue Po' Salad

Baked Alaska

THE FIRST INDEPENDENCE DAY RODEO AT RANCHO LA ZACA, IN 2002, WAS PLANNED in five days. We jury-rigged a CD player into some loudspeakers for music and rodeo announcements. The "official" clock was an old analog model, like the ones mounted in classrooms. Our clown was a skinny local high school kid who borrowed some of his mother's makeup, his father's overalls, and a rainbow Afro wig that my son had once used in a Halloween costume. And our fireworks were from a small cache that had been brought from the Midwest by a friend.

There were twelve competitive events for which trophies were awarded, including a tennis-ball volley on horseback that I threw in for the benefit of Jimmy Connors, who didn't sign up for the event after all. Instead, it was aced improbably by Vincent Gallo, the indie film star, who may never have held either a tennis racket or a pair of reins in his life, but who understood that the winning strategy was simply to keep the ball bouncing. As the guests were leaving, everyone made me promise to do it again next year.

With a full year to plan it, by 2003 I had a much larger event in the works, with a professional clown, the announcer from the county rodeo grounds, and an authorized fireworks show set to music, the only one in our town. We had some experienced riders, too, who brought their ranked competition horses. This year we'll have more than 150 competitors, and the program is more than thirty pages long. We also have trick riders, a uniformed college marching band, and a team of synchronized swimmers performing.

The annual Independence Day rodeo has become a project that the ranch manager, Wyatt Cromer, Stephanie, and I work on part-time year round, and full-time in the six weeks before. The long-term payoff is in the possibility that by encouraging competition in the Western arts, we are helping to keep alive some of the centuries-old equestrian-based traditions of the Santa Ynez Valley. But what keeps me hosting this event year after year is the lump that starts growing in my throat at the sound of the first chords of the national anthem, and from which I get little relief until the last firework has fizzled out.

Red Hot, Pure White, and Justice for All

A tray of red, white, and blue drinks on the Fourth of July—what could be more appropriate? The Red Hot tastes just like the sweet and fiery candy, albeit with a nice vodka kick. The Pure White, made with the Mexican rice milk drink called horchata, is smooth and creamy with a surprising taste of licorice. And the Justice for All, a sort of tropical sangria, is a refreshing cooler at the end of a hot day. The mixer-base for all three of these drinks is sparkling water, which helps rehydrate our rodeo guests. The drinks are especially festive when swizzled with tinsel-topped sticks.

Red Hot

makes syrup for 12 drinks

4 cups sugar

4 cups water

12 cinnamon sticks

3 tablespoons red chili flakes

1 star anise pod

2 cloves

3 used vanilla bean pods, optional
 (only if you have them)

1 teaspoon sea salt

1 cup pure pomegranate juice

¼ cup fresh-pressed beet juice (optional)

Vodka

Sparkling water

In a large, heavy-bottomed saucepan over high heat, combine the sugar, water, cinnamon sticks, red chili flakes, star anise, cloves, vanilla bean pods, if using, and salt to make the red hot syrup. Bring to a boil. Reduce the heat, and simmer for 15 minutes. Pour through a fine-mesh strainer, let cool completely, and stir in the pomegranate juice and beet juice.

For each drink, shake together 3 ounces of red hot syrup and 1 ounce of vodka and pour over ice into a 12-ounce highball glass. Top with sparkling water and serve.

Pure White

makes 1 serving

3 ounces horchata (Mexican rice milk drink; see
 Resources)

1 ounce Sambuca

Sparkling water

Shake the horchata and sambuca together and pour over ice into a 12-ounce highball glass. Top with sparkling water and serve.

Justice for All

makes 1 serving

1 ounce blue curaçao

4 ounces gewürztraminer

1 ounce pineapple juice

Sparkling water

Stir together the curaçao, gewürztraminer, and pineapple juice. Pour over ice into a 12-ounce highball glass, top with sparkling water, and serve.

Planked Salmon with Habanero Pesto

You can find single-use cedar planks at many grocery stores. The wood will blacken and smoke a bit once it hits the fire, and if you tent the cooking salmon with foil, you can capture some of the fragrant cedar in the fish and help the meat cook more evenly at the same time. The fiercely hot pesto is absolutely addictive. Make extra and have a great loaf of bread on hand for dipping. And wear plastic gloves when handling the habaneros!

makes 25 servings as part of a buffet

4 habanero peppers, seeded and chopped	½ cup extra virgin olive oil
1½ cups packed basil leaves, chopped	1 teaspoon sea salt
2 garlic cloves, chopped	3¼-pounds king salmon fillet, skin on and
Juice of 2 medium limes	pinbones removed

In a blender, combine the habaneros, basil, garlic, lime juice, olive oil, and ½ teaspoon of the salt. Pulse the salmon until smooth, 30 seconds to 1 minute.

Pat the salmon dry with a paper towel and rub with the pesto on both sides, using all of the pesto. Place the salmon in a glass baking dish, cover, and marinate in the refrigerator for 1 to 2 hours.

Preheat the grill to medium-high. Place the salmon with the pesto on a cedar plank. Season the salmon with the remaining ½ teaspoon of salt. Tent the salmon with foil and place on the grill over medium heat. Cook until the flesh is firm and medium-rare to medium, about 20 minutes. If the bottom of the salmon is cooking too fast, lower the heat or move the salmon to a cooler spot on the grill.

Antelope with Coffee and Chili Crust

This crust is both very simple and extremely complex—simple to make, but with a rich, layered set of complex flavors and textures, similar to a Mexican mole, with a mellow start on the palate followed by sweetness and then the spicy attack of chili. The crust would also be great on chicken, pork, or even salmon—it's incredibly versatile.

makes 25 servings as part of a buffet

5 tablespoons chili powder	2½ teaspoons coarsely ground black pepper
2½ tablespoons ground coffee	One 5-pound boneless antelope loin
1¼ teaspoons sea salt	(see Resources)
2½ tablespoons light brown sugar	

In a small bowl, combine the chili powder, coffee, salt, brown sugar, and black pepper. Press the crust into the loin, place in a large glass baking dish, and refrigerate for 2 to 4 hours.

Preheat the grill to medium-high. Cook the loin, turning every 6 minutes, until medium-rare, about 20 minutes. Let the loin rest on a cutting board for 5 minutes before slicing and serving.

Grilled Lobster with Green Mango Butter

Some varieties of mango are intended to be eaten unripe, when they taste more like tart citrus than sweet mango. You can find green mangoes at Asian and South Asian markets. If you can't find them, by no means substitute a ripe mango—just omit the mango from the butter.

makes 20 servings as part of a buffet

Apple cider vinegar

Ten 1-pound Maine lobsters

2 green mangoes, peeled, pitted, and chopped

1 bunch cilantro, chopped, plus additional
  sprigs for garnish

Juice of 2 medium limes

1 ½ teaspoons sea salt

2 jalapeños, seeded and chopped

1 cup (2 sticks) unsalted butter, softened

Fill the largest pot you have with water and bring to a boil, adding 2 tablespoons of vinegar per gallon of water. Place the lobsters in the boiling water, turn off the heat, and parcook for 5 minutes. Remove the lobsters from the pot and let cool slightly on a cutting board. Using a heavy knife, cut the lobsters in half from the head to the tail and set aside.

Place the mango, chopped cilantro, lime juice, salt, jalapeños, and butter into the blender. Blend until fairly smooth. The butter can be prepared a day in advance and refrigerated. Bring to room temperature before using.

Preheat the grill to medium-high. Place the lobsters on the grill shell side down and brush the meat with the butter. Grill for 15 minutes, turning the lobsters once or twice during cooking. Transfer the lobsters to a platter, garnish with the cilantro sprigs, and serve. (Make sure to have the proper tools for guests to crack the claw and knuckle shells.)

Bison Riata

All bison is grass-fed, so it's not as fatty as American beef and it actually has a grassy taste that evokes the great American plains—the perfect meat for Independence Day. It is readily available online, and most upscale markets will special-order a fresh rib for you.

makes 25 servings as part of a buffet

3 leeks, halved and thoroughly cleaned

4 rosemary sprigs, needles only

4 garlic cloves

3 tablespoons black peppercorns

1 ½ tablespoons sea salt

One 5-pound bison rib

Start your wood grill or coals to create a nice, low, even heat. (As an alternative cooking method, the roast may be baked in the oven at 250°F.)

In a large, straight-sided sauté pan with a tight-fitting lid, steam the leeks over medium-high heat for 2 minutes (or put them in the microwave with a small amount of water). In a mortar, crush the rosemary, garlic, peppercorns, and salt together into a paste. Rub the bison with the paste and then wrap it in a single layer of leeks. Tie at 2-inch intervals with butcher's twine.

Place the bison over the open fire, with the heat in the closed grill at around 250°F to 275°F. Cook the loin for 20 to 30 minutes per pound, or until the roast reaches an internal temperature of 120° to 125°F, carefully turning the roast 2 to 3 times.

Remove the rib from the fire to a cutting board, tent with foil, and let sit for 20 minutes. Remove the twine and leeks. Julienne some of the leeks for garnish. Slice and serve with the Onion Steak Sauce (see page 188) and the Smoked Mushroom Pinot Salsa (page 187).

Spicy Blackstrap Chicken

Even though you can make this recipe with a regular-size chicken, try to find poussin. Since this is a buffet with several meat options, the smaller-size bird is nice. A poussin is a very young, small chicken that is especially tender and moist.

makes 25 servings as part of a buffet

½ cup unsulfured molasses

¼ cup light brown sugar

¼ cup Tabasco sauce

½ teaspoon whole yellow mustard seeds, coarsely ground

6 poussins (see Resources) or Cornish game hens, split in half and breastbones removed

In a small saucepan, combine the molasses, brown sugar, Tabasco, and mustard seeds. Bring to a simmer for 2 minutes, then remove from the heat to cool. Two hours before grilling, place the poussins in a baking dish, brush with the glaze, cover, and refrigerate. Remove from the refrigerator 30 minutes before grilling.

Preheat the grill to high. Place the poussins on the grill, skin side down, and adjust the heat to medium. Turning often, grill the poussins until cooked all the way through, about 30 minutes. Remove to a platter and serve.

Smoked Mushroom Pinot Salsa

This sauce may be the epitome of our region's wine country cuisine: It's a cross between the classic French wine reduction sauce and the Mexican influences that are such an important part of California cooking. Use this as a condiment for bison, beef, antelope—any full-bodied meat, even a chicken with some spice to it. No smoker? No problem. Simply use regular mushrooms—the salsa is delicious smoked or not.

makes 3 cups

1 bottle pinot noir

2 pounds Chef's Blend Wild Mushroom Mix (see Resources)

3 to 4 tablespoons grapeseed oil

2 shallots, minced

2 garlic cloves, minced

¾ teaspoon sea salt

¼ teaspoon freshly ground black pepper

4 plum tomatoes, peeled, seeded, and roughly chopped

2 tablespoons minced parsley

2 tablespoons finely sliced chives

1 teaspoon minced thyme

½ teaspoon minced rosemary

In a medium saucepan, bring the wine to a simmer. Lower the heat and reduce to about 1 cup of liquid, about 40 minutes.

Trim away any tough stems from the mushrooms and cold-smoke them according to your smoker's instructions. In a large sauté pan heat the oil. Add the mushrooms, shake the pan to loosen them, and cook, stirring, until they have a nice golden color, 2 to 3 minutes. Add the shallots and garlic and cook for 1 minute. Add the reduced wine, salt, black pepper, tomatoes, parsley, chives, thyme, and rosemary. Stir to combine, and serve. The salsa can be prepared a day in advance and refrigerated. Reheat gently before serving.

Oak-Smoked Onion Steak Sauce

We smoke our onions over oak because, of course, we're Oak Savanna, but you could use any wood. And if you don't have a smoker or you're not grilling, you could omit the smoking entirely and this would still be a huge step above gloppy jarred steak sauces.

makes 4 cups

4 medium yellow onions, halved lengthwise then cut lengthwise into ⅛-slices

2 tablespoons grapeseed oil

½ teaspoon sea salt

½ teaspoon freshly ground black pepper

1½ cups low-sodium canned chicken stock

1½ cups soy sauce

1½ cups light brown sugar

1¼ cups apple cider vinegar

¼ teaspoon cayenne pepper

¾ cup Pickapeppa Sauce

Place the onions on a square of foil with 1 tablespoon of the oil and the salt and pepper. Smoke in a low smoker at 225°F for 1 hour.

In a large sauté pan, heat the remaining 1 tablespoon of oil. Add the smoked onions and cook over medium-low heat, stirring often, until the onions are very soft and slightly caramelized, about 10 minutes.

In a medium saucepan, combine the chicken stock, soy sauce, brown sugar, vinegar, and cayenne. Bring to a boil, reduce the heat to low, and simmer for 30 minutes. Add the onions and Pickapeppa Sauce, and stir to combine. The sauce can be prepared up to 3 days in advance and refrigerated. Reheat before serving.

Grilled Vegetables and Corn with Smoked Tomato Mayonnaise

Smoked Tomato Mayonnaise is the creation of Frank Ostini at the Hitching Post II in Buellton, California, just down the road from Rancho La Zaca. It's a combination of mayonnaise and the restaurant's proprietary smoked tomato pesto, a wonderful condiment that belongs in every pantry. If you don't want to come to California and buy a jar, or if you haven't the time to mail-order one, you can try spiking sun-dried tomato pesto with some chipotle chiles in adobo.

makes 25 servings as part of a buffet

2 bunches asparagus, tough ends removed

3 medium heads radicchio, outer leaves removed

1¼ teaspoons sea salt

3 medium fennel bulbs, sliced lengthwise ¼-inch thick

4 medium green zucchini, sliced lengthwise ½-inch thick

4 medium yellow squash, sliced lengthwise ½-inch thick

6 Japanese eggplant, halved lengthwise

3 medium red onions, sliced into ½-inch rounds

15 ears corn, shucked

½ cup plus 2 tablespoons extra virgin olive oil

¼ teaspoon freshly ground black pepper

¼ cup high-quality balsamic vinegar

⅓ cup chopped parsley

Smoked Tomato Mayonnaise (recipe follows)

Bring a 3-quart pot of water to a boil. Add the asparagus and blanch for 30 seconds. Drain and rinse with cold water.

Cut the heads of radicchio into 8 wedges, keeping the cores intact. Season both sides with ¼ teaspoon of salt each. Set aside for 30 minutes.

ABOVE: Bison Riata
RIGHT: Antelope loin with Coffee and Chili Crust

TOP LEFT: Arugula and mozzarella "LaLa" salad

ABOVE: Grilled Vegetables

LEFT: Spicy Blackstrap Chicken

Lay the asparagus, radicchio, fennel, zucchini, squash, eggplant, onions, and corn, in turn, on a baking sheet or sheets. Brush with ¼ cup plus 2 tablespoons of the olive oil. Sprinkle all of the vegetables except the radicchio with ½ teaspoon of salt and ¼ teaspoon of black pepper.

Preheat the grill to medium-high. Place the asparagus in a grilling basket. Grill the vegetables in batches until tender, 3 to 5 minutes per side for everything except the radicchio, which should need only 1 minute.

Remove the vegetables from the grill and place on a serving platter. Drizzle with the remaining ¼ cup of oil and the balsamic vinegar, and sprinkle with the parsley and an additional ¼ teaspoon of salt. Serve with the smoked tomato mayonnaise on the side.

Smoked Tomato Mayonnaise
makes 3 cups

2 cups mayonnaise

¾ cup Hitching Post Smoked Tomato Pesto (see Resources)

In a medium bowl, combine the ingredients and stir. The mayonnaise can be prepared a day in advance and refrigerated.

LaLa Salad

This salad is named LaLa for the main ingredients—the arugula and mozzarella—but it's really a wonderful pasta salad, packed with fresh summer herbs and the refreshing taste of lemon juice, plus little chewy bits of oven-dried tomato.

makes 25 servings as part of a buffet

One 8-ounce package pappardelle dried pasta, preferably from Rustichella D'Abruzzo (see Resources)

1 cup extra virgin olive oil

1 ½ teaspoons sea salt

8 small heirloom tomatoes

2 sage leaves, chopped

1 summer savory sprig, chopped

1 rosemary sprig, chopped

2 oregano sprigs, chopped

2 thyme sprigs, chopped

¼ teaspoon freshly ground black pepper

2 large balls (approximately 8 ounces each) fresh mozzarella, sliced ¼-inch thick

8 ounces good quality pitted green olives, such as Santa Barbara Olive Co. olives, sliced ¼-inch thick (see Resources)

1 cup basil leaves, sliced

4 cups baby arugula, large stems removed

Juice of 1 medium lemon

Cook the pasta in boiling salted water for 5 to 7 minutes; drain well. Return to the pot and toss with 6 tablespoons of the olive oil and ¼ teaspoon of the salt.

Preheat a convection oven to 275°F (300°F for a standard oven).

Slice 4 heirloom tomatoes ½-inch thick and lay in a single layer on a rack placed on top of a foil-lined baking sheet. Brush both sides of the tomato slices with 2 tablespoons of the olive oil and sprinkle with the chopped sage, savory, rosemary, oregano, thyme, ¼ teaspoon of the salt, and the black pepper. Place in the oven to dry until the tomatoes are shriveled but not completely dry, about 2 hours.

Cut the remaining 4 tomatoes into ½-inch chunks and place them in a large bowl with the pasta, oven-dried tomatoes, mozzarella, olives, the remaining ½ cup of olive oil, the basil, arugula, lemon juice, and the remaining teaspoon of salt. Toss together gently and serve.

Minted Cucumber Salad

A light, refreshing salad that's a great addition to a barbecue; the bracing vinegar is the perfect foil for cooked meats. This is best if made a few hours ahead.

makes 25 servings as part of a buffet

8 medium cucumbers, sliced ⅛-inch thick

1 small red onion, halved lengthwise then cut lengthwise into ⅛-inch slices

¾ cup rice wine vinegar

1½ teaspoons sea salt

¼ cup chopped mint

In a small bowl, combine the cucumbers, red onion, vinegar, salt, and mint. Mix well and set aside to marinate for 2 to 4 hours.

Asaca Salad

Native Americans called our region Asaca. When the Spanish arrived, they translated the word into La Zaca, and that's the name of our ranch—Rancho La Zaca. This recipe is an homage to the original residents here.

makes 25 servings as part of a buffet

¾ cup extra virgin olive oil

1 small yellow onion, cut into ¼-inch dice

1 garlic clove, minced

3 cups wild rice

3 cups pecan halves, toasted and chopped

2¼ cups dried cranberries

5 tablespoons chopped parsley

¼ cup finely sliced chives

2 large ripe avocados, pitted, peeled, and cut into ¼-inch dice

7 tablespoons red wine vinegar

2 to 3 teaspoons sea salt

1½ teaspoons freshly ground black pepper

Heat a 3-quart saucepan over medium-high heat. Add 2 tablespoons of the olive oil with the onion and garlic. Sauté until the onion is translucent, about 1 minute. Add the rice and 9 cups of water and bring to a boil. Reduce the heat to low, cover, and cook for 55 minutes. Drain well and set aside to cool.

In a large bowl, combine the rice, pecans, cranberries, parsley, chives, avocados, the remaining 10 tablespoons of olive oil, the vinegar, salt, and black pepper. Mix well and serve.

Red, White, and Blue Po' Salad

We pack as much of the tricolor into this meal as possible, and here it's with three varieties of potato. The grilled onions add a sweetness you don't often find in potato salad, and the tangy mustard-tarragon vinaigrette adds a refreshing bite. Be sure to dress the potatoes while they're still warm so they can absorb the vinaigrette.

makes 25 servings as part of a buffet

6 pounds mixed red, purple, and white potatoes

8 medium sweet onions, halved lengthwise

3½ teaspoons sea salt

1 teaspoon freshly ground black pepper

¾ cup extra virgin olive oil

2 celery stalks, cut into ¼-inch dice

Juice of 3 large lemons

½ cup grainy mustard

2 bunches tarragon, leaves only

In a large pot, cover the potatoes with water. Bring to a boil and cook until tender, about 20 minutes. Drain and let cool slightly. Cut the potatoes into ¾-inch cubes and place them in a large bowl.

Preheat the grill to medium. In a large bowl, toss the onions with ½ teaspoon of salt, ½ teaspoon of black pepper, and ¼ cup of the olive oil. Grill the onions until they are cooked through and have some dark coloring, about 8 minutes per side. Let cool and chop into ½-inch cubes.

Add the onions to the cooked potatoes along with the celery, lemon juice, mustard, the remaining ½ cup of olive oil, the tarragon, and the remaining 3 teaspoons of salt, and ½ teaspoon of black pepper. Stir together gently and serve.

Baked Alaska

The thin layers of ice cream are separated by crunchy graham crackers and pure, fudgy sauce; you can also add sparklers for a bit of drama. Assemble this dessert the day before, and make sure to clear a space in your freezer before you start assembling. This recipe can easily be cut in half; just bake the brownie base in a 9-inch square pan, or you can bake it in the 12 x 9-inch pan and just use half.

makes 30 to 40 servings

Brownies (recipe follows)

6 cups peppermint stick ice cream, slightly softened

1½ cups fudge sauce, plus more for serving (this may be purchased, or use ½ recipe Hot Fudge Sauce, page 151)

One 15-ounce box regular graham crackers

1½ cups egg whites (from approximately 10 large eggs)

¼ teaspoon cream of tartar

2¼ cups sugar

Remove the brownies from their baking pan and remove the paper from the bottom. Cut a piece of cardboard the same size as the brownies and wrap it in a double layer of foil. Place the brownies on the foil-covered cardboard, and place this on a baking sheet that will fit into your freezer. Working quickly, spread the brownie with 2 cups of the peppermint ice cream. Then drizzle ½ cup of fudge sauce on the ice-cream layer. Top with a single layer of graham crackers. Place the tray in the freezer until firm, at least 30 minutes. Repeat the layering process two more times and, at the last layer, also cover the outside edges with graham crackers. Return to the freezer.

In a large bowl, whip the egg whites at high speed with the cream of tartar until they are foamy. Slowly add the sugar and whip until the sugar is dissolved and the whites have tripled in volume and hold stiff peaks. Spread the whipped whites over the ice-cream cake evenly. Using an offset spatula, make a swirling pattern in the meringue; you could also use a piping bag with a large star tip to decorate it in the same way. Freeze for 3 hours. The cake can be prepared to this point a day or two in advance and kept frozen.

To serve, preheat the oven to 500°F. Place the dessert directly from the freezer into the oven and bake until it is well browned, 3 to 4 minutes. Place sparklers in the cake to take it to the table for a dramatic presentation! Serve in slices with extra fudge sauce on the side.

Brownies

makes 2 dozen brownies

5 tablespoons unsalted butter, plus more for greasing the pan

5 ounces Valrhona bittersweet chocolate, chopped

½ cup granulated sugar

¼ cup light brown sugar

2 large eggs

½ teaspoon pure vanilla extract

2 tablespoons unsweetened cocoa powder

¾ cup all-purpose flour

Pinch of sea salt

Preheat the oven to 350°F. Grease a 12 x 9-inch baking pan and line it with parchment paper.

In a double boiler over low heat, melt the 5 tablespoons of butter with the chocolate. Let cool slightly and stir in the sugars, eggs, and vanilla. In a medium bowl, combine the cocoa, flour, and salt. Add the flour mixture to the chocolate mixture and stir until just combined. Pour this into the prepared pan. Bake until the brownies are set in the middle and the edges are just slightly dry, 15 to 20 minutes.

Let cool completely. The brownies can be prepared up to 4 days in advance and stored in an airtight container.

WINE NOTES

Pinot Noir, Clos Pepe, Brewer-Clifton, 2005 (Santa Rita Hills, California)
Pinot Noir, Ten, Sea Smoke, 2004 (Santa Rita Hills, California)
Chardonnay, Oak Savanna Vineyard, 2005 (Santa Ynez, California)

Given the breadth of selection at this delicious buffet, keep it simple—go for a wine with versatility, something that won't be a shrinking violet in the face of all this bold, occasionally spicy food, but something that won't fight with it, either. Is this a call for pinot noir or what? And if you crave a deep and intense flavor here (who wouldn't?) you won't find any better than these from the Santa Rita Hills, the

latest greatest region in the country for the pinot noir grape.

Santa Barbara pinots certainly don't lack power—and you'll need something with some richness to hold court with antelope, bison, and wild game—but they also offer finesse. Their generally soft tannins won't fight with the spicy elements in the dishes, and the fruit will offer a juicy cushion for all those fierce flavors.

On the white side, you'll want something with some stuffing to go with the richness of salmon and lobster, so here's your opportunity to break out one of your fuller, rounder "big-gun" chardonnays, perhaps from California or Australia. This is a big buffet, with lots of sharp flavors and big proteins, so you don't need to be shy with your white choice.

THE GAMES WE PLAY

TEAM PENNING

This game originated in California in the 1970s. It evolved from typical Western cattle ranch work where it is often necessary to separate several cows from a herd into smaller pens for doctoring, transportation, or inoculation. In arena competition, three riders are given a herd of thirty cattle wearing numbered markers from 0 to 9, with three cows per number. The judge calls out one number and, in ninety seconds or less, the three riders must cut the three animals wearing that number from the rest of the herd and put them into a pen, without bringing more than two additional cows back across a foul line in the center of the arena. The team with the fastest time wins.

REINED COW HORSE

This game is often called Dressage for Western Horses, because it requires a horse and rider to move together through a prescribed sequence of maneuvers. But unlike the English equestrian event, which is rooted in riding for sport, the Western event is meant to show the competence of a working horse. Competition consists of three events: herd work, reining work, and cow work. In the herd work, the horse must cut one steer from a small herd and keep it from returning to the herd. In the reining work, the horse maneuvers through a pattern of figure eights, straight runs, lead changes, spins, and sliding stops. In the cow work, the horse must control the movements of a single steer at a dead run along a fence, heading it off and turning it back, then driving it into the center of the arena and riding circles around it until the steer is stopped. Scores are awarded for each of the three events; they are tallied and the rider with the highest score wins. Our neighbor, Michael Lippman, is one of the top riders in the country in the reined cow horse competitions. Of all the Western riding events, reined cow horse is the one I admire the most because it keeps alive historical riding styles and ranch skills that date back to the Spanish *vaqueros* in California.

CUTTING

This is another Western equine sport derived from practical ranch work and the need to separate a cow from the herd. But unlike team penning, where the winners are the team of people who show the most cattle sense and skills, cutting horse competitions are meant to determine which horse exhibits the best cow skills. With a clock running, the rider enters a herd of thirty cows and selects a single cow for the horse to cut out. The rider must then use subtle body language to communicate to his horse the cow he has selected. Next, the rider loosens the reins, but he is not allowed to exhibit further signs of controlling his horse until the horse has satisfactorily cut out the cow and kept it from returning to the herd. In the 2½ minutes before time is called, a

competitive rider typically cuts three cows. The panel of judges awards points to the horse based on the elegance and efficiency of its work. Several of the top competitive cutters in the state come from the Santa Ynez Valley, but the real "capital" of the cutting horse world is in Texas. After thoroughbred racehorses, the highest purses in the equine world are won by cutting horses.

LOS VAQUEROS Y EL TORO DE ONCE

This is the Spanish name for our rodeo bull-riding competition. The rider holds on to a flat braided rope that has been placed around the bull, right behind its shoulders. The bull is then turned loose in the arena. There's no eight-second rule with Rancho La Zaca bull riding: These vaqueros must ride until the bull stops bucking. Riders are judged on style and finesse.

BARREL RACING

Barrel racing is a timed rodeo event that tests cooperation between horse and rider, where the fastest time matters most. At most other rodeos, it is exclusively a ladies' event, but at Rancho La Zaca, men can barrel race, too. Three twenty-gallon barrels are placed far apart, forming the outside points of a triangular course. The riders enter the arena at full speed, ride around each barrel in a cloverleaf pattern, and exit where they entered. Speed is what barrel racing is all about: The riders come as close as they can to the barrels without knocking them over. The same person, Berit Campion, wins this event every year—riding my horse!

"STEAL THE RIBBON FROM THE TAIL OF THE GOAT . . . AND PUT IT BACK ON AGAIN"

This is a foot race that has become a Rancho La Zaca favorite. Ten goats are tied to stakes set around the perimeter of the arena on ten-foot rope leads. Each goat has a colorful grosgrain ribbon tied around its tail. In teams of two, twenty contestants stand in the center of the arena until the starting whistle is blown. One runner

from each team travels on foot from the starting circle to the staked goat. The contestant must capture the goat without harming it or touching the rope, remove the ribbon from its tail, and run the ribbon back to his or her teammate, who sets off to replace it. The fastest team wins.

SADDLE BRONC RIDING

This is the classic rodeo event, which grew naturally from the breaking of wild broncos to use as working cow horses on the Western cattle ranch. Saddle bronc riders dismount with the help of a mounted pickup rider, who comes alongside the bucking bronc and picks the rider up off its back. A panel of judges awards the highest score to the rider displaying the most finesse.

THE FRANKLIN SEAT SWEEPSTAKES RACE

This is the last event in the rodeo. All contestants are asked to exchange $100 (a Franklin) for a poker chip on which their initials are written. The cash is put into a bag and held by the judge. At the starting line, all riders place their poker chip between their seat and the saddle. Then riders are asked to circle the ring at a trot. Periodically, the judge calls a halt, and any rider who has lost his poker chip is eliminated. As the number of riders is diminished, the judge speeds up the pace until only a few riders are left. At this point, the judge may ask the riders to move the chip from beneath them and balance it on another spot, like the brim of their hat. The last rider holding his or her chip is the winner and receives the bag of cash.

MIDWAY

In addition to the arena events, we stage midway event competitions, too. Like the arena events, these are scored and winners receive trophies. The events are: high striker (the traditional carnival game where players use a big rubber mallet to strike a spring-loaded base that sends a weight up a pole); mechanical bull riding; horseshoe toss; knife throwing; steer roping (on foot, using a "dummy" steer); cow milking (with a real cow); and pig kissing (the prize is given for the best photo taken with the piglet).

ELEVENSES:
A DOVE HUNTERS' BRUNCH

Savanna-Style Squab with Corn Bread–Sausage Stuffing

Sweet Potato Hash

French Toast Ooh La La

Warm Spinach Salad

MY FORMER HUSBAND WANTED A SHOTGUN FOR CHRISTMAS. I IDLY THREATENED that no gun would come into our house "as long as I lived in it," but he was determined. Can't beat 'em, so . . .

I signed us both up for shotgun instruction at the Orvis School in Manchester, Vermont. Much to my surprise, it turned out to be a wonderful weekend. Half our time was spent in the classroom, learning about the mechanics of the gun, safety, cleaning, care, and about shot and shells. The other half was in the field, learning how to hit something with a shot. (I would later discover that shotgunning is much like golf: You could do it every day of your life and never be satisfied with the way you played.) Not only did I give my then-husband the gun he wanted for Christmas, but I found a sport I have enjoyed ever since.

Most of the time at Rancho La Zaca we shoot sporting clays, so all we "kill" are biodegradable targets. But occasionally we shoot live birds in the field. In California, we have basically two species of game bird, the valley quail and the mourning dove.

Tom and I have come to adore the large coveys of valley quail that forage among the grasses and sage, and we have names for many of the families who live here: the Sage Gang, the Gully Group, the Triangle Sentinels, the House Covey.

Doves, however, in large numbers, are vineyard pests: Beneath the canopy of leaves, they roost and nest and peck at the sweet grapes. And if only a few grapes in a cluster have been pierced by a bird, the whole cluster can rot. Grape growers use several devices to deter the birds, including gas-fired noise cannons, tinsel strips that flutter in the wind and reflect light, and bird netting, the most labor-intensive option.

We hunt doves at the ranch during the short fall season at the beginning of September, using Beretta and Perozzi 12- and 20-gauge breach-loading shotguns, and taking no more than the limit of ten birds a day. Doves are among the most challenging birds to hunt. Even their ordinary flight pattern is skittish, but the slightest movement or the glint of steel on a shotgun is enough to turn them around.

This brunch is called "Elevenses," and is inspired by the formal English hunt. There, a horn is blown at 11:00 A.M. sharp, signaling a break. A butler, often in full morning clothes and white gloves, presents a hamper of cold cuts, cheeses, and sweets, and a trolley on which is displayed a bracing array of aged ports and single-malt Scotches. These are tossed back from crystal cordial glasses or sterling silver tumblers—shots that are believed by some to be helpful "aim straighteners."

Savanna-Style Squab
with Corn Bread–Sausage Stuffing

A squab is a young pigeon—four weeks old—that has never flown. Its red meat is tender, rich, and lightly gamey in taste. While it is a bit of a spoof to stuff it with a quail egg, the combination of corn bread, sausage, and eggs is a classic, and your guests will be delighted by the little birdy surprise inside. Serve with Sweet Potato Hash (page 206) and, for this brunch, do like the English do at elevenses and serve a fine Scotch with your meal.

makes 4 servings

FOR THE SQUABS

4 squabs, partially deboned (see Resources)

¼ small yellow onion, sliced

¼ small carrot, sliced

4 quail eggs, plus additional, if desired (see Resources)

Corn Bread–Sausage Stuffing (recipe follows)

1 teaspoon sea salt

¼ teaspoon freshly ground black pepper

2 tablespoons grapeseed oil

FOR THE SQUAB SAUCE

2 jalapeños

¼ cup light brown sugar

2 tablespoons rice wine vinegar

½ cup reserved squab stock

1 cup veal demi-glace (see Resources)

¼ teaspoon sea salt

Preheat the oven to 425°F.

MAKE THE SQUABS: Remove the neck and giblets from the squabs and pat the squabs dry. In a small roasting pan, roast the necks until well caramelized, about 30 minutes. Transfer to a medium saucepan with enough water to cover, plus the giblets, a slice of onion, and a slice of carrot. Bring to a boil and simmer for 45 minutes. Pour the stock through a fine-mesh strainer into another saucepan and simmer until reduced to about ½ cup of liquid, skimming off the foam, about 20 minutes.

In a medium saucepan, bring 1 quart of water to a boil. Add the eggs (you may want to cook a few extra, as they are sometimes difficult to peel nicely), stir once, and simmer until soft boiled, about 2 minutes. Remove the pan from the heat and place the eggs in cool water. Peel while still warm, just as you would a chicken egg.

Stuff each squab with ½ cup of the corn bread stuffing. Place 1 soft-boiled egg in each center and add an additional ½ cup of stuffing, keeping the egg in the center. Truss the squab firmly and season the outside with the salt and black pepper.

In a large sauté pan, heat the oil over high heat. Carefully sear both breasts of the squabs until browned, then sear the bottom, about 2 minutes for each side. Place on a baking sheet and then in the hot oven. Immediately reduce the oven temperature to 350°F and roast for 45 to 60 minutes, or until an instant-read thermometer inserted in the stuffing measures 165°F.

MAKE THE SAUCE: Roast the jalapeños over an open flame or under the broiler, turning often, until the skin is blackened, 5 to 10 minutes. Place in a small bowl and cover with plastic wrap until cooled. Peel the jalapeños, remove the seeds, and julienne the flesh.

In a medium saucepan, combine the brown sugar and vinegar. Bring to a simmer over medium heat, then reduce the heat to low and cook to a light syrup consistency, about 3 minutes. Add the reserved squab stock and the veal stock reduction and bring back to a simmer. Simmer for 5 minutes. Right before serving, add the roasted jalapeños and salt.

Remove the strings from the birds and serve the squabs on a platter with the sauce spooned over all.

Corn Bread–Sausage Stuffing

makes enough for 4 squabs

FOR THE CORN BREAD

1 cup whole wheat flour, plus more for the pan

1 cup yellow cornmeal

1 tablespoon baking powder

1 teaspoon sugar

½ teaspoon sea salt

1 cup whole milk

1 large egg, beaten

¼ cup (½ stick) unsalted butter, melted, plus more for greasing the pan

FOR THE STUFFING

1 stick unsalted butter

1 small yellow onion, cut into ¼-inch dice

1 garlic clove, minced

8 ounces breakfast sausage, removed from the casing

1¼ cups low-sodium canned chicken stock

3 tablespoons chopped parsley

2 tablespoons minced chives

1 tablespoon chopped sage

1 tablespoon chopped thyme

½ teaspoon sea salt

⅛ teaspoon freshly ground black pepper

Preheat the oven to 425°F. Butter and flour an 8-inch square or round pan.

MAKE THE CORN BREAD: In a large bowl, sift together the flour, cornmeal, baking powder, sugar, and salt. Add the milk, egg, and melted butter. Stir until just combined. Pour into the prepared pan and bake until the top springs back when lightly touched, 20 to 25 minutes. Let cool and cut into ½-inch squares. Transfer to a baking sheet. Reduce the oven temperature to 300°F and dry out the corn bread in the oven for 30 to 45 minutes.

MAKE THE STUFFING: In a large sauté pan, melt the butter. Add the onion and garlic and cook over low heat until the onion is translucent, 2 to 3 minutes. Add the sausage and cook through, breaking it up as it cooks. Add the corn bread, chicken stock, parsley, chives, sage, thyme, salt, and black pepper. Stir gently to combine. If stuffing the squabs a day ahead, make sure to cool the stuffing completely before doing so. The stuffing can be prepared up to 3 days in advance and refrigerated.

Sweet Potato Hash

2½ tablespoons grapeseed oil

1 white sweet potato, peeled and cut into ¼-inch dice

1 orange sweet potato, peeled and cut into ¼-inch dice

½ teaspoon sea salt

1 small yellow onion, cut into ¼-inch dice

1 red or yellow bell pepper, cut into ¼-inch dice

1 garlic clove, minced

1 tablespoon chopped parsley

1 tablespoon finely sliced chives

1 teaspoon chopped thyme

⅛ teaspoon freshly ground black pepper

Heat a large sauté pan over high heat. Add the oil, sweet potatoes, and ¼ teaspoon of the salt. Cook over high heat for 5 minutes, stirring or shaking the pan often. Reduce the heat to medium and continue to cook, stirring or shaking, until the potatoes are cooked through and well browned, about 5 minutes. Add the onion, bell pepper, garlic, and the remaining ¼ teaspoon of salt. Continue to cook until the onion and pepper are tender, about 5 minutes. Remove the pan from the heat and stir in the parsley, chives, thyme, and black pepper.

French Toast Ooh La La

The brie baked on top of this casserole-style French toast provides the "ooh la la" and the rosemary-scented bacon syrup is a sweet-savory take on the traditional. For a real showstopper, try this with vanilla ice cream for dessert. (And, yeah, leave the bacon on!)

makes 6 servings

FOR THE FRENCH TOAST

2 tablespoons unsalted butter

1 crusty French baguette
(for about six 3-inch slices)

2½ cups whole milk

5 large eggs

2 tablespoons pure maple syrup

¼ teaspoon sea salt

4 ounces Brie, cut while cold into ⅛-inch slices

FOR THE ROSEMARY-SCENTED BACON SYRUP

10 ounces slab bacon, cut into ¼ x ¼ x ¾-inch strips

1 pint strawberries, hulled and quartered

½ cup pure maple syrup

1 tablespoon finely chopped rosemary

MAKE THE FRENCH TOAST: The night before, butter a 2-quart ceramic baking dish. Cut the ends off the French bread and discard. Cut the remaining loaf crosswise into 3-inch slices and place in the prepared pan with a cut side up. They should fill the pan. In a large bowl, whisk together the milk, eggs, maple syrup, and salt, and pour through a fine-mesh strainer over the bread. Cover and refrigerate overnight.

Preheat the oven to 350°F.

Bake the prepared French toast for 45 minutes.

MAKE THE BACON SYRUP: In a medium sauté pan, cook the bacon over low heat until most of the fat is rendered but the bacon is still slightly chewy, about 10 minutes. Drain off all but 3 to 4 tablespoons of the fat and add the strawberries, maple syrup, and rosemary. Warm slightly and serve.

Remove the French toast from the oven and arrange the sliced Brie over the top of the bread. Return the pan to the oven, and bake until the cheese melts, about 5 minutes. To serve, spoon the bacon syrup over the top.

OPPOSITE, TOP: Savanna-Style Squab, with a quail egg inside
BOTTOM: French Toast Ooh La La

Warm Spinach Salad

The egg and bacon are noticeably absent from this warm spinach salad, but are not missed. The pickled shiitakes, apples, and nutty-sweet gjetost cheese are a delicious change. Gjetost (YEHT-ohst) is a Norwegian cheese made from a combination of cow's and goat's milk. The milks are added to whey and cooked until the sugars caramelize, which gives the cheese a sweet, nutty flavor. It is available at some specialty cheese shops and online. A three- or five-year-old Gruyère may be substituted.

makes 4 to 6 servings

1 large bunch spinach, large stems removed, leaves torn into 1- to 2-inch pieces

½ cup Pickled Shiitakes (recipe follows)

1 medium Fuji apple, peeled, cored, and cut into ⅛-inch-thick wedges

2 ounces gjetost cheese, shaved with a vegetable peeler

½ cup Candied Pecans (recipe follows)

1 small shallot, minced

1 garlic clove, minced

¼ cup extra virgin olive oil

2 tablespoons sherry vinegar

1 tablespoon Dijon mustard

¼ teaspoon sea salt

In a large bowl, toss together the spinach, pickled shiitakes, apple, gjetost, and pecans. In a small sauté pan, combine the shallot, garlic, and olive oil. Cook over medium heat until the shallot and garlic begin to bubble and just start to turn brown, about 2 minutes. Remove from the heat and stir in the vinegar, mustard, and salt. Pour over the spinach salad and toss to coat. Serve as soon as possible.

Pickled Shiitakes

makes ½ cup

4 ounces shiitake mushroom caps

2 tablespoons rice wine vinegar

1 tablespoon light brown sugar

1 tablespoon low-sodium canned chicken stock

¼ teaspoon sea salt

Preheat the oven to 350°F. Place the shiitakes in an aluminum foil pouch with the vinegar, sugar, stock, and salt. Tightly close the pouch, place in the oven on a baking sheet, and bake for 25 minutes. Let cool, then julienne and set aside. The shiitakes can be prepared up to 3 days in advance and refrigerated.

Candied Pecans

makes ½ cup

½ cup pecan halves

2 teaspoons light brown sugar

¼ teaspoon extra virgin olive oil

Pinch of sea salt

Preheat the oven to 300°F.

In a small bowl, stir together the pecan halves, sugar, oil, and salt. Spread on a baking sheet and bake until the pecans are completely toasted, 20 to 30 minutes. Let cool and set aside. The pecans can be prepared up to 3 days in advance. Cool completely and store in an airtight container.

WHAT IS AN OAK SAVANNA?

The oak savanna is an ecosystem comprised of widely spaced oak trees above a layer of prairie grasses and broad-leaved herbs. To flourish, a savanna relies on periodic disturbances such as fire, grazing, and drought, which also prevent the land from being overtaken by the oak trees.

In 2001 we experienced one such disturbance: a fire that consumed almost 250 acres of our oak savanna. In spite of the ferocity of the blaze, it destroyed only a tiny fraction of the mature oaks here. (The good news is that from those that died, we were blessed with enough cordwood to last us for a decade or more, so all of our barbecues are cooked over these hot-burning native logs.) Healthy oaks are resistant to these disturbances: These hardy souls often survive for a century or more. Once common in the United States and Europe, and predominant in California, the oak savanna is now a rare ecosystem; it is questionable whether any true and original oak savanna remains.

One unfortunate consequence of the Spanish colonial heritage of grazing cattle in Alta California was the replacement by both man and natural forces of the native perennial grasses with exotic, fast-growing, and short-lived European annuals. Some people attribute the Golden State nickname to the color of the dried grass so prevalent on south-facing hillsides here. But once I learned that it was not native, and that the indigenous grasses remain greener longer (golden-be-damned), I wanted to see if there was any hope of restoring the native grass species on our ranch. I would quickly learn that it isn't easy, fast, or cheap.

First, I consulted native-plant specialist John Anderson, who identified about six remaining species that would typically have grown here before the introduction of grazing cattle. He harvested hundreds of seeds from these grasses and sowed them in a greenhouse. In December, at the beginning of the rainy season, when the diameter of the sprouts was about the size of a quarter, we planted them, concentrating the plants where we thought the natural conditions were most favorable: enough shade and light, low human and animal traffic, and adequate water collection and drainage. Of these plants, only 30 percent survived, and this meager showing was considered by Anderson to be something of a success—and considered by me to be a testament to the difficulty of grassland restoration.

In other more visible and traveled areas, I have been helped by John Greenlee, the guru of grass. "Kill Your Lawn, Plant a Meadow" is the gospel he preaches, and I confess that I am a convert. Under his supervision, we have restored more than fifty acres of perennial grasses and sedges. These natives are drought-tolerant and disease-resistant; some are evergreen and others show seasonal color in their leaves. In areas where we walk, he has planted low-creeping varieties. From that vantage point, we view my favorites, the ones with arching plumage that dances in the slightest breeze and forms complex patterns of shadow and light. The whole meadow composition reminds me of a symphony orchestra, one that plays all day, all year long, and never fails to entertain me.

HARVEST

Meats, Cheeses, Fruits, and Breads on a Barrel Top

Simple Pasta Salad with Basil and Lemon

Roasted Potato and Heirloom Tomato Shuffle

Triple Black Brownies

Gingerbread Squishies

Junk Food Chunkies

another one to celebrate the end of the season. The first party, during mid- to late September, is more of a ceremonial affair, when we invite friends to pick the first ton of chardonnay.

We pick in the early morning, when the air is still cool, which helps keep the grapes fresh until they reach the winery. Fermentation begins the minute the berries are separated from the vine and their sweet juice comes into contact with the yeast that has naturally accumulated on the grape skin. (The white "dust" you see on every bunch of grapes is yeast, not dirt.)

Felipe distributes buckets and grape-picking knives with short, sharp, curved blades. After a few fumbling tries, we get a rhythm down. But even after we do, we notice that Felipe's crew has finished an entire block in the same time we have taken to pick a few rows. Usually it takes about an hour for the twelve of us to harvest a ton of grapes.

When the 5 x 5 container box is full, Felipe is satisfied that we have about a ton. While the forklift carries the grapes to the winery, we return to the house with sticky hands, stained shirtsleeves, and a few cuts and blisters to show for our work. At noon, after a quick siesta and shower, we head to the winery where the grapes have already been hoisted and dumped into the crushing machine. Even though it has not yet been turned on, juice is gushing from the spout, extracted by gravity and weight. Our friends are always surprised at how delicious and sweet the fresh juice tastes, dispelling the myth that wine-grape juice tastes good only when it is made into wine.

As the afternoon goes on, more trucks arrive from the fields with full boxes, the machines are turned on, and crush begins in earnest. Once Andrew is satisfied that everything is working the way it is supposed to, he takes us on a tour of the winery, where we can sample wines held in barrels and tanks from previous vintages. When Stephanie arrives with lunch, our guests are happy to see that it is not a sit-down affair: We are all having too much fun climbing up ladders and siphoning tastes out of barrels. The selection of meats, cheeses, and fruits laid out on barrel tops are all the sustenance we need to carry on here until late afternoon.

Meats, Cheeses, Fruits, and Breads on a Barrel Top

For the most part, everything on this menu is store-bought: great sausages, venison, rabbit, and duck varieties from D'Artagnan (www.dartagnan.com) as well as some great cheeses and breads from a local market.

makes 12 servings

8 ounces or 4 links rabbit and ginger sausage (see Resources)

8 ounces or 4 links duck and Armagnac sausage (see Resources)

8 ounces or 4 links wild boar sausage (see Resources)

Two 8-ounce links wild boar saucisson sec, thinly sliced (see Resources)

12 ounces or 4 links venison and cherry sausage (see Resources)

Seasonal fruits such as grapes, pomegranates, and apples, for garnish

6 ounces grainy mustard

2 ounces plum mustard (see Resources)

2 ounces white Burgundy wine mustard (see Resources)

6 ounces Morbier cheese

1 wheel Cowgirl Creamery Red Hawk cheese (see Resources)

4 ounces Taleggio cheese

4 ounces Montbriac or other soft cheese, such as Brie

6 ounces Rinconada Dairy Pozo Tomme cheese (see Resources) or other hard sheep's milk cheese

6 ounces soft goat's milk cheese

1 loaf focaccia bread, sliced

1 loaf walnut rye bread or other artisanal-quality bread, sliced

8 ounces crackers, such as Cowgirl Creamery organic whole-grain crackers

Preheat the grill to medium-high.

Grill the rabbit, duck, uncooked wild boar, and venison sausages until they are firm to the touch, about 4 minutes per side. Remove from the grill to a cutting board and let rest for 5 minutes. Slice each link into 4 pieces on the bias. Garnish a platter with the fruits and jars of mustard. Arrange whole wedges of the cheeses on the same platter or on a separate platter also garnished with fruits. Arrange the sliced sausage on the platter. Serve with baskets of bread and crackers on the side.

Simple Pasta Salad with Basil and Lemon

Because this salad is so simple, the quality of the ingredients is paramount. Freshly squeezed lemon juice and fresh basil are as important as a high quality extra virgin olive oil. The Rustichella line is among the best artisanal-quality dried pastas, and their trofie is a little 11-centimeter-long rolled cylinder that is super-cute. It can be replaced with rotini or another shape of your choice.

makes 12 servings as part of a buffet

8.8 ounces (250 grams) trofie pasta, preferably Rustichella d'Abruzzo (see Resources)

3 tablespoons fresh lemon juice

Finely grated zest of 1 medium lemon

1 bunch (2 ounces) basil, large stems removed, leaves chopped

⅔ cup freshly grated Pecorino Romano cheese

6 tablespoons extra virgin olive oil

½ teaspoon plus ⅛ teaspoon sea salt

Bring a medium pot of salted water to a boil over high heat. Add the pasta and cook for 20 minutes. Drain, rinse, and let cool. Transfer to a bowl and add the lemon juice, zest, basil, cheese, oil, and salt. Mix well to combine.

Roasted Potato and Heirloom Tomato Shuffle

Grape harvest happens at the very tail end of tomato season—with the first grapes come the last tomatoes. This is a fall variation on the lighter, more summery tomato-mozzarella-basil combination, with a pungent blue cheese and the unusual addition of roasted potatoes for a hearty, earthy note.

makes 12 servings as part of a buffet

2 pounds Yukon Gold potatoes, sliced ¼-inch thick

¼ cup extra virgin olive oil

1 teaspoon sea salt

½ teaspoon freshly ground black pepper

1 teaspoon chopped rosemary

1 teaspoon chopped thyme

4 ounces Point Reyes Blue cheese or Rogue Creamery Smokey Blue cheese (see Resources)

5 medium heirloom tomatoes (about 2 pounds), sliced ¼-inch thick

1 tablespoon chopped parsley

Preheat the oven to 425°F.

In a large bowl, toss the potatoes together with the olive oil, ¾ teaspoon of the salt, ¼ teaspoon of the black pepper, the rosemary, and thyme. Spread out on a sheet pan and roast in the oven until browned, about 25 minutes. Crumble the blue cheese over the top and return to the oven for 3 minutes. Let cool slightly, then "shuffle," alternating potatoes and tomatoes. Sprinkle with the chopped parsley and the remaining ¼ teaspoon of salt and ¼ teaspoon of black pepper.

ABOVE: Roasted Potato and Heirloom Tomato Shuffle

RIGHT: Simple Pasta Salad with Basil and Lemon

Triple Black Brownies

Black olive and cherry is a combination you won't often taste, and rarer still is the opportunity to have this savory-sweet sensation paired with dark chocolate. Try it; you will probably like it. (And if you do, try the olives and cherries another way, with the Venison Tenderloin on page 172.) If you don't, the brownies are sumptuous without the olives, too.

makes 40 brownies

FOR THE BROWNIES

1 ¼ cups (2 ½ sticks) unsalted butter, plus more for greasing the pan

15 ounces Valrhona bittersweet chocolate, chopped

1 ½ cups granulated sugar

¾ cup light brown sugar

7 large eggs

1 ½ teaspoons pure vanilla extract

6 tablespoons unsweetened cocoa powder

2 ¼ cups all-purpose flour

Pinch of sea salt

1 cup dried cherries, chopped

1 cup pitted dry-cured black olives, chopped, plus ¼ cup chopped olives for garnish

5 ounces Valrhona bittersweet chocolate, chopped into coarse chunks (1 cup)

FOR THE GLAZE

6 ounces Valrhona bittersweet chocolate, chopped (1 ⅓ cups)

6 ounces (1 ½ sticks) unsalted butter

Preheat the oven to 350°F. Butter a 12 x 9-inch baking pan. Line the bottom of the pan with parchment paper and butter the paper.

MAKE THE BROWNIES: In a double boiler over low heat, melt the butter and chocolate. Let cool slightly and stir in the sugars, eggs, and vanilla until completely incorporated. In a medium bowl, combine the cocoa, flour, and salt. Add the flour mixture to the chocolate mixture, ½ cup at a time, until combined. Stir in the chopped cherries, the 1 cup of olives, and the chocolate chunks.

Pour into the prepared baking pan and bake until set in the middle and just slightly dry at the edges, 25 to 30 minutes.

MAKE THE GLAZE: In a double boiler over low heat, melt the chocolate and butter. Stir until it is completely smooth, then remove from the heat and pour while still warm over the brownies still in the pan. Let cool until the glaze is set. Cut into 1 ¼-inch squares and garnish each piece with a small chunk of chopped olive. The brownies can be prepared up to a week in advance and refrigerated in an airtight container.

Gingerbread Squishies

These were inspired by a favorite cookie made by Baked in the Sun Bakery on the Caribbean island of St. John. They are take-your-breath-away gingery. But the crispy-chewy texture combo is what makes them so addictive, and the quirky squish during baking is what makes them this way.

makes 24 squishies

½ cup (1 stick) unsalted butter, softened

¾ cup light brown sugar

½ vanilla bean, split and scraped

1 large egg

2 tablespoons finely grated ginger

¼ cup unsulfured molasses

¾ cup boiling water

¾ teaspoon baking soda

2½ cups all-purpose flour

¾ teaspoon sea salt

2 teaspoons ground cinnamon

1 tablespoon ground ginger, plus 2 teaspoons for dusting

3 tablespoons chopped crystallized ginger

Granulated sugar, for pressing

½ cup plus 2 tablespoons seedless raspberry jam

½ cup confectioners' sugar

In a standing mixer, cream together the butter, brown sugar, and vanilla bean seeds until pale and fluffy, about 1 minute. Add the egg and process until combined, then beat in the grated ginger, molasses, and the boiling water. In a medium bowl, sift together the baking soda, flour, salt, cinnamon, and the 1 tablespoon ground ginger. Stir in the crystallized ginger. Slowly add the dry ingredients to the wet ingredients and mix until just combined. Refrigerate for at least 3 hours or overnight.

Preheat the oven to 425°F. Line a baking sheet with parchment paper.

Drop 1 tablespoon or a ½-ounce scoop of dough per cookie onto the prepared baking sheet, spacing them 2 inches apart. Bake for 3½ minutes, then remove the cookies from the oven. With a flat-bottomed glass dipped in granulated sugar to prevent sticking, press (squish!)

evenly until about ¼-inch thick. Immediately return to the oven for 2 minutes.

While still warm, spread 1¼ teaspoons of the jam on the bottom of one cookie and sandwich together with another. Continue baking and filling in batches until all of the squishies are filled. Let cool completely.

Combine the confectioners' sugar and the remaining 2 teaspoons of ground ginger. Place in a sifter and liberally dust the squishies with the gingered sugar. The filled cookies can be prepared up to 3 days in advance and stored in an airtight container at room temperature.

Junk Food Chunkies

Let 'er rip. Every so often, it is downright healthy to hop off your high horse and give in to the primal craving for good (bad?) old American junk food. For these cookies, you can even shop for most of the ingredients at a convenience store (Valrhona excepted), but serve them with pride: These won't compromise your high style one iota. To make the cookies chewier, refrigerate the dough overnight before baking.

makes about 30 cookies

1 cup (2 sticks) unsalted butter, softened

¾ cup granulated sugar

¾ cup light brown sugar

2 large eggs

1 teaspoon Jim Beam whiskey

2¼ cups all-purpose flour

1 teaspoon baking soda

½ teaspoon baking powder

1 teaspoon sea salt

7 ounces Valrhona bittersweet chocolate, chopped into chunks (1½ cups)

1 cup crushed potato chips

1 cup crushed pretzels

½ cup dried cranberries

½ cup chopped roasted salted peanuts

Preheat the oven to 350°F. Line ungreased baking sheets with parchment paper.

In a standing mixer, cream together the butter and sugars until pale and fluffy, about 1 minute. Beat in the eggs one at a time, then add the whiskey. In a medium bowl, sift together the flour, baking soda, baking powder, and salt. Slowly add the flour mixture to the butter-egg mixture and mix until just combined. Stir in the chocolate chunks, chips, pretzels, cranberries, and peanuts.

Drop 2 tablespoons of dough per cookie on the prepared baking sheets about 1 inch apart. Bake until lightly browned on the bottom, 10 to 12 minutes. The cookies can be prepared up to 3 days in advance and stored at room temperature.

WINE NOTES

Viognier, Estate, Andrew Murray Vineyards, 2005 (Santa Ynez, California)
Viognier, Vogelzang Vineyard, Cold Heaven, 2005 (Santa Ynez, California)
Zinfandel, Late Harvest, Dasche Cellars, 2005 (Napa, California)

Since this is a tasting-and-grazing event, we didn't select a white and a red. With the pasta salad, cheeses, and other varied dishes, you want something flexible: Chardonnay is a good choice, but viognier is better because it is so versatile. It is light, clean, and floral with citrus and tropical fruits. These excellent examples come from the Central Coast.

For the dessert course, a late-harvest zinfandel is great with chocolate brownies, and the one from Dasche Cellars, in Napa, is a fantastic choice.

Imagine a sweet, ripe black-cherry and plum purée with notes of exotic spice and vanilla aromas that ooze from the glass. The brownies beg to be dipped in this wine. The zin adds layers of complementary fruits and its nuance takes dessert to another level.

THE SANTA YNEZ VALLEY

by Andrew Murray, winemaker

The Oak Savanna Vineyard lies literally at the heart of the Santa Ynez Valley both in location and in feeling. It was planted about twenty-five years ago to a single variety, chardonnay, on phyloxera-resistant rootstock. In the past the grapes have all been sold to a few neighboring wineries that gladly paid top dollar: This vineyard is blessed with a microclimate and soil profile especially suited to growing grapes.

The vineyard lies within the Santa Ynez Valley appellation, which is essentially a portion of a large east-west canyon that stretches from the San Rafael mountain range in the inland eastern reaches of the valley to the Pacific Ocean in the west. As the daytime temperature rises, cool ocean breezes funnel from the coast and gain velocity as they blow through the valley. This acts as a moderating effect, making it a great place both to grow grapes and to live.

Oak Savanna is at about the limit on the warm side where one might want to grow chardonnay. So we need to pick the chardonnay a bit earlier to preserve freshness in the form of a balanced acidity. The wine is then fermented in French oak barrels on yeast lees for twelve months; we further preserve the freshness by inhibiting malolactic fermentation. The result is a style as wonderfully unique as the Oak Savanna Vineyard itself.

Not content to simply produce a chardonnay, Sandy asked Felipe, calling upon his years of experience, to come up with the three best red varieties to grow on the property, based purely upon the best potential match between climate, soil, and variety. Felipe and Sandy decided upon syrah, sangiovese, and tempranillo. I suggested we create a unique proprietary blend of these grapes, and Sandy hit upon the name One Thousand Hills, which some of the original Spanish settlers called this beautiful place. The roots of this wine are French, Italian, and Spanish, but the final wine is 100 percent Santa Ynez Valley, and more important, 100 percent Oak Savanna Vineyard.

LA COSECHA

Red Chile Beef

La Zaca Chicken Mole

Chorizo Agridulce

Refritos La Zaca

White Rice with Cumin and Bay

Pico de Gallo

Guacamole

Sandra's Cebollas

Flanaranja

Choco Picopans

THE SYRAH AND TEMPRANILLO GRAPES ARE HARVESTED IN MID-OCTOBER. WITH just twelve acres of red grapes, it takes the men only two mornings to pick them. So by lunchtime on the second day, with rows of fruitless and sad-looking spent vines behind them, everyone is ready to celebrate the end of the season in the vineyard. During the first few years Tom and I were here, dining alone at lunch, we could smell the grilled meats wafting from the old picnic area, and hear music and laughter in the distance. We knew Felipe's crew and their families were having all the fun, and we longed to join in. The next year, we hosted the party ourselves. It has become a tradition ever since at Oak Savanna to honor the men who harvest our grapes when their work is finished.

The post-harvest feast has long been a tradition in many wine-growing areas of France: In Burgundy, a bacchanal named La Paulée de Meursault marks the end of the harvest (it's named for the sauté pan, called a *poele*, in which the meal is customarily prepared); and in the Loire Valley, luncheons laid with over-the-top spreads for the grape pickers were legendary. But in recent years, the tradition has waned in France. One reason for the decline may be that mechanical pickers have replaced live work-ers in some areas; another is that women are more involved in the operations of the wineries and therefore have less time to spend in the kitchen preparing decadent lunches.

My Spanish is broken and Tom's is nonexistent, but it doesn't seem to matter very much. At the table, the men are more interested in food than conversation anyway. Taking a cue from the French custom, we bottle some of the first-press juice to taste cer-emoniously with the workers. Then, when the meal is underway, we offer our Oak Savanna wine, which they politely accept, but it's obvious they prefer Corona. The lunch menu includes all their favorite dishes (for ideas and recipes, Stephanie consults some of their wives). A few bring food from home, to share. After everyone has had his fill, we move to the fire pit and Tom passes his favorite Honduran cigars all around. Invariably, the men begin singing, and sometimes they dance.

Red Chile Beef

Who doesn't love braised short ribs? The long, slow cooking process renders the otherwise tough meat into something irresistibly tender that literally melts in your mouth. This recipe uses mild chiles—you get the chile flavor, without the heat—to lend a Mexican twist to a braise that's more often associated with red wine than Mexican ingredients. Be forewarned that when this is in the oven, your kitchen will be swarming with people who want to know what exactly is creating that enticing aroma—and when they will be allowed to eat it.

makes 10 servings

5 pounds boneless beef short ribs (or other braising meat)

1 tablespoon sea salt

3 tablespoons grapeseed oil

1 medium yellow onion, halved lengthwise then sliced lengthwise into ⅛-inch strips

4 garlic cloves, minced

1 teaspoon cumin seeds

¼ teaspoon coriander seeds

4 dried New Mexican chiles, stemmed and seeded, soaked for 30 minutes in warm water

2 dried ancho chiles, stemmed and seeded, soaked for 30 minutes in warm water

5 large plum tomatoes, cored, seeded, and chopped

1 jalapeño, seeded and chopped

One 2-inch piece Mexican cinnamon

2 cups low-sodium canned chicken stock

Preheat the oven to 300°F.

Preheat a large, heavy-bottomed saucepan over high heat. Season the beef with the salt. Add the oil to the pan, then the meat, and sear on all sides until golden brown, 8 to 10 minutes. Remove the meat from the pan and add the onion, garlic, cumin, and coriander. Sauté until the onion is translucent, 2 to 3 minutes. Stir in the chiles, tomatoes, jalapeño, cinnamon, and stock. Return the meat to the pan and bring to a simmer, then cover and place in the oven. (The braise can also be done on the stovetop over very low heat.) Cook until fork-tender, turning the meat halfway through the cooking, about 2 hours.

Remove the meat from the broth and let cool slightly. (The beef can be prepared to this point a day in advance and refrigerated overnight, which will cause the fat to rise to the top of the liquid.) Skim off as much fat as you can. Shred the meat by hand. In a blender puree the broth on high speed until smooth, about 2 minutes. Stir the meat and sauce together and warm over low heat.

La Zaca Chicken Mole

Moles are the richly spiced, extremely complex sauces of Mexico. They can be green, yellow, or red, but the mole most familiar to Americans is the Oaxacan style made with chocolate. This wonderfully layered sauce is a special dish for celebrations. Use the same heavy-bottomed pan (such as a cast-iron skillet) for the crucial step of toasting all the ingredients, which imparts a great char to the vegetables and brings out the aromas of the spices.

makes 10 servings

5 dried ancho chiles, stemmed and seeded

3 dried California or New Mexican chiles, stemmed and seeded

2 dried chiles negros, stemmed and seeded

½ teaspoon cumin seeds

½ teaspoon coriander seeds

¾ teaspoon anise seeds

2 cloves

12 black peppercorns

One ½-inch piece Ceylon cinnamon

⅓ cup white sesame seeds, plus 1 tablespoon for garnish

5 tablespoons lard or nonhydrogenated vegetable shortening

2½ tablespoons raisins

20 whole raw almonds

2½ ounces pumpkin seeds

1 corn tortilla, quartered

5 medium plum tomatoes

5 garlic cloves, unpeeled

1 small yellow onion, cut into 5 chunks

5 cups low-sodium canned chicken stock

3¼ ounces Mexican chocolate, chopped (see Resources)

3 teaspoons sea salt

1 teaspoon freshly ground black pepper

2 large (3 to 4 pounds each) chickens, each cut into 8 pieces

2 tablespoons chopped cilantro

In a medium bowl, soak all of the chiles for 30 minutes in warm water.

In a small, heavy-bottomed sauté pan, separately toast the cumin, coriander, anise, cloves, peppercorns, cinnamon, and sesame seeds over medium-low heat until each spice releases its aroma and starts to color. Set aside to cool. Grind separately in a spice grinder to a fine meal, being careful not to turn the sesame seeds into a paste.

In the same heavy-bottomed pan, melt 1 tablespoon of the lard over medium-low heat. Add the raisins, almonds, pumpkin seeds, and tortilla and cook until the almonds are toasted and the raisins are plumped, about 6 minutes. Remove from the pan and set aside.

In the same heavy-bottomed pan over medium-low heat, roast the tomatoes whole until just beginning to blacken, about 12 minutes; remove to a bowl. In the same way, roast the whole garlic cloves and onion chunks until just beginning to blacken, about 8 minutes. Peel the garlic and coarsely chop along with the onion and tomatoes.

In a medium, heavy-bottomed saucepan, heat 1 tablespoon of the lard. Add the ground spices with the seeds, raisins, almonds, and tortilla, along with the chopped garlic, onion, and tomatoes. Sauté over medium-high heat until heated through, 2 to 3 minutes. Add the drained chiles and the chicken stock and simmer for 1 hour.

Let cool slightly and blend with the chocolate. Season with 1 teaspoon of the salt and ½ teaspoon of the black pepper.

Preheat the oven to 350°F.

In a large, ovenproof saucepan, heat the remaining 3 tablespoons lard. Season the chicken pieces on all sides with the remaining 2 teaspoons of salt and ½ teaspoon of black pepper. Brown the chicken on all sides for about 3 minutes per side. Pour the mole over the chicken and bring to a simmer. Cover and place in the oven for 1 hour. Remove the chicken and place it on a serving platter. Pour the mole over the chicken and sprinkle with the reserved sesame seeds and the cilantro for garnish.

FROM TOP: La Zaca Chicken Mole, Red Chile Beef, White Rice with Cumin and Bay

Chorizo Agridulce

For this sweet-and-sour sausage entrée, be sure to use true Mexican fresh chorizo, not the dried Spanish kind, which is like a pepperoni.

makes 10 servings

¼ cup grapeseed oil

2 medium yellow onions, halved lengthwise then sliced lengthwise into ⅛-inch strips

2 tablespoons unsalted butter

1 jalapeño, thinly sliced

Juice of 2 limes

½ teaspoon sea salt

¼ teaspoon freshly ground black pepper

4 pounds fresh chorizo in natural pork casings (see Resources)

Cilantro sprigs, for garnish

In a large sauté pan, heat the oil over medium-high heat. Add the onions; turn the heat to low and brown slowly, about 45 minutes, stirring every 10 minutes to prevent the onions from sticking to the pan. Add the butter, jalapeño, and lime juice. Stir and remove from the heat. Season with the salt and black pepper.

Meanwhile, preheat a grill to high. Slice the chorizo into 3- or 4-inch lengths. Grill until cooked all the way through, 15 minutes. Arrange on a platter and cover with the onions. Garnish with the cilantro sprigs.

Refritos La Zaca

Soaking the beans twice overnight really makes a difference, resulting in much creamier beans when you mash them. *Refritos* means "refried," meaning that not only do you soak them twice, you also cook them twice. This may seem like a lot of effort for a bean dish, but it's actually very easy—it just requires a couple nights' advance thought—and it will change the way you think about *frijoles*.

makes 10 servings

2 pounds dried pinto beans

1 small yellow onion, quartered

1 head garlic, halved

4 oregano sprigs

½ cup lard or nonhydrogenated vegetable shortening

3 teaspoons sea salt

1 teaspoon freshly ground black pepper

Two days ahead of time, place the beans in a large pot and cover with 2 inches of water. Soak the beans overnight in the refrigerator.

Drain the beans. Place them back in the pot and cover with 2 inches of water. Place over high heat and add the onion, garlic, and oregano. Bring to a boil, then reduce the heat to low and simmer until the beans are tender, about 45 minutes. Turn off the heat and allow the beans to cool. Remove the onion, garlic, and oregano, then place the beans, covered, in their cooking liquid in the refrigerator overnight. The beans become creamier with this process.

Heat the lard in a large, heavy-bottomed saucepan over medium-high heat. Add the beans with ½ to 1 cup of their liquid and mash with a potato masher. (Or mash the beans in a food processor and add them to the hot lard.) Reduce the heat to medium and cook, stirring constantly, until the beans are fully softened, about 20 minutes. Season with the salt and black pepper. The beans can be prepared up to 3 days in advance and refrigerated. Reheat before serving, adding water to soften and seasoning as necessary.

White Rice with Cumin and Bay

The classic Mexican technique for rice begins with toasting the rice in lard, which is indispensable for imparting that unique taste of rice south of the border. If you don't use the lard, it just won't taste like Mexican rice.

makes 10 servings

3 tablespoons lard

1 garlic clove, minced

½ small yellow onion, diced (about ¼ cup)

1 teaspoon cumin seeds

2 bay leaves

2 cups long-grain white rice

1 teaspoon sea salt

Heat the lard in a medium saucepan. Add the garlic and onion and sauté over medium heat until translucent, about 5 minutes. Add the cumin and bay leaves and sauté for 2 minutes. Stir in the rice and coat with the lard.

Add 2 ½ cups of water and the salt and bring to a simmer. Reduce the heat to low, cover, and cook for 18 minutes. Turn off the heat and let sit, covered, for an additional 10 minutes. Fluff with a fork and serve.

Pico de Gallo

This is so simple to make, and when fresh, like this, it elevates even a simple Mexican meal. If you have any left over, save it overnight in the fridge. In the morning, use it to top scrambled eggs served with a warm corn tortilla.

makes 4 cups

6 plum tomatoes, cored, seeded, and cut into ¼-inch dice

½ red onion, minced

2 jalapeños, seeded and minced

1 bunch cilantro, chopped

Juice of 2 limes

1 teaspoon sea salt

In a medium bowl, stir all of the ingredients together and adjust the seasoning to taste. The salsa can be prepared 2 days in advance and refrigerated.

Guacamole

makes 3 cups

5 Hass avocados, halved and pitted

2 jalapeños, seeded and minced

Juice of 2 limes

3 tablespoons minced red onion

1 bunch cilantro, chopped

½ teaspoon sea salt

Score the avocado in the shell with a paring knife at ½-inch intervals, both ways in a cross-hatch pattern. Scoop the chunks out into a medium bowl. Add the jalapeños, lime juice, red onion, cilantro, and salt. Coarsely mash with a fork or stiff whisk. Adjust the seasoning to taste. The guacamole can be prepared a day in advance. Press plastic wrap directly onto the prepared guacamole and refrigerate.

Sandra's Cebollas

This recipe is from Sandra Hernandez, Felipe's wife. It is a wonderful spicy complement to the beef (page 229). Make sure to very finely cut the onions to soften them properly in the salt and vinegar.

makes 3 cups

2 medium yellow onions, halved lengthwise then sliced lengthwise into ⅛-inch strips

1 tablespoon sea salt

3 tablespoons rice wine vinegar

1 habanero chile, seeded and julienned

In a medium bowl, combine all the ingredients and let sit for at least 4 hours at room temperature. The onions can be prepared a day in advance and refrigerated.

Flanaranja

Creamsicle, anyone? This version of flan is simply decadent, with hints of orange and vanilla.

makes 10 servings

2 cups half-and-half

1 cup whole milk

1 cup heavy cream

½ vanilla bean, split and scraped

Two 2-inch lengths of orange zest

1 Ceylon cinnamon stick (3 inches)

1 cup plus 6 tablespoons sugar

3 large whole eggs

2 large egg yolks

½ teaspoon sea salt

Preheat the oven to 325°F.

In a medium saucepan, bring the half-and-half, milk, cream, vanilla bean pod and seeds, orange zest, and cinnamon to a simmer. Turn off the heat and allow to sit for 30 minutes.

In a small heavy-bottomed saucepan over medium-high heat, place 1 cup of the sugar and ⅓ cup of water and cook, until the mixture reaches a deep caramel color, about 10 minutes. Wash down the sides of the pan with a pastry brush dipped in water while cooking to avoid crystallization. Divide the caramel evenly among ten 4-ounce ramekins or one 3-quart baking dish, turning to coat the bottom.

In a small bowl, whisk the whole eggs, yolks, salt, and the remaining 6 tablespoons of sugar. Whisk into the milk mixture. Pour through a fine-mesh strainer then divide among the ramekins. Line a roasting pan with several layers of paper towel or a kitchen towel. Place the ramekins or baking dish in the roasting pan, making sure the dishes don't touch. Place the pan in the oven, then pour scalding hot water into the pan so it comes two-thirds of the way up the sides of the custard dish. Bake until the custard is set but has a slight gelatin-like jiggle to it, about 30 minutes. Carefully remove the ramekins or dish from the water bath and refrigerate for 12 hours or overnight.

To serve individual flans, run a small knife around the edge of the flan and invert onto the serving plate; tap lightly if necessary. A large flan may be served in its baking dish or inverted onto a large, deep serving dish.

Choco Picopans

These delicious shortbread cookies are filled with crunchy cacao bean nibs. Most upscale grocers sell these little bits of unprocessed chocolate; think of them as a guilt-free alternative to the chocolate chip.

makes 30 cookies

1 cup (2 sticks) unsalted butter, softened

½ cup plus 2 tablespoons turbinado sugar

¼ vanilla bean, split and scraped

1½ cups all-purpose flour

½ cup whole wheat pastry flour

½ cup cacao nibs (see Resources)

In a mixer, cream the butter, the ½ cup of sugar, and the vanilla seeds until light and fluffy, about 2 minutes. Blend in the flours until just combined; stir in the cacao bean nibs. The dough will be slightly crumbly. Form the dough into two 1½-inch-diameter logs. Wrap in plastic and refrigerate for 1 hour.

Preheat the oven to 350°F.

Cut the logs crosswise into ¼-inch-thick disks. Place on two parchment-lined baking sheets, brush very lightly with water, and sprinkle with the additional 2 tablespoons of sugar. Bake until the bottoms are golden brown, 12 minutes. Remove from the oven and let cool completely on a wire rack. The cookies can be prepared up to 3 days in advance and stored in an airtight container.

ABOVE: Choco Picopans
LEFT: Flanaranja

FELIPE HERNANDEZ,
OUR VINEYARD MANAGER

Felipe Hernandez is the vineyard manager at Oak Savanna. Around the valley, he is known as *Don* Felipe, and spoken of by both his peers and subordinates with conspicuous emphasis on the well-deserved and hard-earned title of respect.

In 1972, Felipe came from Jalisco, Mexico, into the United States by the most common route: He jumped the border fence. A friend who lived in the valley had told Felipe there might be some jobs with the newly formed Santa Ynez Grape Growers, an association of farmers that included Brooks and Kate Firestone. Felipe still remembers the long hot days he spent planting grapes during those first years, and how Kate would often appear in the fields late in the afternoon with a tray of cold drinks. Besides grape planting, during his "off hours" Felipe worked whatever odd jobs he could find, including mowing the lawn at the residence of the owner of La Zaca.

The original Zaca plantings were vast, and because of the size, several managers were needed to oversee the different blocks. By 1977, Felipe was managing the hillside plantings, which needed tending by hand, since the steep terrain made working by machine impossible. The hillside terrain was eventually parceled off from Zaca and is what comprises the Oak Savanna Vineyard today. By the 1980s, Felipe was so valuable to the grapes that he was asked to move into a little house on the property that had been built for him and his family. Several of his viticultural "inventions" have become standard Santa Ynez grape growers' practice, including the interplanting of rows with grain and grass crops, bird netting applications, grafting techniques, and vineyard hygiene standards.

Today Felipe is the manager of Oak Savanna Vineyard, a co-owner of the neighboring Koehler Vineyard, consultant to a handful of other wineries in the valley, and the vintner for his own wine label, called Feliz Noche. He is the father of five, including four grown children, all of whom have gone to college. Two are engineers, one is a registered nurse, and the other (a daughter!) is an aspiring FBI agent. His youngest, Little Felipe, is only ten years old.

To me and to Tom, Felipe represents the American Dream. But like everyone who knows him, we just abbreviate the superlatives and call him Don Felipe.

DINNER FOR DEAD POETS

Mincemeat Purses
". . . they dined on mince and slices of quince."
—EDWARD LEAR

Roasted Pork Loin Stuffed with Braised Cabbage
"Of shoes—and ships—and sealing wax—
Of cabbages—and kings—
And why the sea is boiling hot—
And whether pigs have wings."
—LEWIS CARROLL

Blackberry Dacquoise Cake
"Nobody in the lane, and nothing, nothing but blackberries."
—SYLVIA PLATH

"I DON'T EVEN LIKE POETRY," SAID ONE GUEST. "I AM CLOSE TO EARNING MY DOCTORATE, with a specialty in Coleridge," said another. The invitation for Dinner for Dead Poets requested that each guest come dressed as a poet, or, translated more liberally, as the subject of a poem. All the women who were invited quickly discovered that there have been few female poets at all, and none who were stylish. Several of the men admitted that it was fun to have had an excuse to reread poems forgotten since high school. One of the wives revealed that her husband had been reading poems aloud before going to bed each night, an activity she might like to continue even after the dinner.

Once we were seated at the table but before the first course was served, "Ovid" volunteered to start the poetry readings, since his verse, from *Metamorphosis*, foretold the future of poets. After that, we proceeded through the readings in the historic order in which they were written. As the wine was being poured, the Sufi mystic "Rumi" and I deliberated which one of us came next. I did. The eighth-century Chinese poet Li Po wrote of illumination while under the influence of wine and moonlight—appropriate since we, too, had plenty of both on this night of the full moon in October.

The female guests who came dressed as Emily Dickinson and Madame "Fanny" Laurent LeCoulteux (the muse of Louis XIV's court poet, André de Chénier) benefited from their proximity to Hollywood costume shops. I didn't know that the real Miss Dickinson would have never attended such a party, since she spent fifty years in self-imposed confinement; in contrast, our "Miss Dickinson" is the author of a nationally read social column.

"Hiawatha," like the rest of us, maintained character all evening long. But then just as dessert was being served, she got the most laughs when, during her reading of Longfellow's "The Song of . . . ," she cast off the Hudson Bay trapper's coat she had been swaddled in to reveal the beaded chamois bikini—and little else—that she wore underneath.

The most elegantly dressed women were the muses of Rilke and Bulgakov, and they were escorted by the dark dandies "Charles Dickens," "Ambrose Bierce," and "Oscar Wilde." Eerily, the wry guest who read lines from Kurt Cobain's grunge rock classic "Smells Like Teen Spirit" looked like a contemporary of the nineteenth-century trio. The distinctions between who belonged in what century blurred. Great poets, we all agreed, are a messed-up lot.

Mincemeat Purses

". . . they dined on mince and slices of quince."—EDWARD LEAR

The traditional mincemeat pie doesn't actually have meat—just suet—and was used to stretch the scant bit of animal into a meal at Christmastime. That's not exactly appealing. So this mincemeat pie has actual meat—rich short rib, plus smooth chicken liver mousse—but is constructed in the classic fashion, as individual-serving pastries, albeit tiny ones. The chicken liver pâté is good enough to be enjoyed on its own, spread on a cracker or toast; prepare it the morning of or a day ahead, so it has time to firm up.

makes 12 servings

FOR THE MEAT
8 ounces boneless beef short ribs

½ teaspoon sea salt

¼ teaspoon freshly ground black pepper

2 tablespoons grapeseed oil

1 small yellow onion, cut in small dice

1 small carrot, cut in small dice

1½ cups low-sodium canned chicken stock

3 tablespoons brown sugar

1 cinnamon stick

1 star anise pod

3 cloves

6 black peppercorns

FOR THE FILLING
1 tablespoon grapeseed oil

½ small yellow onion, cut in small dice

1 apple, peeled and cut in small dice

½ cup chopped dark raisins

½ cup chopped prunes

1 tablespoon apple cider vinegar

1 tablespoon chopped parsley

¼ teaspoon sea salt

⅛ teaspoon freshly ground black pepper

6 sheets phyllo dough, thawed

4 ounces (½ cup) clarified butter, melted (page 100)

4 tablespoons bread crumbs or cracker crumbs

Chicken Liver Pâté (recipe follows)

2 tablespoons quince paste

¾ cup Buttermilk Dressing (recipe follows)

3 teaspoons extra-vecchio balsamic vinegar (see Resources)

1 cup micro herbs or tiny herb salad, including micro chives or cut chives

1 to 2 teaspoons crunchy salt, such as Maldon

Preheat the oven to 300°F.

MAKE THE MEAT: Heat a small, ovenproof sauté pan over high heat. Dry the meat with a paper towel and season it on both sides with the salt and black pepper. Add the oil to the pan, then the meat, and sear it on all sides, about 1 minute on each side. Remove the meat from the pan and add the onion and carrot. Cook until lightly browned, about 3 minutes. Add the chicken stock, brown sugar, cinnamon, star anise, cloves, and peppercorns and bring to a simmer. Return the meat to the pan, cover, and place in the oven until the meat is fork-tender, about 2 hours. Remove the meat from the braising liquid. Pour the liquid through a fine-mesh strainer into a small saucepan and cook over medium-low heat until reduced to a syrupy consistency, 8 to 10 minutes. Shred the meat and combine with the reduced liquid.

MAKE THE FILLING: In a medium sauté pan, heat the oil over medium-high heat. Add the onion and apple and sauté until lightly browned, stirring often, about 5 minutes. Add the shredded meat, raisins, prunes, vinegar, parsley, salt, and black pepper and mix well.

Lay out the phyllo sheets near a work surface that you can cut on; cover the phyllo with a towel. The towel can be misted with a spray bottle, but don't dampen it under the faucet with water, which would make the phyllo too wet and possibly cause it to stick together. Place one sheet of phyllo on the work surface, brush it generously with the melted clarified

butter, and sprinkle evenly with 1 tablespoon of the bread crumbs. Lay the second sheet on top and again brush with the butter and sprinkle with 1 tablespoon of the bread crumbs. Lay the third sheet on top and brush with butter, then press it gently all over. Cut this into 6 even squares. Fill each square with $1\frac{1}{2}$ tablespoons of the filling. Gather together all of the edges, and press in the middle. Set aside on a baking sheet. Repeat with the remaining 3 sheets of phyllo. You will have extra filling, which freezes nicely. The pies can be prepared to this point a day in advance. Cover them with very lightly dampened paper towels and plastic wrap and place them in the refrigerator until you are ready to bake them.

Preheat the oven to 400°F. Bake the pies until golden brown, about 12 minutes.

Place a slice of chicken liver pâté on each plate. Place a baked mince pie on top, then place ½ teaspoon of the quince paste on each plate in three spots around the pie. Drizzle each plate with 1 tablespoon of the buttermilk dressing and ¼ teaspoon of the vinegar. Garnish with a large tablespoon of the micro herb salad and a sprinkle of crunchy salt.

Chicken Liver Pâté

makes 12 servings

8 ounces chicken livers, trimmed of any membrane

½ teaspoon sea salt

⅛ teaspoon plus 1 pinch of freshly ground black pepper

2 teaspoons grapeseed oil

1 shallot, minced

½ Fuji apple, peeled and cut into ¼-inch dice

1 tablespoon brandy or cognac

4 tablespoons cold unsalted butter, cut into chunks

1 tablespoon minced chives

1 tablespoon chopped parsley

½ cup chopped pecans, toasted

Blot the livers dry with a paper towel and season with ¼ teaspoon of the salt and the ⅛ teaspoon of black pepper.

Heat a medium sauté pan over high heat. Add the oil and seasoned livers. Sear on all sides until browned by shaking the pan and turning them with a fork, 1 to 2 minutes. Add the shallot and apple and cook until the livers are medium rare, about 2 minutes. Remove the pan from the heat and add the brandy, then return the pan to the heat for 30 to 60 seconds to allow the alcohol to burn off.

In a food processor, combine the liver mixture and butter and puree until the butter is completely incorporated and the liver pâté is fairly smooth. Press the pâté through a sieve to remove any membrane. Stir in the chives and parsley, and season with the remaining ¼ teaspoon of salt and the pinch of black pepper.

Transfer the chicken liver pâté to a piece of plastic and form a log shape ¾ inch in diameter, using the plastic. Tighten by twisting both ends to make a firm log and remove any air bubbles. Refrigerate until the pâté is firm, at least 3 hours and up to 3 days.

Just before serving, unwrap the chicken liver pâté and roll it in the nuts. Slice the pâté into twelve ¾-inch disks.

Buttermilk Dressing

makes 1 cup

½ cup buttermilk

¼ cup Garlic-Herb Mayonnaise (page 51)

2 tablespoons extra virgin olive oil

1 teaspoon fresh lemon juice

1 tablespoon finely sliced chives

1 tablespoon chopped parsley

1 teaspoon chopped thyme

In a small bowl, whisk the buttermilk and mayonnaise together until smooth. Stir in the remaining ingredients until just combined.

Roasted Pork Loin Stuffed with Braised Cabbage

"Of shoes—and ships—and sealing wax—
Of cabbages—and kings—
And why the sea is boiling hot—
And whether pigs have wings."—LEWIS CARROLL

There are three types of pork here: loin, pork sausage, and bacon, as well as two types of cabbage—a tribute to "pigs and cabbages." Thank you, Lewis Carroll, for your inspiration, from the poem "The Walrus and the Carpenter."

makes 12 servings

One 6-pound boneless Berkshire pork loin, butterflied twice by the butcher (see Resources)

3 tablespoons extra virgin olive oil

2 medium yellow onions, diced

1 garlic clove, minced

3 tablespoons unsalted butter

2 cups drained chopped sauerkraut

½ teaspoon sea salt

¼ teaspoon freshly ground black pepper

4 links (1¼ pounds) Italian pork sausage, casings removed

½ cup sliced chives

¼ cup chopped parsley

3 tablespoons grapeseed oil

3 sage leaves

3 thyme sprigs

2 rosemary sprigs

2 cups low-sodium canned chicken stock

Potato Puree (recipe follows)

Braised Cabbage and Onions (recipe follows)

Bacon and Pickled Golden Raisin Vinaigrette (recipe follows)

Pound the pork loin to a ½-inch thickness so that it forms a 36 x 12-inch rectangle. Keep the pork loin chilled until you are ready to stuff it. In a medium sauté pan over medium-high heat, heat the olive oil. Add the onions and garlic, reduce the heat to medium, then add the butter. Sauté until the onions are light golden brown and soft, about 8 minutes. Add the chopped sauerkraut and cook over low heat for 10 minutes. Season with the salt and black pepper and spread out on a rimmed baking sheet to cool quickly.

Lay out the pork loin with the fat side farthest away from you. Spread the sausage meat over the loin in an even layer, leaving about ½ inch at the top and bottom, but going all the way to the left and right edges. Spread an even layer of the seasoned sauerkraut over the sausage and sprinkle with the chives and parsley. Starting from the side nearest you, roll up the pork loin and tie firmly with butcher's twine every 2 inches.

Preheat the oven to 300°F.

Heat a large, shallow roasting pan over high heat. Add the grapeseed oil and sear the pork loin on four sides until lightly browned, 8 to 10 minutes. Add the sage, thyme, rosemary, and chicken stock. Roast for 3 hours, then let cool for 30 minutes before slicing. Serve with the potatoes, braised cabbage, and vinaigrette.

Potato Puree

5 medium russet potatoes, peeled and cut into
  1-inch chunks

1 ½ teaspoons plus ¾ teaspoon sea salt

½ cup heavy cream

2 tablespoons extra virgin olive oil

6 tablespoons (¾ stick) unsalted butter,
  softened

⅛ teaspoon freshly ground white pepper

In a large stockpot, place the potatoes and the 1½ teaspoons of salt. Cover with cold water and bring to a boil. Cook until the potatoes are tender all the way through, 30 to 40 minutes. Drain well.

In a standing mixer fitted with a paddle, blend the potatoes on medium-high speed with the cream, olive oil, and butter. Season with the remaining ¾ teaspoon of salt and the black pepper.

Braised Cabbage and Onions

makes 12 servings

½ cup grapeseed oil, more if needed

1 head (3½ pounds) green cabbage, outer
  leaves removed, cut into 12 wedges with the
  core attached

1 ½ teaspoons sea salt

¾ teaspoon freshly ground black pepper

1 large yellow onion, diced

2 thyme sprigs

1 sage sprig

1 to 2 cups low-sodium canned chicken stock

Preheat the oven to 350°F.

In a large sauté pan heat the oil over high heat. Place the cabbage wedges in a single layer in the pan and brown each side for about 4 minutes. Season each side with salt and black pepper as you go, and add more oil if the pan gets too dry. You may need to do this in batches. Transfer the cabbage to a large roasting pan.

In the same pan, sauté the onion over medium heat until translucent, 4 to 5 minutes. Spoon the onion over the cabbage in the roasting pan. Add the thyme and sage and cover the cabbage with the chicken stock to a ¼-inch depth. Cover, place in the oven, and braise until tender, about 1 hour. (You may also add the seared cabbage and onion to the pork roasting pan during the last hour of cooking. Make sure to add more chicken stock if needed.)

Bacon and Pickled Golden Raisin Vinaigrette

makes 3 cups

1 shallot, minced

1 garlic clove, minced

2 teaspoons extra virgin olive oil

½ cup golden raisins

½ cup white wine vinegar

½ cup low-sodium canned chicken stock

1 rosemary sprig

1 thyme sprig

1 oregano sprig

1 teaspoon sea salt

6 bacon slices, cut into ½-inch pieces

1 ½ cups veal demi-glace (see Resources)

In a small saucepan, sauté the shallot and garlic in the olive oil over medium heat until tender, about 2 minutes. Add the raisins, vinegar, chicken stock, rosemary, thyme, oregano, and salt. Bring to a simmer and remove from the heat. Let the mixture sit for at least 1 hour before continuing.

Place the bacon slices in a cold medium sauté pan over medium-low heat. Turn and cook until the bacon is mostly crispy, 15 minutes. Drain off all but 2 tablespoons of the fat. Add the veal stock reduction and the pickled raisins with their juice. Heat through. The vinai-

RIGHT: Layers of cake, blackberry jam, crisp meringue, goat cheese cream, and blackberry curd, in a tribute to Sylvia Plath

Blackberry Dacquoise Cake

"Nobody in the lane, and nothing, nothing but blackberries"—SYLVIA PLATH

This is a meringue layer cake, with a twist in deference to the dead poet's line "nothing but black-berries": a blackberry curd, blackberry vinegar in the meringue, and even fresh blackberries in the garnish. Nothing but blackberries indeed.

makes 12 servings

FOR THE BLACKBERRY CURD
2 tablespoons fresh lemon juice

1½ cups blackberries

2½ tablespoons granulated sugar

2 large egg yolks

3 tablespoons unsalted butter, cut into pieces

FOR THE CRUST
½ cup (1 stick) cold unsalted butter,
  cut into ¼-inch chunks

1 cup all-purpose flour

2 tablespoons confectioners' sugar

Pinch of sea salt

¾ cup blackberry jam

FOR THE CAKE
5 tablespoons unsalted butter, melted,
  plus more for the pan

1 cup all-purpose flour, sifted,
  plus more for the pan

3 large eggs

½ cup granulated sugar

1 tablespoon fresh orange juice

FOR THE MERINGUE
½ cup walnut halves

⅓ cup plus ½ cup granulated sugar

¼ teaspoon sea salt

½ cup egg whites (from 4 eggs),
  at room temperature

2 teaspoons blackberry vinegar or
  raspberry vinegar

FOR THE GOAT CHEESE CREAM
8 ounces fresh goat cheese

4 tablespoons heavy cream

2 tablespoons granulated sugar

FOR THE GARNISH
½ cup black currant jelly

2 cups blackberries

½ cup chopped toasted walnuts

MAKE THE BLACKBERRY CURD: In a blender, puree the lemon juice and blackberries. Pour through a fine-mesh strainer into a glass measuring cup. In a small heatproof bowl combine ½ cup of the puree with the granulated sugar and egg yolks. Reserve the remaining puree. Place the bowl over boiling water and whisk the mixture very quickly until it starts to thicken and steam rises, 4 to 5 minutes, being careful not to overheat the eggs so they don't curdle. (You can remove the bowl from the heat to check the mixture at any time.) Clean the edges of the bowl with the whisk while constantly whisking. Remove the bowl from the heat and whisk in the butter. Chill for at least 4 hours to set, or up to 2 days.

MAKE THE CRUST: Preheat the oven to 350°F. In a food processor pulse the butter, flour, confectioners' sugar, and salt until the dough forms a ball, 3 to 5 minutes. Press the dough into a disk, wrap it in plastic, and refrigerate for 1 hour.

On a sheet of parchment paper, roll the dough into a 4 x 12-inch rectangle. Use the rolling pin to give the top a final go-over to make sure it is very even. Transfer the dough and parchment to a baking sheet and refrigerate for 20 minutes. Then bake until golden, about 15 minutes. Remove from the oven and refrigerate until you are ready to assemble the cake.

MAKE THE CAKE: Preheat the oven to 325°F. Line a 13 x 9-inch baking pan with parchment paper, then butter and flour the paper.

In a medium heatproof bowl, whisk together the eggs, granulated sugar, and orange juice. Place the bowl over a pan of boiling water and whisk until very warm and the sugar is dissolved, 2 to 5 minutes. Remove the bowl from the heat and whisk by hand or with a mixer until cool and the mixture has tripled in volume, about 4 minutes. Very gently fold in the 1 cup of flour, then the 5 tablespoons of melted butter. Pour the batter into the prepared cake pan and use an offset spatula to spread it out evenly. Bake until golden, 20 to 25 minutes.

MAKE THE MERINGUE: Preheat the oven to 200°F. On a piece of parchment paper, trace two 4 x 12-inch rectangles. Transfer the paper to a baking sheet. In a food processor, grind the walnuts, the ⅓ cup of granulated sugar, and the salt until the nuts have the fine texture of polenta, about 4 minutes. It should be mealy, but do not let it form a paste.

In a standing mixer, beat the egg whites and vinegar on medium-low speed until soft peaks form, about 2 minutes. Increase the speed to high and slowly add the remaining ½ cup of granulated sugar in a steady stream. Beat until the meringue holds very stiff peaks, 3 to 4 minutes. Fold in the nut mixture. Divide the meringue evenly between the two traced rectangles, and spread it with an offset spatula. Make sure that the thickness of the meringue is as even as possible. Neaten the edges with the spatula or your finger so the meringue fits perfectly into the rectangle form. Bake until dry and crisp, about 2 hours.

MAKE THE GOAT CHEESE CREAM: Just before assembling the dessert, warm the goat cheese, cream, and granulated sugar in a heatproof bowl set over boiling water until spreadable, 3 to 5 minutes.

MAKE THE GARNISH AND ASSEMBLE THE CAKE: In a small saucepan, warm the black currant jelly and gently stir in the blackberries. Let cool slightly. Cut the cake into two 4 x 12-inch strips. Spread about 3 tablespoons of the blackberry jam onto the crust. Place a slice of cake on the crust and spread 3 tablespoons more of the jam on the cake. Place a layer of meringue on top and spread with about half of the goat cheese cream. Repeat, with the cake, jam, meringue, and goat cheese cream. On the top layer of goat cheese cream, spread the blackberry curd and arrange the jelly-coated blackberries on top. Spread the remaining jam over the sides of the cake and press the toasted walnuts on the sides. Serve with the remaining sauce from the blackberry garnish.

WINE NOTES

Apple Ice Wine "Frimas," La Face Cachée de la Pomme, 2003 (Quebec, Canada)
Pinot Noir, Woollaston Estate, 2005 (Nelson, New Zealand)
Dulce Monastrell, Bodegas Olivares, 2003 (Jumilla, Spain)

One of our favorite wine-and-food pairings of all time was the combination of this apple ice wine with the "mince and quince." This special wine is made in Quebec from Spartan and McIntosh apples, which are harvested frozen, just like the grapes used in ice wines—in either case, water is removed from the fruit in the form of ice crystals, leaving behind a super-concentrated fruit juice that is fermented into a sweet, unctuous nectar.

Because of the natural crispness of the apples, the resulting ice wine remains very high in acidity, which balances its considerable sweetness. While it is honeyed and rich, it nevertheless has a light touch on the palate. It echoes the flavors of the quince and apples while masking the saltiness of the liver with its sweetness—and the acidity in the wine leaves you refreshed after each bite.

An elegant pinot noir was a classic choice for the pork loin, whose raisin and bacon vinaigrette lends some fruity intensity. The pinot from Woollaston Estate combines some of the fruit-forward richness found in California pinots with some of the earthy, mineral qualities of French Burgundy. It's a good-sized pinot, one with enough finesse for pork but enough ripeness for the sweet and sour fruit elements.

The Olivares Monastrell Dulce is a late-harvest mourvèdre from Spain that tastes like something between a Banyuls from France and port, but it's softer and easier on the palate. This is also a great cigar wine, because while port has a lot of tannin, this doesn't, so it gives you a refreshing, lingering sweetness in your mouth when you're smoking.

THANKSGIVING

Spit-Roasted Turkey and Gravy

Parsnip-Potato Puree

Settler's Spoonbread

Seared Wild Mushrooms

Brussels Sprouts with Walnuts and Vinaigrette

Pods and Roots

Rebel Greens

Apple Finocchio

Bounceberry Sauce

Sweet Po' Bikkies

Pumpkin Crème Brûlée

Sourdough Bread Pudding with Jack Daniel's Custard Sauce

"Whatever Red's Open" Oranges

IT IS MIDNIGHT, AND THE CONVERSATION AT THE DINNER TABLE IS STILL SO SPIRITED you'd think it was a wrap party for the combined casts of *Meet the Press* and *The Tonight Show*. There are fourteen of us here, and I have just pulled the cork on the last bottle in a case of wine. This would be cause for worry if it were not for the fact that we have been at this for a little more than six hours now. Anyway, we're all spending the night here. This is our family on Thanksgiving.

It has always been my favorite holiday. Thanksgiving is free of the pressures of gift giving, devoid of religious or civic ceremony, and requires no dramatic annual self-reinvention. Thanksgiving is so perfectly focused: It's the only day of the year when our agenda is dedicated to one idea, the family meal. Heaven!

My basic menu never changes: turkey, stuffing, gravy, parsnips, Brussels sprouts, bread pudding, and at least one other dessert. However, when we started holding Thanksgiving dinner at the ranch, we quickly realized that cooking the turkey outdoors on our big rolling grill not only freed up the oven for all the other dishes, but several smaller and more tender turkeys could be roasted on it, all at one time. Of course, when Stephanie worked her magic on these holiday favorites, our groaning board set a new standard.

For us, though, what is on the plate is never more amazing than who is at our table. And at no time is this more obvious to me than in the minutes after midnight when, by all rights, we should be sated with food, wine, and conversation. But we go on. Someone else notices that we are out of wine. "Don't worry!" Bo says, "I'll run down to the cellar and get a bottle of some of the old stuff." The rest of us laugh, because we know that this means some treasured bottle we have been saving for a special occasion, and that, for us, the night is still young. It is at this moment that I know what I am most thankful for on Thanksgiving.

Spit-Roasted Turkey and Gravy

At Rancho La Zaca, our Thanksgiving turkeys come from Heritage Foods USA, which markets the products of farmers dedicated to preserving both the past and the future by raising heirloom birds, like the Red Bourbon turkey we prefer. We spit-roast over an open flame, so Southwestern ingredients are natural: The bird is rubbed with chipotle chiles and sage. Wyatt Cromer, the ranch manager at Rancho La Zaca, mans the spit starting before sunrise, and tends the birds and the fire all day, until dinner. But when he joins us at the table, even he agrees it's worth the effort: The birds are smoky and tender from the long roasting process.

makes 15 servings

One 18-pound American Heritage Red Bourbon turkey (see Resources)

1 cup (2 sticks) unsalted butter, plus 6 tablespoons, softened

1 bunch sage, large stems reserved and leaves minced

1 bunch chives, finely sliced

2 chipotle chiles in adobo, chopped

2 small shallots, 1 minced, 1 cut in thirds

2 garlic cloves, 1 minced, 1 halved

3 teaspoons sea salt

¾ teaspoon freshly ground black pepper

½ large carrot, halved lengthwise

½ celery stalk, halved lengthwise

6 cups low-sodium canned chicken stock

5 tablespoons all-purpose flour

Fourteen hours (or more) before serving the bird, prepare a bed of coals. Rinse the turkey under cold, running water. Remove the neck and gizzards and reserve. Cut away any excess skin. Dry the turkey well.

Using your hands, gently separate the skin from the breast meat. In a medium bowl, stir together the 1 cup of softened butter, the sage, chives, chipotles, minced shallot, minced garlic, 2½ teaspoons of the salt, and the black pepper. Rub ⅓ cup under the skin of each breast. Rub the remaining seasoned butter on the inside of the turkey and a thin coating on the outside. Truss the turkey firmly with butcher's twine.

Wrap the turkey in several layers of foil and arrange on the spit spindle; make sure it is firmly in place. Roast the bird for about 12 hours, replacing the coals as necessary. Keep the temperature of the turkey between 250°F and 300°F. You should check its temperature every so often to make sure it is cooking and the temperature is rising. The turkey should be slowly cooked until an instant-read thermometer inserted at the thigh joint registers 165°F. During the last 40 minutes of roasting, remove the foil to brown and crisp the skin. Let the turkey rest for 30 minutes before serving.

While the turkey is cooking, preheat the oven to 400°F. Place the neck in a small roasting pan in the oven. Roast until golden brown, about 45 minutes. Remove the neck from the pan and add about ½ cup of water, scraping up any browned bits in the pan. In a medium saucepan, place the neck pan liquid, remaining shallot and garlic, the carrot, celery, 4 sage stems, and the giblets. Cover with the chicken stock and bring to a simmer. Simmer, uncovered for 1 hour. During the last 5 minutes of cooking, melt the remaining 6 tablespoons butter in a medium saucepan over low heat. Add the flour and whisk together. Continue stirring for 2 to 3 minutes. Pour the stock through a fine-mesh strainer; you should have about 4 cups. Slowly add the hot stock to the hot roux (butter-flour mixture), whisking to avoid lumps. Bring this gravy to a simmer over low heat and cook for 15 minutes, stirring. Season the gravy with the remaining ½ teaspoon of salt.

Parsnip-Potato Puree

This is an earthy, sweet alternative to mashed potatoes. As with a mound of mashed potatoes, a dimple in the top makes the perfect spot for a gravy pool.

makes 8 cups; serves 15

4 pounds parsnips

3½ teaspoons sea salt

1 star anise pod

1½ pounds russet potatoes, peeled and
  cut into 1-inch chunks

½ cup heavy cream

¼ cup (½ stick) unsalted butter

½ teaspoon freshly ground white pepper

Peel the parsnips and cut into ¼-inch slices. Place in a large saucepan with enough water to cover. Add 2 teaspoons of the salt and the star anise and bring to a boil. Reduce the heat to medium and simmer until tender, about 30 minutes.

Meanwhile, place the potatoes in a medium saucepan with water to cover and ½ teaspoon of salt. Bring to a boil, reduce the heat to low, and simmer until tender, about 20 minutes.

Drain the parsnips and the potatoes, which can be combined at this point. Discard the star anise. Put them through a food mill or ricer. Stir in the cream, butter, white pepper, and remaining 1 teaspoon of salt. The parsnip-potato puree can be prepared 1 day in advance and refrigerated. Reheat gently and adjust the seasoning before serving.

Settler's Spoonbread

Since our turkey is spit-roasted and can't be stuffed, this spoonbread is a substitute for the in-bird bread crumb kind. It is an old-fashioned American dish you don't see much anymore.

makes 15 servings

4 tablespoons (½ stick) unsalted butter,
  plus more for greasing the pan

Flour, for the pan

1 tablespoon extra virgin olive oil

1 small yellow onion, cut in small dice

1 celery stalk, cut in small dice

1½ cups whole milk

2¼ cups half-and-half

½ teaspoon sea salt

1½ cups cornmeal

5 large eggs, separated

½ cup heavy cream

⅛ teaspoon cream of tartar

4 ounces high-quality blue cheese,
  such as Maytag or Point Reyes, crumbled

¾ cup dried cranberries

Preheat the oven to 375°F. Butter and flour a 9-inch square pan.

Heat the olive oil in a medium, heavy-bottomed saucepan. Add the onion and celery and cook over low heat for 2 minutes. Add the milk, half-and-half, salt, and the 4 tablespoons of butter, and bring to a simmer. In a steady stream, whisk in the cornmeal and stir with a wooden spoon for 3 to 4 minutes. Remove from the heat. In a small bowl, whisk together the egg yolks and cream, and stir into the cornmeal mixture.

In a standing mixer, whip the egg whites and the cream of tartar on high speed until stiff peaks form. Fold a third of the egg whites into the cornmeal mixture to lighten it, then gently fold in the remaining egg whites along with the blue cheese and cranberries. Pour the mixture into the prepared pan and bake until lightly browned on top and puffy, 35 to 40 minutes.

TOP: Spit-Roasted Turkey with Gravy; Pods and Roots

Seared Wild Mushrooms

To get a nice sear on the mushrooms, cook them over very high heat in a single layer. Be careful not to crowd the pan; depending on the size, you might need to do the searing in batches. It is easiest to use a nonstick pan and merely wipe it dry with a paper towel in between batches.

makes 15 servings

4 pounds mixed wild mushrooms,
  such as chanterelle, oyster, black trumpet,
  and blue oyster (see Resources)

6 tablespoons grapeseed oil

3 shallots, minced

3 garlic cloves, minced

4 tablespoons (½ stick) unsalted butter,
  cut into pieces

2½ tablespoons fresh lemon juice

1 teaspoon sea salt

½ teaspoon freshly ground black pepper

¼ cup minced parsley

¼ cup finely sliced chives

1 tablespoon minced thyme

1 tablespoon minced sage

Clean the mushrooms by brushing away any dirt and trim away any tough stems. In a large sauté pan, heat the 6 tablespoons of oil over high heat. Add the mushrooms and shake the pan to loosen them. Cook, stirring, until golden, about 5 minutes; the moisture should be evaporated from the mushrooms. Add the shallots and garlic and cook for 1 minute. Add the butter, lemon juice, salt, black pepper, parsley, chives, thyme, and sage and stir to combine. The mushrooms can be prepared up to 3 days in advance and refrigerated. Reheat before serving.

Brussels Sprouts with Walnuts and Vinaigrette

What makes these Brussels sprouts special is the vinaigrette—sharp, grainy mustard and bright fresh-squeezed lemon juice—plus the addition of crunchy toasted walnuts. Be sure not to add the vinaigrette until right before serving to preserve the Brussels sprouts' color and texture.

makes 15 servings

3 pounds Brussels sprouts

3 tablespoons grapeseed oil

1 small shallot, minced

1 garlic clove, minced

3 thyme sprigs, plus 1 tablespoon chopped
  thyme

1 teaspoon sea salt

¼ cup extra virgin olive oil

2 tablespoons fresh lemon juice

1½ tablespoons grainy mustard

¼ teaspoon freshly ground black pepper

½ cup walnut halves, toasted and chopped

Bring a large pot of water to a boil. Trim the Brussels sprouts of any tough outer leaves and cut an X on the bottoms. Blanch the sprouts in the boiling water for 1 minute, then drain. Do not put in an ice bath.

In a large sauté pan, heat the oil over high heat. Add the Brussels sprouts and shake the pan. Cook, shaking occasionally to turn the sprouts, until they have a dark roasted color on several sides, about 3 minutes. Add the shallot, garlic, the 3 thyme sprigs, and ¾ teaspoon of the salt, and cook for 30 seconds. Reduce the heat to low, add ⅓ cup of water, and cook until the water evaporates and the sprouts are tender in the center, 5 to 7 minutes.

In a small bowl, stir together the olive oil, lemon juice, mustard, chopped thyme, black pepper, and the remaining ¼ teaspoon of salt. Pour over the sprouts and stir gently. Transfer to a serving dish and sprinkle with the walnuts.

Pods and Roots

You may not think of vanilla as an apt flavor to pair with root vegetables, and in fact your guests will probably not be able to identify the vanilla flavor (or the cardamom), but they will definitely know there's something special about this dish. The vegetables sweeten as they caramelize, and the vanilla pairs perfectly with the natural sugars. If you can't find baby vegetables, just cut large ones into bite-size chunks.

makes 15 servings

2 pounds baby beets, tops trimmed

1 vanilla bean, split and scraped

1 pound baby rutabagas, peeled and cut into
  wedges

2 pounds baby carrots, tops trimmed, peeled

1 pound baby parsnips, tops trimmed, peeled

2 pounds baby turnips, tops trimmed, peeled

¼ cup vanilla oil (see Resources)

2 green cardamom pods, black seeds removed
  and crushed

1 teaspoon sea salt

¼ teaspoon freshly ground black pepper

1 tablespoon fresh lemon juice

3 tablespoons chopped parsley

Preheat the oven to 425°F.

Put the beets on a large square of foil with the vanilla bean pod. Wrap tightly and place on a baking sheet in the oven. Roast until the beets are tender and the skin can be easily peeled, about 1½ hours. Remove from the oven, let cool slightly, and peel.

In a large bowl, combine the rutabagas, carrots, parsnips, turnips, vanilla bean seeds, vanilla oil, cardamom seeds, salt, and black pepper, and stir to coat. Spread the vegetables on a rimmed baking sheet in a single layer and roast until they are slightly caramelized on the outside and tender inside, 20 to 25 minutes. Transfer to a serving bowl. Add the beets, lemon juice, and parsley and toss to mix. Serve.

Rebel Greens

Collard greens are typically a Southern dish that goes great with roasted turkey. These are doused in vinegar, honey, and bacon.

makes 15 servings

5 bunches collard greens (3 to 3½ pounds)

2 tablespoons extra virgin olive oil

5 thick-cut bacon slices, cut into ¼-inch pieces

1 medium yellow onion, diced

3 garlic cloves, minced

3½ cups low-sodium canned chicken stock

1 cup apple cider vinegar

1 cup raw honey

4 tablespoons (½ stick) unsalted butter

1 teaspoon sea salt

½ teaspoon freshly ground black pepper

Cut out and discard the stem of each collard leaf. Cut the greens into 1-inch strips. Wash the greens in a large amount of water. Remove them from the water but do not shake away the excess.

In a large, heavy-bottomed pot, heat the olive oil. Add the bacon, onion, and garlic and cook over low heat until the onion and bacon are tender but not crispy, about 20 minutes. Add the washed collards and let them cook down, stirring, for 5 minutes. Add 1½ cups of the stock, ½ cup of the vinegar, and ½ cup of the honey. Cover and continue cooking for 1 hour. Add the remaining 2 cups of stock, ½ cup of honey, ½ cup of vinegar, and the butter. Cook until the greens are tender, about 1 hour. Season with salt and pepper and serve.

TOP LEFT: Pods and Roots

ABOVE: Parsnip-Potato Puree

LEFT: Brussels Sprouts with Walnuts and Vinaigrette

Apple Finocchio

The braised apple-fennel combination is a great sweet-savory accompaniment to turkey. Make sure to get a good sear on the fennel and don't let the apples cook too long, to ensure they stay snappy and crunchy—this isn't applesauce you're making.

makes 15 servings

5 fennel bulbs, tops trimmed and tough outer layer removed

2 tablespoons grapeseed oil

¾ teaspoon sea salt

4 thyme sprigs

2 sage sprigs

2 rosemary sprigs

1 cup low-sodium canned chicken stock

2 tablespoons extra virgin olive oil

14 lady apples, peeled

1 tablespoon honey

¼ teaspoon freshly ground black pepper

Preheat the oven to 300°F.

Cut the fennel into quarters, through the core. Heat the grapeseed oil in a large sauté pan. Add the fennel, cut side down, and cook over high heat until nicely browned, 2 to 3 minutes. Turn and cook on the other cut side for 2 to 3 minutes. Add ¼ teaspoon of the salt along with 2 thyme sprigs, 1 sage sprig, 1 rosemary sprig, and ½ cup of the stock. Cover with foil or a pan lid, and bake until tender, about 1 hour.

Heat the olive oil in a medium sauté pan over high heat. Add the apples and shake while cooking until nicely browned on a few sides, 4 to 5 minutes. Reduce the heat to low and add ¼ teaspoon of the salt, the remaining 2 thyme sprigs, 1 sage sprig, 1 rosemary sprig, ½ cup of stock, and the honey. Cover and simmer until tender but not mushy, 12 to 15 minutes. Remove the fennel from the oven and toss gently with the roasted apples. Season with the remaining ¼ teaspoon of salt and the black pepper.

Bounceberry Sauce

When cranberries are fully ripened and ready to eat, not only do they turn that beautiful shade of red, they also bounce!

makes 4 cups

Three 12-ounce packages cranberries

1 cup sugar

½ cup fresh orange juice (from 2 oranges)

One 2-inch cinnamon stick

1 thyme sprig

¼ teaspoon sea salt

⅛ teaspoon freshly ground white pepper

Bring all of the ingredients to a boil in a medium, heavy-bottomed saucepan. Reduce the heat to low and simmer until at least half of the cranberries are broken, about 5 minutes. Remove from the heat and chill before serving. The sauce can be prepared up to 4 days in advance and refrigerated.

Sweet Po' Bikkies

Most kids love sharing in the preparation of a holiday meal. If they are old enough to read, they can make these biscuits all by themselves (with some adult supervision during the baking).

makes 24 biscuits

One 13-ounce sweet potato

2 cups all-purpose flour

2 teaspoons baking powder

¾ teaspoon sea salt

6 tablespoons (¾ stick) cold unsalted butter,
  cut into ½-inch chunks

½ cup buttermilk

2 tablespoons thinly sliced chives

1 tablespoon chopped sage

¼ cup whole milk

Preheat the oven to 375°F. Line a baking sheet with parchment paper.

Place the sweet potato on a rimmed baking sheet or baking dish and roast until tender, about 1½ hours. Let cool, cut in half, and scrape out the inside; discard the skin. Mash the flesh with a fork until smooth.

Increase the oven temperature to 450°F. In a large bowl, combine the flour, baking powder, and salt. Drop in chunks of the cold butter and cut in with 2 knives, a pastry blender, or by rubbing the butter and flour between your fingers until the butter and flour pieces are the size of peas. Coat and separate the butter pieces as you work; do not allow the butter to melt or form a paste. Mix in the buttermilk, ¾ cup of the mashed sweet potato, chives, and sage with a wooden spoon or fork just until the dry ingredients are moistened. Gather the dough into a ball and knead it gently against the sides and bottom of the bowl 5 to 10 times, pressing any loose pieces into the dough until the bowl is fairly clean.

On a lightly floured surface, roll or press out the dough into a square or rectangle ¾ inch thick. Using a 1¾-inch-diameter round cookie cutter, cut out the biscuits and place on the prepared baking sheet at least 1 inch apart. Brush the tops with the milk and bake until golden brown on top and deeper golden brown on the bottom, 12 to 14 minutes.

Pumpkin Crème Brûlée

This crème brûlée is an alternative to pumpkin pie. The preparation is for portions in tiny dishes, so each person can have a little taste of this very rich and sumptuous dessert.

makes 10 servings

1 small sugar pumpkin (about 3 pounds)

2 cups heavy cream

2 cinnamon sticks

10 cloves

1 bay leaf

1 star anise pod

½ vanilla bean, split and scraped

2 large whole eggs

9 large egg yolks

½ cup sugar, plus 4 to 7 tablespoons for sprinkling

Preheat the oven to 400°F. Line a shallow baking dish with foil.

Cut the pumpkin in half and place it, cut sides down, in the prepared baking dish with 4 tablespoons of water. Roast until tender, about 45 minutes. Peel the pumpkin and puree the flesh in a food processor. Reduce the oven temperature to 325°F and dry out the puree in the oven until it is the consistency of refried beans, about 45 minutes. Let cool.

In a medium saucepan, bring the cream to a boil with the cinnamon, cloves, bay leaf, star anise, and vanilla bean pod and seeds. Remove from the heat and let steep for 45 minutes.

Reduce the oven temperature to 250°F. In a large bowl, whisk together the whole eggs and egg yolks, and add 1½ cups of the pumpkin puree and the ½ cup of sugar. Pour the steeped cream through a fine-mesh strainer into the egg mixture and whisk for 1 minute. Divide this mixture among ten 4½-ounce crème brûlée molds or ramekins and divide the molds between two shallow baking dishes. Boil 6 cups of water and pour the water into the baking dishes until it almost reaches the top of the molds (but be careful not to get water in the custards). Bake until the custards are set, about 45 minutes. Remove the molds from the water bath and chill for 3 hours or overnight.

To serve, sprinkle 1 to 2 teaspoons of sugar in an even, thin layer over the top of each custard. Caramelize the tops with a torch or under the broiler until the sugar is completely melted and golden brown.

Sourdough Bread Pudding
with Jack Daniel's Custard Sauce

Bread pudding may not be a traditional Thanksgiving dessert, but the cranberries lend a seasonal touch, and the orange zest and whiskey make this something of a solid, sweet hot toddy. Be sure to leave the crust on the bread, and bake until the edges of the bread cubes brown up nicely—these crusty browned edges are irresistible.

makes 15 servings

FOR THE BREAD PUDDING

10 tablespoons (1 ¼ sticks) unsalted butter, softened

One 1-pound loaf artisanal sourdough bread, in 1-inch slices

5 cups whole milk

½ cup plus 2 tablespoons sugar, plus 2 to 3 tablespoons for sprinkling

5 large eggs

Finely grated zest of 1 orange

5 tablespoons Jack Daniel's whiskey

¾ cup dried cranberries

FOR THE JACK DANIEL'S CUSTARD SAUCE

½ cup whole milk

½ cup half-and-half

½ cup heavy cream

3 tablespoons plus 2 teaspoons sugar

Finely grated zest of 1 orange

4 large egg yolks

1 tablespoon Jack Daniel's whiskey

Pinch of salt

MAKE THE BREAD PUDDING: Butter the bread slices on both sides, using up to 1 stick of the butter. Keep the bread slices together and cut the bread into 1-inch chunks. In a large bowl, whisk together the milk, the 10 tablespoons of sugar, the eggs, orange zest, and 3 tablespoons of the whiskey. Add the bread cubes and the cranberries. Place a plate on top of the mixture to keep the bread submerged in the custard and refrigerate. Let sit for 2 hours or overnight. Stir once or twice to evenly moisten all of the bread with the custard.

Preheat the oven to 350°F. Butter a deep 3-quart baking dish with the remaining 2 tablespoons of butter and sprinkle with the remaining sugar. Shake out any excess sugar. Spoon the bread cubes into the dish, pressing them down to fit and mounding the bread over the top. Pour any excess custard into the baking dish and douse the top with the remaining 2 tablespoons whiskey. Bake on a rimmed baking sheet until the pudding is crusty and golden brown on top and a tester comes out clean, 55 minutes.

MAKE THE JACK DANIEL'S CUSTARD SAUCE: Fill a 4-quart bowl halfway with ice and 2 cups of water. Place a 2-quart metal bowl inside the 4-quart bowl. In a small saucepan, combine the milk, half-and-half, cream, 2 tablespoons of the sugar, and the orange zest, but do not stir. Bring to a simmer. In a medium bowl, whisk together the egg yolks and the remaining 1 tablespoon plus 2 teaspoons of sugar. Temper the yolks by slowly whisking in the hot milk mixture, then return to the saucepan. Place over medium-low heat and cook, stirring constantly with a wooden spoon, until the custard begins to steam and coats the back of the spoon, about 4 minutes; be careful not to curdle the egg yolks. Immediately pour into the bowl in the ice bath and cool, stirring occasionally. Pour the custard through a fine-mesh strainer. Stir in the whiskey and salt. Serve with the warm bread pudding. The sauce can be prepared up to 2 days in advance and refrigerated. Bring to room temperature before serving.

"Whatever Red's Open" Oranges

It seems there is always an open bottle of red wine in the fridge at Rancho La Zaca. And in the fall, we find ourselves blessed with a basket of oranges harvested from Jackie Rosa's tree. So, a dessert was born. Besides filling your house with an unmistakable holiday fragrance, this happens to be great with the Sourdough Bread Pudding (page 269). Make the oranges early in the day to allow the flavors to meld.

makes 15 servings

5 Valencia oranges, peeled with no pith remaining

2½ cups red wine

1 cup sugar

2 cinnamon sticks

1 star anise pod

5 cloves

10 black peppercorns

Two ⅛-inch ginger slices

In a medium nonreactive saucepan, combine the oranges, wine, sugar, cinnamon, star anise, cloves, peppercorns, and ginger. Bring to a boil, then simmer over low heat for 45 minutes, turning the oranges halfway through. Remove the pan from the heat and let the oranges infuse at room temperature for 3 hours. Turn the oranges every so often as they sit. Slice the oranges ½ inch thick and serve. The oranges can be prepared 2 days in advance and refrigerated, unsliced, after infusing. Slice and bring to room temperature before serving.

WINE NOTES

Chablis, Les Clos, François Raveneau, 2000 (Chablis, France)
Riesling, Ürziger Würzgarten, Kabinett, Dr. Loosen, 2000 (Mosel, Germany)
Shiraz, Run Rig, Torbreck, 2002 (Barossa Valley, Australia)

Chardonnay and riesling tend to be the traditional white wines of Thanksgiving, and either would work, though riesling is the slightly better choice with the sweet potatoes, pumpkin, and turkey. We chose a kabinett-level riesling like the Ürziger Würzgarten from Dr. Loosen, which is one of the best Thanksgiving wines around—

off-dry, clean, crisp and spicy, and served well chilled. For chardonnay, we selected one of the top producers in France, François Raveneau, for his deep, rich, and structured wines that are equal parts power and layered levels of aromatics and nuance.

When choosing a red to go with the cranberry sauce or the turkey, look for a

rich and tangy syrah that doesn't have too much tannin. We went a little (OK, way) over the top with the Run Rig Shiraz from Torbreck—a mouthful of deep and intensely flavored black fruits that stains the teeth. Pure decadence!

A HISTORY OF FOXEN CANYON ROAD, LOS OLIVOS, CALIFORNIA *by Jim Norris, Santa Ynez Valley Historian and Publisher, Olive Press*

Foxen Canyon Road is a place of broad vistas, clear ocean-cooled air, pine-topped mountain ridges, bright roadside wildflowers, green-then-golden hills, pastured livestock, historic *ranchos* (including Rancho La Zaca and Oak Savanna Vineyard), and some of the finest land in Santa Barbara County for growing wine grapes.

The history of Foxen Canyon Road reads like something out of a Hollywood script, as evidenced by the many faces it has worn: Indian trade route, mission trail, military route, road for cattle drives, stage route, Los Angeles to San Francisco coastal highway, and the focal point of today's wildflower tours and winery trail.

For more than 10,000 years, the resident Native Americans used the present road as a trade route. A large village site called *asaca* was located at what is now the intersection of highways 101 and 154. This name would be adapted by the Spanish to La Zaca. With the establishment of the Santa Ines Mission in 1804, local Indians gathered at the mission, and many villages were eventually abandoned. Western agriculture and free-roaming cattle and horses were introduced, grazing under the Santa Ines Mission brand.

After Mexican independence in 1821, retired military officers were granted large coastal ranchos and the so-called pastoral period began. Cattle grazed "on a thousand hills," and the hide, tallow, and horn trades flourished. Ship captains and crew members, landing here after long sea voyages, were understandably enamored of the dark-eyed señoritas, and this resulted in many marriages. Some of the settlers converted to Catholicism and became Mexican citizens, while many Americans also became rancho owners.

BENJAMIN WILLIAM FOXEN

Foxen Canyon Road was named for English mariner Benjamin William Foxen, who was also known as Guillermo Domingo and Don Julian. Born in Norwich County, England, in 1796, he joined the British navy in his youth, then went into the shipping business for himself, trading hides and tallow between Boston and California, which he first visited in 1817. In 1831, after the required conversion to Catholicism, Foxen married Maria Eduarda del Carmen Osuna. They settled in what is now Santa Barbara County. In 1837, Governor Alvarado awarded Foxen the Rancho Tinaquiac (meaning "Little Far Stream") on what is now Foxen Canyon Road.

Of the adobe ranch house there, Foxen's daughter, Mathilda, wrote:

When my father and mother first went to live in Foxen Canyon there were a great many bears. They built a little two-roomed adobe with a flat roof, tule, and mud. The bears were so bad, my father and mother had to sleep on top of the roof.

Foxen built a large adobe ranch house and barns, as well as a blacksmith shop. In this shop he made a cattle branding iron in the shape of an anchor to commemorate his life at sea, which is used today on the label of Foxen Winery.

JOHN C. FREMONT ON FOXEN CANYON ROAD

As the concept of Manifest Destiny spread west, traders and trappers began arriving in the still-Mexican territory of California. Tensions developed between these settlers and the dominant Mexican or Spanish ranchers, called Californios. In 1846, the Bear Flag uprising in Sonoma first established a Republic of California.

As a member of the United States Topographical Corps, Lieutenant Colonel John C. Fremont was already in California, and he soon led a 423-man ragtag "army" of trappers, soldiers, mariners, and Indians south to connect with Commodore Stockton in Los Angeles, further defining the republic. In December 1846, Fremont traveled south from the San Francisco area along today's Foxen Canyon Road, and stayed at Benjamin Foxen's ranch. Assisted by Foxen and his son, and collecting horses as he traveled, Fremont slogged through a rainstorm, over a trail east of the present-day San Marcos Pass, before slipping and sliding down the south side of the Santa Ynez Mountains.

On December 28, he "captured" Santa Barbara without firing a shot. On January 13, 1847, he accepted the Californios' surrender at Cahuenga. California became the thirty-first state in 1850.

The discovery of gold at Sutter's Mill near Sacramento in 1848 speeded California's statehood. Many eager forty-niners from the East and Mexico traveled along Foxen Canyon Road on their way north to the goldfields—to "see the elephant." Little more than ten years later, in 1861, a mail stage was established on Foxen Canyon Road, part of the route between San Francisco and San Diego. The stage carried many new arrivals—entrepreneurs and homesteaders—to the area.

THE RANCHOS OF FOXEN CANYON ROAD

Between 1795 and 1846, the governors of Alta California approved approximately forty grants for ranches in what is now Santa Barbara County; Foxen Canyon Road cut across six of these. The 4,458.10-acre grant for Rancho La Zaca was awarded in 1838 by Governor Alvarado to Antonio Paljalchet, a leader of the Native Americans at Santa Ines Mission. It is said that he homesteaded with his wife and children on the shores of Zaca Lake, even though the lake was not part of the grant. Today, the original grant lands are held in five parts: Zaca Ranch (Fleming), Rancho La Zaca (Hill), Foxen Canyon Ranch (Hayer), Rancho Riata (Roven), and Zaca Mesa Wineries (Cushman).

CHRISTMAS EVE

Hot Rum Sting

Open Fire–Roasted Chestnut Soup

Roasted Stuffed Goose with Huckleberry Gastric

Turnip Pavé

Herb Salad with Beet-Vanilla Vinaigrette

Christmas Trifle

WHEN OUR KIDS WERE LITTLE, WE WOULD POUR ALL OF OUR HOLIDAY ENERGY INTO Christmas morning. Now the children are all grown, and we're grandparents only this year, so in order to hear the pitter-patter of tiny feet at holiday time, we've been forced to rely on the generosity of younger friends who are parents. We don't miss it so much we're willing to invade Christmas morning, but enough so that we were prompted to start this holiday tradition—children most welcome—on Christmas Eve.

A Christmas Eve *posada* ("shelter" in Spanish) is a tradition in Mexico: a reenactment of the search for rooms by Mary and Joseph on the first Christmas Eve. Our procession, held at the historic Misión La Purísima, in Lompoc, is led by Callum and Estelle Murray, dressed in biblical costume, and accompanied by Babalu, our miniature donkey. By candlelight we move from door to door, down the long gallery, singing the begging songs in Spanish. At each room, we are refused, also in song, by other carolers inside. But upon knocking on the door of the sanctuary, we are admitted. And after singing the last joyful verse of the Spanish song ("Enter Wanderers!"), we all burst into the traditional English Christmas carols, the tunes we all know.

A social hour follows the posada, during which the young children are invited to break a piñata filled with candy. Usually that is enough for the little ones and their parents to head home, with visions of sugarplums dancing in their heads. Then we empty-nesters sit down to a Christmas Eve dinner that has been prepared in the mission kitchen.

Hot Rum Sting

Leave it to tropical fruits to bring spice and spike to your winter holidays. This hot drink is a welcome change from the more traditional but heavy eggnog, and a refreshing variation on the ubiquitous hot apple cider.

makes 16 servings

2 pineapples, peeled, cored, and cut into ½-inch chunks

3 mangos, peeled, pitted, and cut into ½-inch chunks

1 quart fresh orange juice

Juice of 6 Key limes

1 vanilla bean pod, no seeds (optional)

2 cinnamon sticks

6 cloves

1 star anise pod

2 cups high-quality dark rum, such as Mount Gay Extra

In a blender, puree the pineapple and mango in batches with the orange and lime juices until smooth, about 1 minute. Pour the puree through a medium-mesh strainer into a large saucepan. Heat over medium heat and add 1 cup water. Stir in the vanilla bean pod if using, cinnamon, cloves, and star anise. Bring to a boil, reduce the heat to the lowest possible setting, and steep for 30 minutes. Stir in the rum and serve warm.

Open Fire–Roasted Chestnut Soup

Roasted chestnuts are a must on any Christmas menu, and unexpected to find in the soup. This one is enhanced with the flavors of bacon, maple, and crème fraîche.

makes 12 servings

3 pounds chestnuts in the shell or 6 cups frozen (see Resources)

2 tablespoons unsalted butter

1 small yellow onion, diced

2 garlic cloves, minced

1½ teaspoons minced ginger

10 sage leaves

2 thyme sprigs

8 cups low-sodium canned chicken stock

½ cup heavy cream

Bacon Maple Chutney (recipe follows)

½ cup crème fraîche

2½ tablespoons finely sliced chives

To peel the chestnuts, preheat the oven to 450°F or prepare a fire in a fireplace. Make an X incision on the smaller end with a paring knife and lay flat on a rimmed baking sheet or a chestnut roasting pan and roast for 5 to 8 minutes, shaking or stirring. Let cool slightly and peel.

In a medium stockpot over medium heat, melt the butter. Add the onion, garlic, and ginger and sauté until the onion is translucent, about 4 minutes. Add the chestnuts, sage, and thyme and cook for 2 minutes. Add the stock and bring to a boil, then reduce the heat to a simmer. Cook over medium heat until the chestnuts are very tender and have started to break into pieces, 30 to 40 minutes.

Let the soup cool briefly. Remove the sage leaves and thyme sprigs and add the cream. In a blender, working in batches, puree the soup until it is smooth and creamy, 2 to 3 minutes per batch. Pour through a fine-mesh strainer. Return the blended soup to the pot and bring back to a simmer to serve.

Ladle 1 to 1½ cups of hot soup into each bowl and garnish with 1 tablespoon of the chutney and 2 teaspoons of the crème fraîche. Sprinkle with the chives and serve. The soup can be prepared a day or two in advance and refrigerated. Thin it with a little chicken stock or water, gently reheat, and readjust the seasoning before serving.

Bacon Maple Chutney

makes about ¾ cup

Grade B maple syrup is more flavorful than Grade A, plus it is slightly less expensive. Buy slab bacon in an 8-pound piece from Niman Ranch (see Resources), cut it into 8-ounce chunks, and freeze it: You'll always have great bacon at your disposal.

6 thick-cut bacon slices, cut into ¼-inch pieces	1 tablespoon Grade B maple syrup
1 small shallot, minced	1 tablespoon sliced chives
1 garlic clove, minced	¼ teaspoon freshly ground black pepper

In a medium sauté pan, cook the bacon over low heat until crisp, 10 to 15 minutes. Drain off any fat. Add the shallot and garlic to the bacon in the pan and cook for 1 minute. Stir in the maple syrup and cook for 30 seconds. Remove the pan from the heat and add the chives and black pepper. The chutney can be prepared up to 4 days in advance and refrigerated. Reheat gently before serving.

Roasted Stuffed Goose
with Huckleberry Gastric

People often complain about goose, "It's too rich." We say, "You can never be . . ." Oh, never mind. Face facts: Goose is fabulously rich, meaty, and succulent. In this recipe, the fat permeates the meat and the dried fruit and foie gras stuffing is made moist, and richer still, by the savory meat drippings. To cut all this super-richness down to size, pair your goose with a sweet-sour sauce, called a gastric, and serve with the Turnip Pavé. And for the luscious stuffing, use any leftover foie gras in the freezer. The foie gras melts into the rich challah and highlights the dried fruits' flavors.

makes 12 servings

Two 10- to 12-pound Heritage Foods USA geese (see Resources)

½ small yellow onion, cut into 1-inch wedges

½ carrot, halved lengthwise

Dried Fruit and Foie Gras Stuffing (recipe follows)

4 teaspoons salt

1 teaspoon freshly ground black pepper

Huckleberry Gastric (recipe follows)

Turnip Pavé (recipe follows)

Micro celery, for garnish (optional)

Preheat the oven to 450°F.

Remove and reserve the goose necks and giblets. Cut off excess fat from around the cavities (reserve for rendered goose fat if you like). Place the necks on a small rimmed baking sheet with the onion and carrot, and roast for 30 minutes. Remove the necks and vegetables to a medium saucepan. Pour about ½ cup of water into the baking sheet and scrape up any browned bits. Pour into the saucepan. Cover with additional water and bring to a boil. Reduce the heat to low and simmer for 2 hours, skimming off any fat. Pour through a fine-mesh strainer and reserve to use in the huckleberry gastric.

Reduce the oven temperature to 400°F.

Rub ¼ cup of the reserved fruit from the stuffing under the skin of each goose breast; loosely stuff the remaining fruit stuffing in the body cavities. Season each goose with 2 teaspoons of the salt and ¼ teaspoon of the black pepper. Truss the goose firmly with butcher's twine. Roast in the bottom third of the oven for 1 hour. If the skin starts to become too brown, cover with foil, then remove the foil for the last 15 minutes of roasting. After 1 hour, reduce the oven temperature to 350°F and continue roasting until an instant-read thermometer inserted at the thickest part of the leg joint registers 165°F, about 1½ hours.

Let the geese rest for 20 minutes. If carving the geese tableside, slice the meat directly off the bone. If carving in the kitchen, cut the entire breasts off the bone, then slice them on the bias. This way, every piece of meat has an equal amount of crispy skin.

Place ¼ cup of the stuffing just off center on each plate. Place 1 square of turnip pavé on the plate, angled next to the stuffing. Place about 3 slices of leg meat on top of the stuffing, and follow with 2 or 3 slices of breast meat. Spoon 3 to 4 tablespoons of the huckleberry gastric over the goose, and garnish the turnip pavé with a few celery leaves, if using.

Dried Fruit and Foie Gras Stuffing

One 1-pound loaf challah bread, preferably a day old

½ cup unsalted butter

1 small yellow onion, diced

1 celery stalk, diced

1 garlic clove, chopped

1 cup pitted prunes, chopped

1 cup dried apricots, chopped

¾ cup dried Morello cherries, chopped

1 cup dried Bing cherries, chopped

¾ cup dried cranberries

2 cups low-sodium canned chicken stock

8 ounces raw foie gras, cut into ½-inch chunks (see Resources)

1½ teaspoons sea salt

½ teaspoon freshly ground black pepper

1 cup pecan halves, toasted and chopped

3 thyme sprigs

3 tablespoons chopped parsley

2 tablespoons sliced chives

1½ teaspoons chopped sage

Preheat the oven to 300°F.

Cut the bread into ½-inch cubes and spread out on a rimmed baking sheet. Dry out the cubes in the oven for 45 minutes.

In a large sauté pan, melt the butter over low heat. Add the onion, celery, and garlic, and cook over low heat until the onion is translucent, about 8 minutes. Add the prunes, apricots, both types of cherries, the cranberries, and 1 cup of the stock. Simmer over low heat until almost all of the liquid is gone, about 10 minutes.

Remove 1½ cups of the mixture, let cool slightly, then blend in a blender until smooth; set aside to use for seasoning the goose prior to roasting. Keep the remaining fruit in the sauté pan.

Season the foie gras with ¼ teaspoon of the salt and ¼ teaspoon of the black pepper. Heat a medium sauté pan over high heat, and sear the foie gras until brown on all sides, about 1 minute total, shaking the pan and using a spatula to turn the foie gras pieces. Add the seared foie gras to the dried fruit mixture in the sauté pan along with the dried bread cubes. Heat for 5 minutes. Add the remaining 1 cup of stock, the pecans, thyme, parsley, chives, sage, and the remaining ¾ teaspoon of salt and ¼ teaspoon of black pepper. Stir until combined and heated through. The stuffing can be prepared a day in advance and refrigerated.

Huckleberry Gastric

1½ cups frozen purple wild mountain huckleberries, thawed, juices reserved (see Resources)

½ cup sugar

½ cup huckleberry vinegar (see Resources)

1½ cups reserved goose stock (from Goose recipe)

2 tablespoons unsalted butter

¼ teaspoon sea salt

In a medium saucepan, simmer the huckleberry juice over medium heat until syrupy and reduced to about 3 tablespoons. Combine the juice with the sugar and cook until caramelized, about 5 minutes more. Add the vinegar and simmer until thick and syrupy, about 5 minutes. Stir in the goose stock and reduce by a third, about 10 minutes. Remove from the heat and whisk in the butter. Stir in the huckleberries and salt. The gastric can be prepared up to 3 days in advance and refrigerated.

Turnip Pavé

Pavé comes from the French word for "paving stone," and it's a preparation of uniform, shingled slices weighted down to compress the slices and hold them together, so it can be served in an attractive and neat-looking square slice. It's best to make this dish the day before and chill in the refrigerator, which helps the portions hold their shape.

makes 12 servings

7 tablespoons unsalted butter

2 tablespoons chopped chives

1 tablespoon chopped thyme

4 tablespoons chopped parsley

4 pounds turnips, peeled and thinly sliced, preferably on a mandoline

¾ teaspoon sea salt

¾ teaspoon freshly ground black pepper

½ cup heavy cream

Preheat the oven to 350°F. Line a 9-inch square baking pan with foil so there are 2 inches of extra foil hanging off 2 opposite ends; grease with 2 tablespoons of the butter.

In a small bowl, combine the chives, thyme, and parsley. Begin layering the buttered pan with the turnips: Make 2 layers of shingled slices, covering the entire pan; sprinkle with ⅛ teaspoon of the salt, ⅛ teaspoon of the black pepper, 1½ tablespoons of the mixed herbs, 1 tablespoon of the butter (in bits) and 2 tablespoons of the cream. Repeat with the remaining ingredients to make 4 layers of turnips, ending with a layer of salt, black pepper, herbs, butter, and cream. Top with parchment paper, then fold in the edges of the foil to cover. Cover with another layer of foil. Place another 9-inch pan with weights in it directly on top. Bake until the turnips are tender when poked with a knife, about 1 hour and 15 minutes. Keep the weights on while cooling to room temperature, then refrigerate with the weights for at least 4 hours but preferably overnight.

Gently remove the pan and weights and the parchment from the turnip pan and trim about ¼ inch of the pavé from around the edges. Slice into 12 squares. Reheat before serving for about 12 minutes in a 350°F oven.

MISIÓN DE LA PURÍSIMA CONCEPCIÓN DE LA SANTÍSIMA VIRGÍN MARÍA

La Purísima Mission State Historic Park, located in Lompoc, California, was the eleventh of twenty-two Spanish missions established in the state. Father Presidente Fermin de Lasuén founded Misión de la Purísima Concepción de María Santísima (Mission of the Immaculate Conception of Most Holy Mary) on December 8, 1787. The local Indians built the original adobe buildings whose ruins remain to this day. At this site, several thousand Chumash Indians were baptized and put to work raising crops and livestock to great success.

In 1812, known as El Año de los Temblores, or "The Year of the Earthquakes," a devastating earthquake damaged much of the original La Purísima. Father Mariano Payeras was granted permission to rebuild the mission four miles away on a new site where there was a better water supply, climate, and proximity to the travel route El Camino Real. After the move, La Purísima thrived once again. Approximately one thousand Chumash converts lived on the grounds, and it became a school and a training center in the arts of weaving, pottery, leatherwork, and other crafts. Most notably, it was a profitable ranch, and twenty thousand cattle, sheep, and other livestock grazed the lands.

In 1834, California's missions were ordered to become secularized. In 1845, La Purísima was sold for one thousand dollars to Juan Temple, a man from Los Angeles. The property changed ownership and was used for various purposes for the rest of the nineteenth century; it then began to suffer from decline and neglect. The Union Oil Company donated the mission to the public in 1933, but by that time it was in complete ruins. The County of Santa Barbara, the State of California, the National Park Service, and the Civilian Conservation Corps joined together in 1934 to preserve and reconstruct the historic and picturesque landmark. They restored the buildings and grounds, and furnished them in the style of the early nineteenth century.

Today, La Purísima sits on 1,928 acres, a fraction of the original 300,000-acre property. Ten of the original buildings have been fully restored and furnished authentically, including the two chapels and the padre's kitchen. The park rangers give tours, and volunteers enact Mission Life Days demonstrating typical crafts, activities, and industries. They also stage Village Days, allowing visitors to try their hand at activities the Chumash Indians brought to the mission, like grinding acorns, basket making, arrow making, and games.

Herb Salad with Beet-Vanilla Vinaigrette

This salad is liberally spiked with an original smoked raw milk blue cheese from the Rogue Creamery in Oregon. Beet and cheese salads have become popular in the last few years, but this one is a breed apart.

makes 12 servings

FOR THE VINAIGRETTE

1 medium beet, juiced (or ½ cup fresh beet juice purchased from a health food store or juice bar)

½ vanilla bean, split and scraped

2 tablespoons raw unfiltered honey

3 tablespoons fresh lemon juice

2½ tablespoons hazelnut oil

7 tablespoons extra virgin olive oil

½ teaspoon sea salt

⅛ teaspoon freshly ground black pepper

FOR THE SALAD

1 cup hazelnuts

6 heads escarole, tough outer green leaves removed, yellow part chopped into ½-inch squares

¼ bunch flat-leaf parsley, stemmed

½ bunch basil, stemmed, large leaves torn in half

½ bunch tarragon, stemmed

1 bunch dill, torn into small sprigs

½ bunch mint, stemmed

½ bunch chives, sliced ¾-inch long

1 tablespoon fresh lemon juice

2 tablespoons extra virgin olive oil

½ teaspoon sea salt

¼ teaspoon freshly ground black pepper

⅓ pound smoked blue cheese, crumbled (see Resources)

Preheat the oven to 300°F.

MAKE THE VINAIGRETTE: Skim the foam off the top of the beet juice. You will need ½ cup of juice.

In a blender, combine the beet juice, vanilla seeds, honey, lemon juice, hazelnut and olive oils, salt, and black pepper. Pulse until just combined, about 30 seconds.

MAKE THE SALAD: Place the hazelnuts on a rimmed baking sheet, place in the oven, and bake until the skin is loosened from the nuts, 12 to 15 minutes. Let cool slightly, then rub the skins off the nuts and cut each in half.

In a large bowl, toss the escarole and all the herbs together with the lemon juice, olive oil, salt, black pepper, and ½ cup of the vinaigrette. Spoon 1 to 1½ tablespoons of vinaigrette on each plate and top with 1 cup of the salad. Top each salad with 5 to 7 hazelnut halves and 1 tablespoon of crumbled cheese.

Christmas Trifle

This trifle is pretty traditional: Walnut oil cake is layered with a delicate orange cream, walnut brittle, oranges, and raspberries. La Nogalera Walnut Oil (see page 291) is pretty special, and well worth it to go out of your way to purchase.

makes 12 servings

¼ cup unsalted butter, melted, plus more for greasing the pan

½ cup all-purpose flour, plus 2 tablespoons for dusting the pan

6 large eggs, separated

1 cup sugar

1 vanilla bean, split and scraped

Pinch of sea salt

½ cup ground walnuts

¼ cup La Nogalera Walnut Oil (see Resources)

2 pints raspberries

3 Valencia oranges, segmented, juice reserved

⅓ cup Grand Marnier

Orange Cream (recipe follows)

1½ Coconut-Walnut Brittle (recipe follows)

Preheat the oven to 350°F. Prepare a 13 x 9-inch cake pan by greasing and lining the bottom with parchment paper. Grease the parchment as well and dust with 2 tablespoons of the flour.

In a standing mixer, beat the egg yolks, ½ cup of the sugar, and vanilla seeds until the mixture is light, 5 to 8 minutes. In a separate large bowl, beat the egg whites and salt until they hold stiff peaks. Sift the ½ cup of flour over the egg yolk mixture and gently add the ground walnuts, the ¼ cup of melted butter, and the walnut oil. Fold a third of the beaten egg whites into the yolk and flour mixture. Fold in the remaining two-thirds of the whites just until combined.

Pour the batter into the prepared cake pan and bake until lightly browned, 15 to 18 minutes. The trifle can be prepared to this point a day in advance and covered with plastic wrap. Cut into ½-inch chunks before assembly.

In a medium bowl, combine the raspberries, orange segments and juice, the remaining ½ cup of sugar, and the Grand Marnier. Marinate in the refrigerator for 1 to 2 hours before assembling the trifle.

In a large champagne flute, begin by layering 3 pieces of cake and gently pressing down. Sprinkle with ½ tablespoon of the coconut-walnut brittle, 1 tablespoon of the marinated fruit, and 1 tablespoon of its juice. Top this with 2 tablespoons of the orange cream. Repeat with the remaining ingredients until the flute is filled, finishing with a layer of cream and brittle. This can be prepared 1 to 2 hours in advance and refrigerated before serving.

Orange Cream

makes about 4 cups

1 cup half-and-half

2 cups heavy cream

1 cup whole milk

9 large egg yolks

6 tablespoons sugar

1 tablespoon pure vanilla extract

1 tablespoon fresh orange juice

Finely grated zest of 1 orange

Fill a 4-quart bowl halfway with ice and 2 cups of water. Place a 2-quart metal bowl inside the 4-quart bowl.

In a medium saucepan, heat the half-and-half, 1 cup of the cream, and the milk to just before boiling. In a large bowl, whisk the egg yolks and sugar until combined. Slowly pour the hot cream mixture into the yolks while whisking vigorously. Return to the saucepan over

low heat and cook, stirring constantly, until the sauce coats the back of a wooden spoon, 12 to 18 minutes.

Remove the pan from the heat and stir in the vanilla, orange juice, and zest. Transfer to the 2-quart metal bowl in the ice bath and whisk for 2 minutes; let cool completely. The orange cream can be prepared a day in advance and refrigerated until assembly. Just before serving, whip the remaining 1 cup of cream to firm peaks, then fold into the cold orange cream.

Coconut-Walnut Brittle

makes 3 cups crushed brittle

1 tablespoon walnut oil	2 cups walnut halves
1 cup sugar	½ teaspoon baking soda
¼ cup light corn syrup	1 cup shredded unsweetened coconut
½ teaspoon sea salt	1 teaspoon pure vanilla extract

Brush a baking sheet lightly with the walnut oil. In a small saucepan, combine the sugar, corn syrup, salt, and ½ cup of water. Using a candy thermometer, bring the mixture to 240°F and add the walnuts. Continue cooking until the mixture is 300°F, then add the baking soda, coconut, and vanilla. Remove the pan from the heat, pour the mixture onto the prepared baking sheet, and let cool. Break into small crumbled pieces using a mallet or rolling pin to make about 1½ cups. Extra brittle can be stored in an airtight container for up to 4 days.

WINE NOTES

Chardonnay, Reserve, Firestone Vineyard, 2004 (Santa Ynez, California)
Riesling, Vineyard Select, Firestone Vineyard, 2005 (Central Coast, California)
Red Table Wine, The Ambassador, Firestone Vineyard, 2001 (Santa Ynez, California)
Viognier, Late Harvest, Curtis Winery, 2005 (Santa Ynez, California)

We chose a flight of wines from our neighbors, the Firestones (who also own Curtis Winery), for this menu, and discovered some wonderful matches along the way. The riesling had the exotic aromatics to play with the dill, tarragon, basil, and other elements of the herb salad, while the richer, toastier chardonnay found harmony with the ginger-tinged chestnut soup. It has become fashionable to dismiss big oaked-aged chardonnays as being unfriendly with food, but here is an instance where a luscious white with a nice nutty richness is just the thing.

With our gamey, fruity goose, Firestone's powerful Bordeaux-style blend, the Ambassador, got the call. It is deep and dark with an earthy savor, like the goose, but has plenty of vibrant Santa Barbara fruit to play off the garnishes. We also called the riesling back into action here and found that it, too, had some affinity for the goose. Goose is rather fatty, and the acidity of the riesling proved a nice foil.

To play up the exotic citrus notes in the trifle, we chose a late-harvest viognier. This is an explosion of floral aromas wrapped in a luscious, oily package, almost a dessert in itself. We also tried a little with the herb salad and found that it complemented the sweetness of the beet-vanilla vinaigrette while also offering a sweet contrast to the salty blue cheese.

LA NOGALERA WALNUT OIL

Stephanie claimed that it was her favorite local food product besides the wine. I have learned that when she speaks in superlatives, I should listen. She retrieved a can of La Nogalera Walnut Oil from the refrigerator and explained that the oil is extremely temperature-sensitive; it must be kept refrigerated and it expires within a relatively short time after opening. She drizzled some over a porous slice of sourdough bread and handed it to me. The oil began seeping through the doughy holes and a cool slick ran down my fingers, warming to skin temperature by the time it reached my wrist. This was when I discovered the joys of walnut oil sandwiches, a guilty pleasure I've justified as breakfast or an afternoon snack, among other things.

According to Jose Baer, the owner of Rancho La Vina and the walnut groves from which La Nogalera is made, I need feel no guilt at all: Walnut oil has no cholesterol and is high in omega-3 fatty acids, as well as vitamin E (only fish oil and flaxseed oil have superior health benefits, but it's a sure bet I will never crave either of those!).

History informs so much of our regional excellence. So I should not have been surprised to learn during a visit to Baer's hundred-year-old groves that he is a descendant of the original Spanish colonial family who settled this ranch, a part of the original Santa Rosa Land Grant, centuries ago. California is the only American state to grow walnuts and make walnut oil, a relatively common ingredient in the cuisines of Europe and some Middle Eastern countries. Jose's ancestors bought 10,000 trees with money they'd made selling sheep they had herded all the way across the United States to introduce sheep to the Pacific Coast settlements.

Like grapes, walnut trees will grow in almost any climate if irrigated. But the finest grade of edible nuts grows in conditions identical to those of one of the finest wine grapes, pinot noir; that's why the award-winning wines from Sea Smoke Cellars claim La Vina origin on the label. Pointing to the steep hillsides above the walnut grove, which lies on the flats between the Santa Rosa Road and the Santa Ynez River, Jose says those grapes are grown right up there.

La Nogalera differs from other walnut oils because it is made from walnut meat, without the shells and hulls, and from the same quality nut he sells in premium halves for baking. While Jose ships the walnuts out of the county to be processed into oil, the final product bears an orchard appellation, just like some estate-grown wines do; Hibbits, Concord, and Canyon are the three orchard locations. (My palate is not so refined that I could discern a difference among the three.) The second "secret" to Jose's process is that the walnuts are toasted before cold pressing, and I know this is what attracts me to it: The flavor of roasted nuts is one I crave the way other people might yearn for potato chips.

PARTY PLANNING NOTES
&
RESOURCES

WEDDING PICNIC

{pages 9–19}

I wanted a bucolic feel for this picnic, so I used only a few special pieces of silver to accent the more rustic picnic wares, including an antique "loving cup" that was given to us as a wedding gift. It is distinguished by its two handles, and looks a little bit like a trophy cup. Dealers of fine antique silver often have them. My favorite source for small, unusual nineteenth-century sterling objects like this is Alice Kwartler, 123 East 57th Street, New York, NY, 212-752-3590.

The ten-sided silver cups and the silver box are vintage Hermès. The auction house Wright's regularly has sales of fine twentieth-century decorative objects like these (www.wright20.com).

RESOURCES

STEAMED SALMON WITH NASTURTIUM MAYONNAISE: Banana leaves can be purchased at Mexican or Asian markets.

RELEASING A NEW VINTAGE

{pages 21–41}

This wine tasting dinner was held outdoors in late summer, but it could be done at any time of year, and is probably more practical in a real dining room with easier access to the kitchen.

I dragged my George Nakashima dining table and chairs down to the dock, where they fit perfectly. For lighting, I adapted an idea from my friend Robert Isabell, who attaches Japanese paper ball lanterns to long, thin bamboo stakes from the garden shop, then sticks the stakes into the ground, so they bend and bob gracefully with their lighted lanterns on the end. The electrical cords are wrapped around the stakes. Instead, I hung 16-inch lanterns in the trees by the dock. Low-wattage orange lightbulbs inside the lanterns created a magical effect when their soft glow became apparent at twilight. You can find paper lanterns at www.shojidecor.com.

I never have cut flowers on the table for a wine and food tasting because the fragrance of cut flowers can confuse our noses. Instead, we used succulents which were bought in pots from the nursery and simply removed from the pot, and then clustered around some quartz votives. Tony Duquette designed the original candle holders; reproductions of them are available at Hollyhock, a shop I love in West Hollywood, California (for more information: www.hollyhockinc.com) or at ABC Carpet & Home in New York (www.abchome.com). The stemless wineglasses are Riedel "O." The red porcelain dinner plate (for the lamb) and the white one (cheese and dessert) are from Rupert Spira.

To plan my seating for formal dinners, I always use a vintage Hermès leather table chart that I found at an antiques shop in Santa Barbara when we first bought the ranch. A similar one can be purchased at Scully & Scully in New York (www.scullyandscully.com).

The biggest surprise happened at sunset, when steam began rising from the pond and it was so thick that we felt like we were sitting on a cloud. No one who was there that night has forgotten that moment.

A similar, simpler tasting would be what *Wall Street Journal* wine columnists Dorothy J. Gaiter and John Brecher call "Open That Bottle Night," where single bottles that you might have been saving for any number of reasons (for a special occasion, or maybe you're unsure if it's any good, or even where it came from) get opened and enjoyed (or not!). Either way, everyone has fun and learns something.

RESOURCES

CRAYFISH AND BROTH: Crayfish are available by mail from www.farm-2-market.com. Oak Savanna Chardonnay can be purchased at www.oaksavannawine.com.

OLIVE AND BACON RELISH: Artisanal smoked bacon can be purchased from the Grateful Palate, www.gratefulpalate.com.

BRAISED LAMB RIBS WITH HOMINY: Hominy is dried corn kernels that have been treated with an alkali. Hominy can be purchased at www.ranchogordo.com and at Mexican markets.

WILD MUSHROOM SAUTÉ: Wild mushrooms can be purchased at www.earthy.com.

POINT REYES BLUE CHEESE WITH CHERRY, ROSE, AND CRUSHED TELLICHERRY PEPPERCORNS: Rose syrup is available at Indian grocers or www.kalustyans.com. Point Reyes blue cheese is available at www.cowgirlcreamery.com.

OAXACAN MOLE SORBET: Dried chiles can be purchased from the online catalog at www.gourmetsleuth.com

MUSCOVADO ICE CREAM: Muscovado sugar is a dark brown, unrefined sugar from Africa. It is available at many upscale grocers and online from www.kalustyans.com.

FANDANGO: A FIESTA LUNCHEON

{pages 43-63}

This buffet would be great served at home at any time of year (in winter, drop the melon from the Watermelon Pyramid and make a great salad by tossing together the rest of the ingredients; the peaches in the churros become poached pears). Make sure your guests know that it is a Spanish evening; some will surely dress the part, even if just in a small detail, like wearing a shawl, an off-the-shoulder top, or a full skirt.

If you want to splurge on such an evening, it would be fun to bring in a flamenco guitarist to play during the cocktail hour, until everyone is seated at the table. This is an easy live musical act to stage because it can be a single musician with a guitar and does not require any special set-up or amplification.

RESOURCES

MIGAS: Spanish smoked hot paprika can be purchased at www.tienda.com.

FRIED GOAT CHEESE WITH HONEY: White Hawaiian honey can be purchased at many upscale grocers and www.volcanoislandhoney.com.

GARBANZO BEANS WITH FRIED ONION AND BLOOD SAUSAGE: Blood sausage can be purchased at www.tienda.com.

CATALONIAN PORK TENDERLOIN: Spanish smoked paprikas can be purchased at www.tienda.com.

SPICY SEARED SCALLOPS: Sweet smoked paprika can be purchased at www.tienda.com.

OLIVE OIL ICE CREAM: Arbequina extra virgin olive oil, such as Pons Spanish olive oil, can be purchased at many upscale grocers and at www.tienda.com.

BACHELOR PARTY

{pages 65-79}

This hearty menu was perfect for our bachelor party, but could easily be served at a gathering of men and women, too. You could precede it with some sporting event of your own: a couples golf or tennis tournament, for example.

After outdoor meals, in the evening, warmth and conversation around the fire pit—often over drinks or cigars—is the perfect way to wind down. If your outdoor space doesn't have a fire pit, there are very good portable ones. A range of designs is available at www.kitchensource.com/outdoor-fireplaces/welcomefirerings.htm.

The "hammered" flatware we use at most of our outdoor events is a set I found at Crate & Barrel called Revolution. We have 150 five-piece place settings of it, and it has paid for itself many times over, since renting flatware is so expensive and the pattern selection is often limited. The napery we used is from Mexico. On a recent trip there, I found these fringed cotton napkins for less than

a dollar apiece and bought 150 of them, which should be enough to last through many large parties. The serving plates and dinner plates are Mexican Patamban pottery. See La Cosecha (page 303) in this chapter for details.

RESOURCES

SPICY WATERMELON MARGARITA: Chipotle chile powder can be purchased at www.penzeys.com.

CORTE CARNE DE BUFFALO: Buffalo steaks can be purchased at many upscale grocers and at www.dartagnan.com.

GRILLED ANCHO-ORANGE QUAIL WITH WHEATBERRIES: Partially deboned quails can be purchased at www.dartagnan.com.

MEXICAN FRUIT CUP: Mature coconuts should not be used as a substitute for young coconuts. Young coconuts can be puchased at www.melissas.com.

BEACH RIDE

{pages 81-93}

We have done a beach ride at least once a year since we first bought the ranch. It has taken some time to get the details right, but I think we have finally mastered it. We do our ride at Shell Beach, near Pismo Beach, California.

For picnic "furniture," we use hay bales and some big pillows I had made for use as part of my outdoor entertaining kit. They are covered in white stain-resistant Sunbrella fabric with Velcro closures,

so they can be used in any setting (you may notice them in several other chapters, including Indian Feast, page 95, and Dinner for Two, page 159).

This is basically a one-pot supper. At the end of the night, we were left with nothing to carry home except the pot, ladle, napkins (I always use cloth at the beach because paper gets too soggy and can easily blow away), and empty beer bottles. The rest was either consumed or discarded into the fire. It all fit into the stainless steel Coleman cooler, which is both attractive and functional.

The disposable dishes and cutlery are made of bamboo. They are slightly more expensive than their paper and plastic equivalents, but they are more attractive, and since they are made entirely from the bamboo plant, truly biodegradable. They may be ordered online at www.napastyle.com and other sources.

This menu could be easily adapted and is perfect served indoors by a fire in winter or at a dining room table at any time of year. Serve the salad as a first course; for the second, the chowder in bowls with sourdough croutons and a fine Chablis; and end with a different dessert, like the chocolate cake found in Releasing a New Vintage (page 37) or the pear tart in Truffle Dinner (page 111), and you'll have a meal that could be prepared well in advance.

RESOURCES

CALIFORNIA COASTAL CHOWDER: Ray's Own Brand, a Central Coast sausage company, carries a fantastic linguiça-style sausage called salchicha. It can be purchased at www.raysownbrand.com.

SEA URCHIN BUTTER: Prepared sea urchin, often called uni, can be purchased from Catalina Offshore Products, www.catalinaop.com.

S'MORES WITH HOMEMADE MARSHMALLOWS AND VOSGES CHOCOLATE: Vosges chocolates may be purchased at fine grocery stores or through the Vosges website, www.vosgeschocolate.com.

INDIAN FEAST
{pages 95–109}

This event was several months in planning—we had to coordinate with the very busy professional schedules of the elephants from Have Trunk Will Travel (www.havetrunkwilltravel.com). The animals are often used in films, commercials, and television, but they are also available for rent for special events such as ours, in southern California.

I invited my guests using an invitation I made with a vintage photograph of an elephant and elegant riders tipped onto some handmade Indian paper I found at Kate's Paperie in New York. I did not explicitly tell the guests in advance that there would be real elephants. I did ask everyone to wear saris, and most complied, while others wore caftans, sarongs, and other beautiful Indian clothes.

For the floral arrangements and decorations at this event, I called upon Mindy Rice (www.mindyrice.com), who produces many special events in southern California. She used fabrics and props that I have collected on my own travels to India (similar items can be purchased online). For the tablecloth, we used a half-dozen saris, layered one over the other to give some cushioned padding to the table. I found the little stools for less than ten dollars apiece at an Indian furniture shop in New York.

At the ranch, big outdoor umbrellas don't hold up very well in our offshore winds, so when we need shade over our outdoor dining tables we use these pergolas, which I had made from scrap 6 x 6 redwood lumber, left over from a deck building project. Each module is ten feet square, and I use them in multiples to create a "room" anywhere I need one. They are held together with bolts, and can be assembled or broken down by two people in a few minutes. For this party, Mindy painted them using water based paint that can be washed off with a garden hose after the event. Over the pergolas, she draped gauze fabric, which she dyed hot pink. I always keep bolts of natural-color gauze on hand to use as party décor. Where the posts met the ground, Mindy made decorative motifs out of dried peas, lentils, and carrots, by carefully pouring the different colors into concentric rings. She used water-based ground marking paint in spray cans and dry tempera to stencil more Indian motifs on the posts and the ground.

If you want to capture the feeling of India, the flowers you use and the ways you use them are important. Pink and orange should be your dominant colors, and masses of marigolds should constitute the bulk of the flower arrangement, which might also include, as ours did, mums, gladiolus, and carnations. The arrangements are tight masses of flower heads shaped into a ball. Petals and blossoms may also be strewn or strung casually on the tabletop, on the ground, or floated in the water. This is reminiscent of the devotional flower offerings that are commonplace in Indian religious ceremonies.

This menu could certainly be served indoors, at a dinner table, but I think it is better suited to an outdoor party. Somehow, sitting at a low table on stools or pillows just makes the occasion feel more exotic. The more décor you want to add, the better. Fortunately, it is possible to find Indian items at reasonable prices all over the United States. Don't forget to play Indian music; I downloaded about an hour's worth of Nusrat Fateh Ali Khan and Ravi Shankar songs, and played them on a continuous shuffle loop at low volume over battery operated iPod speakers, which I hid under the table. It wasn't loud enough to interrupt conversation, but the subliminal effect of the distinctive percussion added to the ambience.

RESOURCES

All of the Indian spices used in these recipes are available at www.kalustyans.com.

SEARED DUCK BREAST WITH THREE CHUTNEYS: Micro herb mixes can sometimes be found at upscale markets—check carefully for freshness. Often, www.earthy.com has them; call for availability. Or compose your own mix using a selection of soft, tender herb shoots. Chevdo mix and other Indian snack mixes can be purchased at www.kalustyans.com.

COCONUT CHUTNEY: Freshly grated coconut can be purchased at an Indian market, but make sure you select the unsweetened fresh grated coconut, not the dessicated coconut. Sometimes the frozen product is even better, as the fresh coconuts at mainstream grocers tend to be old and are often rancid.

MINT AND COCONUT RICE: For freshly grated coconut, see Coconut Chutney, above.

VINDALOO HARICOTS VERTS AND WHITE ASPARAGUS: Fresh curry leaves can be purchased at www.kalustyans.com. Baby white asparagus can be purchased at Earthy Delights: www.earthy.com. For freshly grated coconut, see Coconut Chutney, above.

CAULIFLOWER KARI: White split gram beans are available at Indian grocers or from www.kalustyans.com. Fresh curry leaves are available at Indian grocers or from www.kalustyans.com.

MASALA APPLE CAKE WITH CARDAMOM ICE CREAM: Whole tea masala is available from www.kalustyans.com.

TRUFFLE DINNER
{pages 111–125}

It is really only possible to hold this dinner during the month of November in California, when white and black truffles are available. Because the ingredients are so precious and costly, this is a meal to share with only a small number of people—your dearest friends. Even though it was just the four of us at home, the formality of the dinner begged for dressing up.

On the tabletop, I used unique and precious handmade objects that I have acquired one by one over many years. The vases are from a collection of mid-century modern pottery, most of which was designed by the Danish ceramicist Axel Salto. I am especially drawn to his green glazes and the unusual shapes he made. They are mostly unsuitable for flowers, but since this is another meal where the smell of flowers might interfere with the heady aromas of dinner, I used these vases for odd groupings of seeds, pods, vegetables, odorless live orchids, and leaves.

The sterling tumblers with gold vermeil inside are made in London by William and Son (info@williamandson.com) and the sole decoration on their simple form is four randomly placed silver hallmarks. While I love to use them as wine cups, I have also given them as gifts for babies and children, another cup every year—by the time they are old enough to drink wine, they will have a full table service.

The crystal stemware was made in the late nineteenth century, but has a very modern design sense. I collected it, piece by piece, at shops in London, and I have only about twenty pieces in all. A similar style can be found in the crystal forms of Elsa Peretti, whose contemporary tabletop designs are sold at Tiffany & Co.

The truffle shaver set that I own is still being produced by G. Lorenzi, on Via Montenapoleone, in Milan (www.lorenzi.it). The most important part of the set is the truffle shaver—look for one with the highest quality stainless steel shaver blade, as an inferior one will make a mess of your truffle. Shavers are found at most fine chef supply stores.

My crystal and silver honey bee is another antique, but I have spotted similar ones in specialty shops. Even if you can't find one just like this, other beautiful and unique crystal, silver, and porcelain honey pots are the kind of thing it can be fun to hunt antique shops for—in the last two hundred years, there have been many charming designs for this highly specialized service piece.

For a formal dinner like this one, I like each guest to have a personal salt cellar and pepper grinder at their place, which gives a ritualistic luxury to the seasoning of food. The cellars are vintage Georg Jensen, from my collection. The pepper grinders can be found at Scully & Scully (www.scullyandscully.com) or at some kitchen supply shops.

RESOURCES

BRAISED RABBIT WITH TAGLIATTA AND WHITE TRUFFLES: Rabbit legs may be ordered from D'Artagnan, www.dartagnan.com. Fresh white truffles can be purchased in season from www.francvin.com.

CHICKPEA PASTA: Chickpea flour can be purchased from www.bobsredmill.com. Upscale grocers often carry micro and tiny lettuce mixes, and farmers' markets have an inspirational variety of greens, herbs, and edible flowers. Micro greens are also available at www.earthy.com; call for availability.

LOBSTER WITH BRAISED PORK BELLY AND BLACK TRUFFLE SALAD: Pork belly can be purchased at www.nimanranch.com, and is often available at Asian markets. Black truffle oil can be purchased from www.francvin.com. Fresh black truffles can be purchased in season from www.earthy.com. Yokoi's brown rice and malt vinegar can be purchased at www.katagiri.com. It is a fine, drinking-quality vinegar.

PEAR TARTS WITH WHITE TRUFFLE WHIPPED CREAM AND RAW HONEY: Almond nougat is a crunchy almond, honey, and egg-white candy. It can be purchased from www.tienda.com, where it is called turrón de Alicante.

FATHER'S DAY
{pages 127–139}

Fourteen to twenty people is a great number for a party, but it is often hard to find a way to seat that number using conventional furniture. To solve that problem, I put together a garden party kit that I plan to use for many years: two 40" x 8' folding tables; felt table pads; silk awning stripe table cloths; and a matching canopy with poles and rope. Whenever I want to have a group this size, I have everything I need except the chairs, and practically any party rental chair you find will go with this set-up.

The flowers are simply cut American Beauty roses. I put them into a mismatched collection of silver mint julep cups.

Because Father's Day is a gift-giving occasion, I decided to give every guest something memorable to take home. The mounted butterfly boxes on which we served the terrine are from Evolution in New York (www.theevolutionstore.com). After lunch, we cleaned them off with Windex, wrapped them in tissue, and put each in a small shopping bag. Barnaby got a unique gift: a handmade pimp cup with his name spelled in colorful sparkling crystals. This one came from Debbie the Glass Lady (contact Deborah Harrison at 773-684-5036, for more information).

The place cards were hand calligraphed by Bernard Maisner on his hand-painted and gilded butterfly bookmarks, and can be ordered online at www.bernardmaisner.com. I printed the luncheon menu on the back of each bookmark. I often have Bernard calligraph printed menus with the name of each guest because it gives the guest a lovely personalized souvenir to take home. I always do assigned seating for tables of eight people or more.

The china on which I served the Soft Shell Crabs is by Bernardaud and available at Takashimaya in New York. The dessert plates are hand painted with images of bugs and moths by Ted Meuhling and are available at Moss, New York (www.mossonline.com).

The recipes in this chapter may seem complicated, but just about everything can be made the day before, giving the hostess plenty of time to spend at the table with guests. When I have children at a grown-up dinner, I always ask them to help with some small chores, like clearing the table and offering more water or tea. I think this makes them feel important and gives them more of an investment in the day.

The best thank-you I received was from Barnaby: a charcoal portrait of me and my dogs.

RESOURCES
FOIE GRAS AND KUMQUAT TERRINE: Foie gras can be purchased from www.dartagnan.com or www.earthy.com. A terrine mold can be purchased at www.jbprince.com.
ALMOND CAKE: Bob's Red Mill almond meal can be purchased at www.bobsredmill.com.

TREASURE HUNT AND FAMILY COOKOUT
{pages 141–157}

I have been doing treasure hunts for kids' parties for twenty years in the city, the country, public parks, neighborhoods, and back-yards. Kids love them. Some adults do, too. When I am planning a treasure hunt, first I decide how many stops I want the kids to make, which is determined by the amount of time and space you have. Then I figure out where the treasure will be hidden and what tools and clues they will need to find the treasure, and I work back-ward from there. In the case of our treasure hunt, for example, they needed to collect a ladder, a key, and a shovel, in that order, along the way, so the three clues before the end had to do with finding those items. I also wanted them to explore and enjoy as much of the ranch as possible, so I made sure that the clues took them into the horse corrals, the chicken coop, and the pond. We had kids from toddlers to twelve-year-olds in our group, so to make sure everyone was a valuable member of the team, I assigned cer-tain "executive" jobs to the older ones at the outset, like scribe, mathematician, reader, and driver, so the littler kids could do some of the labor of running, climbing, and digging without getting trampled. In addition to physical challenges like climbing trees and swimming across the lake to find clues, they also had to solve some riddles, unscramble jumbled words, and navigate using the sun before finding the candy-filled treasure chest.

You can hold treasure hunts for little kids in an area like a public playground or a backyard. The smaller the space, the more the clues will have to involve mental challenges, not physical solutions. It is fun to have treasure hunts and scavenger hunts for adults, too, and these may even involve traveling some distance on foot or by bicycle or car.

For our buffet dinner, we used a set of spatterware tin dishes. These are great because they are indestructible, an important con-sideration when hosting large groups of kids. Tinware and spatterware are available at www.coxcountrygifts.com. I wrapped simple red bandannas around the cutlery as napkins and tied them together with raffia.

Our hot fudge sundae cart, painted in a Mexican tole design, was made by Terry Fealey, a talented neighbor who is both a mini-livestock enthusiast herself and a theatrical set maker. You could make a rustic hot fudge sundae display of your own using a galva-nized tub filled with ice and stuffed with open quarts of ice cream and scoops. Put all of the toppings on the side, and, like we did, let everyone make their own. That was the fun part—kids making sundaes for their parents and each other, parents sneaking back for multiple helpings.

Hay bales make great, no-fuss furniture. On them, I place Pendleton blankets decorated with vintage-style Native American designs (www.pendleton-usa.com). We have about a dozen of these wool blankets, which we almost always use at our evening parties. They make great picnic blankets, chair covers, tablecloths, and cool-weather wraps.

Kids love camping outdoors, and I have always loved it because it is much less hassle than hosting indoor slumber parties. Our tepees come from Reese Tipis in Montana (www.reesetipis.com). They were hand painted by Terry Fealey in designs inspired by some I found in a book. You could have an outdoor sleepover without tepees by ask-ing each family to bring their own tent and bedroll.

The biggest surprise of the day was how well the kids enter-tained themselves after the treasure hunt was over. I had thought I needed fireside entertainment, so I hired a folksinger with a guitar and printed a sheet of campfire songs and ghost stories. But the kids were so busy with their own games that they spent little time fireside. It was the adults who did almost all of the singing.

RESOURCES
BRAISED AND BARBECUED PORK SPARERIBS:
www.gourmetsleuth.com has a wide selection of dried chiles in their online catalog.

DINNER FOR TWO
{pages 159–167}

This romantic dinner could be easily duplicated in almost any loca-tion that has romantic associations for you. Most of the food (except for the french fries) can be ordered and assembled in advance, and would make a great picnic dinner. It's a perfect meal to carry in a basket to Central Park for a summer concert.

Our rowboat is a replica of a 14-foot Whitehall, and was made by students at the Northwest School of Wooden Boat Building (www.nwboatschool.org). The original Whitehall was used as a ferry boat in New York harbor during the late nineteenth and early twentieth centuries. New Whitehalls made with fiberglass hulls can be found through Whitehall Rowing and Sail (www.white hallrow.com). Ours is named the *Tru Luv,* just like the one owned by Ronald and Nancy Reagan, whose California ranch was also located in the Santa Ynez Valley.

The sterling silver lobster picks are more pieces from my col-lection of Georg Jensen "Bernadotte." The caviar bowl is made of horn and is from G. Lorenzi in Milan. I try to make romantic occa-sions memorable by using antiques and personal treasures for serving and decorating.

Our Kansas limestone grape posts came from Pat Pinckney at Specialty Stone, in Petaluma, California (www.specialtystonellc.com).

RESOURCES
NAKED CAVIAR: Farmed osetra caviar can be purchased at www.caviar-direct.com.
STONE CRAB CLAWS: Fresh claws can be purchased in season from www.joesstonecrab.com.

VINTNERS' POTLUCK

{pages 169–177}

For the best potlucks, choose guests who share some common interest or bond. In this case, it was friends who make wine, and the potluck was an opportunity for a tasting. I have also organized potlucks based on specific ingredients, for the occasions of a garlic festival and an heirloom tomato harvest. For one of the most fun potlucks I have ever hosted, I asked everyone to bring a dish prepared from a recipe they found on the back of a box. That buffet had everything from sophisticated risottos to Rice Krispies Treats.

To invite guests to a potluck, I always send a written invitation because the information is more complicated than the usual what, when, and where. I have to let them know it is a potluck, what the focus is, what facilities and accommodations we have for on-site preparation of their dish, and the number of people each dish should serve. I do not make the assignments of what to bring in the invitation; I do that at the time of the RSVP, using a simple chart to keep track. The categories often include hors d'oeuvres, green salad, red meat, fish dish, vegetable side, starch side, cheese, and dessert. When all the responses are in, I decide which dishes I can provide to fill in any weaker categories.

In advance, you should plan how you are going to deal with everyone's leftovers and dirty serving pieces. It's best if you can get them washed and dried before the evening is over, but that is rarely practical and not much fun either. Instead, I have on hand a few wide rolls of aluminum foil and plastic wrap, and some kitchen-size garbage bags with drawstring tops. This way, people can wrap their own dishes the way they want and use the bags to keep the whole thing contained during the drive home.

Most of the details you will need to host a blind wine tasting are given in the text of the chapter (page 176), but there are a few more details that may be useful. You should get a supply of brown kraft paper bags like the ones used by wine shops and grocery stores. It may be possible for your merchant to give you enough for your wine tasting. If not, you can find them online, but they are almost always sold in huge quantities. Don't make the mistake I did the first time I held a blind tasting and try to use lunch bags. They barely cover the shoulders of most wine bottles and the bottoms are so bulky that the wine bottles are prone to tipping over. In a pinch, you can always wrap the bottles in newspaper.

To give my wine tasting a uniform look, I had a rubber stamp made at Kinko's with the name of the party, the date, my name and that of my co-host, and a blank space for writing the bottle number. I met each guest at the door, took their wine, noting whether it was white or red, bagged it, then stamped it and numbered it in sequence: 1R, 2R, 1W, 2W, with R for reds and W for whites. I also pre-printed the score sheets by making a table on the computer with three columns—for "Wine #," "Score," and "Notes"—for the guests to fill in.

Since each of our wines was made by someone in the room, I did not have the additional job of providing a factual set of wine notes to distribute at the end of the evening. But if you are putting together a more typical wine tasting, using a variety of store-bought wines, having this list ready to distribute after all the scores have been tallied can provide some of the best fun of the evening.

I list grape variety, maker, year, region, and price. If you want to take this one step farther, you could Google the wines and print out reviews and comments from wine critics to share with your guests. It never fails to entertain a party when guests score an inexpensive wine better than a Grand Cru, and it's always satisfying to find that a particularly famous wine is truly worth the price.

The Black Cherry Confit and Quince Paste shown are imported by the French Farm. Email your zipcode to ffinfo@frenchfarm.com for retailers in your area.

RESOURCES

VENISON TENDERLOIN WITH CHERRY-OLIVE CHUTNEY: Venison is available through Broken Arrow Ranch, www.brokenarrowranch.com. Pea shoots are available at Earthy Delights, www.earthy.com, and also frequently at farmers' markets and upscale grocers.

CHEESE BOARD WITH KALAMATA AND KUMQUAT BREADSTICKS: Rinconada Dairy Pozo Tomme can be purchased at www.rinconadadairy.com. Cowgirl Creamery Mount Tam can be purchased at www.cowgirlcreamery.com. Point Reyes Blue cheese can be purchased at www.ptreyescheese.com. Cypress Grove cheeses can be purchased at www.cypressgrovechevre.com.

FEATURED SANTA BARBARA COUNTY VINTNERS:
Andrew Murray Vineyards, www.andrewmurrayvineyards.com
Au Bon Climat, www.aubonclimat.com
Calzada Ridge, www.calzadaridge.com
Cold Heaven, www.coldheavencellars.com
Consilience, www.consiliencewines.com
Curtis Winery, www.curtiswinery.com
Firestone Vineyards, www.firestonewine.com
Foxen, www.foxenvineyard.com
Great Oaks Vineyard, www.greatoaksranch.com
Hartley Ostini Hitching Post, www.hitchingpost2.com
Koehler Winery, www.koehlerwinery.com
Oak Savanna Vineyard, www.oaksavannawine.com

INDEPENDENCE DAY BLAST

{pages 179–201}

Our July 4th party is our annual pull-out-the-stops event. If you can do just one big bash a year, I would recommend this over having an annual Christmas party. It has none of the hectic season surrounding it and best of all your friends and their families will likely be free, making it the perfect time to entertain.

A rodeo is essentially a field day competition on horses. Have your own field day by inviting all your guests to compete in games everyone can play, like Balloon Brigade, Egg-and-Spoon Relay, Three-Legged Race, Ring Toss, Sack Race, Badminton, Tug O' War, and Volleyball.

Décor for July 4th is flags, flags, and more flags. I found that this uniformity makes it simple to decorate every year, but that it also looks crisper and stronger than having little bits of décor here and there. Sometimes I hang the flags from a length of nylon rope tied between uprights; other years, I tack them onto flagpoles made from wooden dowels. The key to a good look is to create massive groupings of them. For example, buy dozens of handheld flags and stick them as densely as you can into pots of live daisies. Make as many of these pots as your table can hold for a stunning centerpiece.

One of the high points of everyone's day on July 4th at Rancho La Zaca is the sunset parade. You can easily organize a parade of your own using the young guests at your party. In advance, be sure to stock up on kazoos and Uncle Sam hats for as many people as you expect to participate (but don't bring these out until the parade is just about to begin otherwise the kids will be kazooed out—and so will you—before parade time.) Designate one member of your party as the drum major or field commander, and have the kids follow him or her in marching formation. Even if the parade lasts for only five minutes, kids are always thrilled to have a chance to perform. Have cameras ready, because the photo ops from your parade, no matter how big or small it turns out to be, will be priceless.

Our drinks are self-serve and available all day long. We use galvanized washtubs with a hole drilled in the bottom for drainage, fill them with ice, and then tie a bottle opener on a string to the handle. Be sure to have garbage cans near every tub so the empty bottles and cans don't pile up. For large gatherings like this, I always stock the smallest servings of beverages I can find, so people can switch drinks freely without waste. I also stock water at a ratio of one to one: one bottle of water for one of any other beverage. If water is as readily available as any other drink option, it encourages everyone to stay hydrated throughout the day.

We made our outdoor buffet tables from planks of weathered 6" x 8' barnwood supported by aluminum sawhorses from the hardware store. Using 5 planks to make each tabletop, these are easily stored and moved and can be broken down and set up by one person. The barnwood is attractive enough that no tablecloth is required.

I had our invitation designed in the style of an old-fashioned newspaper. With this format, I am able to give our guests all the information they need—what to wear, a schedule for the day, a description of all the rodeo events, a rodeo sign-up sheet, a map of the property, and a list of local hotels (we have friends who travel for the party; some even plan their summer vacation around it).

The beginning of our fireworks display is announced by the arrival of washtubs of giant sparklers, some lit, stuck in a small quantity of sand. Everyone takes at least one of these, and when the sparkler is done, they snuff the hot end in the sand. Even if you don't have additional fireworks, these sparkling tubs make an exciting display. Our fireworks are designed by Pyro Spectaculars: www.pyrospectaculars.com.

For big gatherings like this one, I use hemstitched linen napkins that I purchased at a restaurant supply store, and had embroidered by machine with the ranch monogram, RLZ. In the long run, this solution has proven less expensive than renting napkins. Paper is not an option—with our late-afternoon breezes, they would all just blow away.

RESOURCES

PURE WHITE: Horchata can be found at most grocery stores in the alternative dairy section.

ANTELOPE WITH COFFEE AND CHILE CRUST: Antelope can be purchased at www.brokenarrowranch.com.

SPICY BLACKSTRAP CHICKEN: Poussins are available through www.dartagnan.com.

SMOKED MUSHROOM PINOT SALSA: Chef's Blend Wild Mushroom Mix is available at Earthy Delights, www.earthy.com, and at some gourmet grocers.

SMOKED TOMATO MAYONNAISE: Hitching Post Smoked Tomato Pesto can be purchased at www.hitchingpost2.com.

LALA SALAD: Rustichella D'Abruzzo pastas are the finest of Italian artisanal pastas and are available at many upscale grocers across the country, or substitute another high-quality imported brand. Santa Barbara Olive Co. olives can be purchased at www.sbolive.com.

ELEVENSES:
A DOVE HUNTERS' BRUNCH
{pages 203–213}

This brunch could be served indoors or out, and with its hearty menu is probably best suited for fall. As a simple outdoor meal with a vineyard view, all we needed for the setting were assorted linens and serving plates. The reversible glasses are from William Laman (www.williamlaman.com). This easy meal would also make a great tailgate brunch before the game or for fall leaf viewing.

My Parsons Jack Russell terriers are Lucky, Ruby Begonia, and Jinx. Ruby is the only one of the three who will retrieve birds—the other two are afraid of the guns.

RESOURCES

SAVANNA-STYLE SQUAB WITH CORN BREAD–SAUSAGE STUFFING: Partially deboned squabs can be purchased from

www.dartagnan.com. Quail eggs may be purchased from www.dartagnan.com and are also available at most Asian grocers and some upscale grocers. Veal demi-glace can be purchased at Earthy Delights, www.earthy.com.

HARVEST
{pages 215–225}

Visiting a vineyard at harvest is an unforgettable experience. You can often see the harvest activities in full swing and up close during that time, particularly at smaller wineries. Pack a picnic like ours, since many vineyards have picnic grounds available for use by the public. To plan a picnic and wine tasting of your own in our area, visit the Santa Barbara County Vintners' Association (www.sbcountywines.com), where you can find links to the wineries and maps coded to show which wineries have picnic grounds.

Wine barrel tops make great cheeseboards. You can buy wine or whiskey barrel tops similar to ours at Kentucky Barrels (www.kentuckybarrels.com).

RESOURCES

MEATS, CHEESES, FRUITS, AND BREADS ON A BARREL TOP: All the sausages can be purchased at www.dartagnan.com. Plum mustard can be purchased at www.francvin.com. White Burgundy wine mustard can be purchased at www.francvin.com. Cowgirl Creamery Red Hawk cheese can be purchased at www.cowgirlcreamery.com. Rinconada Dairy Pozo Tomme can be purchased at www.rinconadadairy.com.

SIMPLE PASTA SALAD WITH BASIL AND LEMON: Rustichella d'Abruzzo trofie pasta can be puchased at http://farawayfoods.com, or substitute another high-quality imported brand.

ROASTED POTATO AND HEIRLOOM TOMATO SHUFFLE: Point Reyes Blue cheese can be purchased at www.ptreyescheese.com. Rogue Creamery Smokey Blue cheese can be purchased at www.roguecreamery.com

LA COSECHA

{pages 227–239}

During harvest, we often use bunches of grapes and vines, sometimes mixed with flowers, as centerpieces.

We served our lunch on paper plates. To dress them up, I have a set of Indian basket plate holders that we used as chargers underneath. The serving pieces are glazed Mexican terra-cotta pottery made in a style called Patamban, after the town in Michoacán, Mexico, where it is made. Distinguished by the dark brown and green glaze, no two pieces match exactly, but they all mix. I have collected them over the years, most of them for less than ten dollars apiece on eBay and through trips to Mexico, and at flea markets and yard sales. Other equally attractive styles of Mexican pottery are Tlaquepaque and Bandera. You can see more of my collection of these pieces in the Bachelor Party (pages 64–79).

RESOURCES

LA ZACA CHICKEN MOLE: Abuelita is a good brand of Mexican chocolate. It can be purchased at www.mexgrocer.com.

CHORIZO AGRIDULCE: Fresh chorizo can be purchased at www.unclecharleyssausage.com.

CHOCO PICOPANS: Cacao nibs are available at www.rawfood.com and at many gourmet and health food stores.

DINNER FOR DEAD POETS

{pages 241–253}

This Halloween dinner theme was originally conceived when we were going to be traveling in Europe with a group of friends. For a "costume," everyone found some small but distinctive accessory to evoke their chosen poet's character. When we're closer to home, we can create more elaborate costumes, but no matter how costumed we are, it's just as much fun.

I held this party in the winery because it was the only room that could be completely transformed. I made a space within a space using the 10' x 10' pergolas I use at other events for shade. I draped the pergolas in gauze, dyed black for an eerie effect. I had originally planned to have the dinner outdoors, where a haunting dead tree and the full moon would have set the scene.

For an elegant menu such as this one, I always produce a complete set of formal dinner stationery, including a mailed invitation, place cards, and menus. In this case, I used funeral wreaths with the name of the poet written on ribbon as "place cards" behind each chair, since I knew in advance which poet each guest would portray.

For menus, I made ten identical lifesize black-and-white photo prints of an X-rayed skull. I printed on a thick matte photo paper, so it was fairly rigid. I then trimmed each photo straight across the bottom, directly underneath the chin. Then I glued a tongue depressor and another piece of paper to the back of the photo print, onto which the menu, calligraphed by Bernard Maisner

(www.bernardmaisner.com) had already been printed. When the glue was dry, I cut out the rest of the skull shape, including eye holes, to make menu masks.

I have used this same idea for birthday parties. Replace the skull with a lifesize headshot of the honoree. If it is a surprise party, it can be a stunning effect to pass these out to guests in advance of the arrival of the honoree; it is very funny to walk into a room full of people who are all masked to look like you.

On the tabletop, we used arrangements of white roses interspersed with dried seedpods and bay leaf branches that had been painted black. The quartz crystal candelabra were handmade for me by the Mermaid's Palace in Petaluma (www.themermaidspalace.com). The black stemless wineglasses are from a collection by Riedel meant for "blind" wine tasting. The martini glasses are "Vega" from Baccarat and the smoky black goblets are from Crate & Barrel. The dishes on which the first and second courses were served are Mottahedeh Festival Black Service Plate and Vienna Evening Filigree Service Plate and the scene depicts an adult and child playing a party game. An albino peacock from my collection of taxidermy helped set the scene, and a suitably morbid touch came from dropper bottles with labels such as "100-year-old blood"—actually filled with extra-vecchio balsamico left over from the Mince and Quince.

The poets represented at our party are: Ovid, Li Po, Rumi, Mikhail Bulgakov, Rainer Maria Rilke, Ralph Waldo Emerson, Ambrose Bierce, Oscar Wilde, Charles Dickens, Emily Dickenson, André de Chénier, and Kurt Cobain.

RESOURCES

MINCEMEAT PURSES: Extra-vecchio balsamico vinegar can be purchased at most gourmet groceries and at www.francvin.com.
ROASTED PORK LOIN STUFFED WITH BRAISED CABBAGE: Berkshire pork loin can be purchased at www.heritagefoodsusa.com
BACON AND PICKLED GOLDEN RAISIN VINAIGRETTE: Veal demi-glace can be purchased at Earthy Delights, www.earthy.com.

THANKSGIVING

{ p a g e s   2 5 5 – 2 7 3 }

For Thanksgiving, when each guest likes to tailor his or her dinner to their liking, I set a buffet. This allows dinner conversation too, since no one has to pass the turkey, please.

The wavy candle centerpieces on the table are collectibles designed by Jean Royère. The antique dishes were designed by Eva Zeisel for Castleton. Fantastic reproductions of these designs have recently been made by Crate & Barrel. Our stemware is "Montaigne Optic" by Baccarat, the stemless wine glasses are Riedel "O," and the colored cut-crystal tumblers are from Moss in New York (www.mossonline.com). The linens are from E. Braun and are embroidered with a monogram designed for me by Caroline Brackenridge (www.monograminc.com). The silver is "Bernadotte" by Georg Jensen.

RESOURCES

SPIT-ROASTED TURKEY AND GRAVY: Heritage turkey breeds are available at www.heritagefoodsusa.com. It is best to order your turkey in September or October.
SEARED WILD MUSHROOMS: Specialty mushrooms are often available at upscale grocers and are readily available online. Two sources for chanterelles are D'Artagnan, www.dartagnan.com, and Earthy Delights, www.earthy.com.
PODS AND ROOTS: Vanilla oil can be purchased at many gourmet groceries or at www.vanillafromtahiti.com.

CHRISTMAS EVE

{ p a g e s   2 7 5 – 2 9 1 }

This mission, like many other historic buildings, is available to rent for private parties. The biggest surprise was that the rangers—this is a state park—allowed us to use the mission furniture as well as the original mission kitchen, with its wood-burning *horno* oven, to cook the meal.

Our California Christmas tree is a living *Quercus agrifolia* (California live oak) which I grew from an acorn in a plastic pot

that I cover in burlap when I use it for the holidays. The ornaments have been collected over a lifetime of travels to Mexico, but similar ones can be found at almost any shop in the U.S. or Mexico that sells Mexican crafts. The big crêpe-paper flowers on the tree were purchased at www.directfrommexico.com.

We made individual candleholders for each guest following a design we saw at Hacienda de Los Santos, in Alamos, Mexico, whose annual Posada was the inspiration for this occasion. We cut 10" lengths of PVC pipe and, using florist tape, secured silk poinsettia leaves and a glass hurricane to the end of each one. With fresh candles put inside, we can use these for many years. The tree and the flowers for this event were designed by Trisha Fountaine (Tricia Fountaine, 805-565-2060).

The funniest moment of the party occurred when our miniature donkey, Babalu, started singing along with the carolers. We all cracked up when, after watching intently and inquisitively as we held the long vowels in the first verse of "O, Holy Night," he decided to join in.

On the table, the three blue-and-white pattern plates are based on the Blue Canton export china that was brought to colonial America by ship captains who had stopped in Asia. Many fine china manufacturers produce versions of these patterns today, and Mottahedeh has a wonderful design (www.mottahedeh.com). The crystal is Waterford. These heavy, leaded glasses made a wonderful chime when clinked together after the toast, unlike the "ping" you hear with contemporary balloon glasses. It was an unexpected and delightful beginning to this holiday dinner.

The hammered chargers are copper-based ones that I had silver plated by a local jeweler many years ago. The copper underneath begins to show through after a little wear, and I like this rustic and slightly humble effect. In recent years I have seen similar ones for sale in fine tableware shops.

RESOURCES

OPEN FIRE–ROASTED CHESTNUT SOUP: Frozen chestnuts can be purchased from Earthy Delights, www.earthy.com.
BACON MAPLE CHUTNEY: Niman Ranch slab bacon is available at www.nimanranch.com.
ROASTED STUFFED GOOSE WITH HUCKLEBERRY GASTRIC: Geese can be purchased from www.heritagefoodsusa.com.
HUCKLEBERRY GASTRIC: Frozen huckleberries can be purchased at Earthy Delights, www.earthy.com. Huckleberry vinegar can be purchased from Priest Lake Berry Patch, 208-443-0802.
HERB SALAD WITH BEET-VANILLA VINAIGRETTE: Smoked blue cheese can be purchased at most cheese shops. For more information and to purchase, see www.roguecreamery.com.
CHRISTMAS TRIFLE: La Nogalera Walnut Oil can be purchased at www.lanogalerawalnutoil.com.

PHOTO CREDITS

The author and publisher wish to thank the following copyright holders for permission to reprint photographs in this book:

ERIC SCOTT, ERIC SCOTT PHOTOGRAPHY, (WWW.ERICSCOTTPHOTO.COM), pages ii, iii, iv, 2, 6, 12 (bottom left; bottom right), 18, 42, 44, 47 (all), 48, 53 (all), 54 (all), 58, 64, 66, 67, 68 (all), 72 (all), 75, 79 (all), 80, 82, 84 (all), 87, 88 (all), 90, 91, 93, 99, 108, 110, 112, 114 (all), 117 (all), 118, 122, 124, 125, 126, 128, 130 (all), 133 (all), 134, 137, 140, 142, 145 (all), 146 (all), 149, 150 (all), 152 (all), 154 (all), 155, 156, 157, 158, 160, 162, 165 (all), 166, 167, 168, 170, 174 (all), 175, 176, 178, 180, 182 (all), 185 (all), 186 (all), 189 (all), 190 (all), 192, 195 (all), 196 (all), 197, 198, 199, 200 (all), 201 (all), 202, 204, 207, 208 (all), 211, 212, 214, 216, 217, 221 (all), 226, 231 (all), 232, 235 (all), 237, 240, 242, 244, 246 (all), 249 (all), 250 (all), 254, 256, 259 (all), 260 (all), 263 (all), 265, 272 (all), 274, 276, 278, 279 (all), 280, 284, 289 (all), and 291.

LUCA TROVATO, LUCA TROVATO PHOTOGRAPHY, (WWW.LUCATROVATO.COM), pages vi, 12 (top), 17, 20, 22, 23, 25, 26 (all), 29, 31, 32, 33, 35, 36 (all), 50, 57, 61, 71, 76, 94, 96, 98, 101 (all), 102, 105, 106 (all), 173, 219 (all), 222, 267, 268, 283, 286, 294, 295, 296, 298, 299, 301, 304, 305, and 314; front cover.

M AND M, INC. MACDUFF EVERTON, (WWW.MACDUFFEVERTON.COM), pages 19, 39, 41, 224, 225, 228, 238, 239, 253, and 292.

ROXANNE LOWIT, (WWW.ROXANNELOWIT.COM), pages 8, 10, and 15 (all).

DAVID CAMERON, page 5.

CROCKER ART MUSEUM, page 63.

ACKNOWLEDGMENTS

With my deep thanks to:

- My family for being so patient, helpful, supportive, and always fun throughout this project: Tom Dittmer; Bo Pittman; Jason, Allison, and Casey Dittmer; Alexis, Chris, Casey, and Peyton Gaughan.

- Stephanie Valentine, whose extraordinary talents in the kitchen I am thrilled to share with others at every possible opportunity, hence the idea (and the courage) to produce this book. Thank you today and every day for the bounty you put on our table and now, through this collection of extraordinary recipes, on the tables of an even greater number of people than we will ever have plates and wineglasses for.

- The photographers who captured all the energy and beauty of the Santa Ynez Valley and the gorgeous people who live and play here: Eric Scott Smith, MacDuff Everton, Luca Trovato, and Roxanne Lowit.

- Laura Sandler, who has been my right hand through every stage of this book's production. We had many memorable laughs and only a few dramas. (We *will* have a dinner under that dead tree someday before it falls down.)

- The extraordinary staff of Oak Savanna Vineyard and Rancho La Zaca, who have made every one of these events possible, in particular, to vineyard manager "Don" Felipe Hernandez and ranch manager Wyatt Cromer (a.k.a. The Blackberry Buckaroo), but also to Nellie Aragon, Juan, Samuel, and Yaya; Jackie Rosa; Carrie Tinkham; and Ashley Mulligan.

- Andrew Bradbury, of Clō in the Time Warner Center, New York, who has shown us all some exciting new ways to enjoy wine.

- My nearest neighbors and friends, who, by being there, made every one of these occasions more fun than I ever dreamed: Brooks and Kate Firestone; Adam, Kate, Nick, Maddie, Matthew, and Peter (the Rabbit) Firestone; David, Polly, Ella, Georgina, and Tamsyn Walker; Kendall Conrad and David, Fanny, and Luisa Cameron; Barnaby and Mary Conrad; Tani Conrad and Helen Gazin; Andrew, Kristen, Callum, and Estelle Murray; Michael and Nancy Lippman; Whitney and Jim Kelley; Carol Ann Elwell; Richard and Pamela Harris; and Chris and Wendy Reynolds.

- More dear friends, not so near, but who always managed to be there when I called on them: Katherine Ross, Gabrielle Sage and Michael Govan, Cat Doran, Nina Griscom, Lionel Piraino, Amanda Ross, and Joan Kron.

- The esteemed vintners of Santa Barbara County, including, once again, Andrew Murray, owner of Andrew Murray Vineyards and winemaker for Oak Savanna Vineyard, as well as Chuck Carlson (Curtis), Jim Clendenen (Au Bon Climat), Morgan Clendenen (Cold Heaven), Dick and Jenny Doré (Foxen), Frank Ostini (Hitching Post), and Brett Escalera (Consilience), as well as vineyard owner Peter Koehler (Koehler Winery).

- The creative people who have helped me and whose considerable talents are evident in the details: floral designers and decorators Mindy Rice, Renae Brubaker, and Tricia Fountaine; and calligrapher Bernard Maisner.

- County historians and owners of Olive Tree Press, Jim and Lynne Norris.

- The Santa Barbara County Sheriff's Department SWAT team and Sergeant Mike Perkins.

- Chris Pavone. First, I need to thank you for your persistence in tracking me down, and then for all your encouragement, guidance, and the welcome incision with a sharp pencil that followed. I am glad we didn't take the mink-covered path. The production of this book has illuminated some adventurous new directions for both of us. Jan Derevjanik for her elegant art direction; Katherine Camargo for her keen attention to detail; and Nicki Clendening for her belief in me from the beginning.

- My grandmother, Alice Marie Jayet Walther, who, by her elegant example, showed me at a very impressionable young age the joys of making any moment into a memorable occasion.

SANDY HILL
RANCHO LA ZACA, 2007

INDEX